15 ⁰⁰

D1442887

COMMODITY SPECULATION
– With Profits In Mind

By

L. Dee Belveal

Published by

COMMODITIES PRESS
a division of BELVEAL & CO., INC.
3100 Country Lane — Wilmette, Illinois 60091

By the author of the
Commodity Trading Manual

Library of Congress Catalog Card Number: 67-30004

Printed in the United States of America

Commodity Charts
by
FUTURES PUBLISHING CO.
608 South Dearborn
Chicago

*Crop Report and Farm
Program Data*
by
McCORD-LAZARE PRINTING CO.
708 Wrightwood Avenue
Chicago

Plate 1   *Courtesy, Corn Industries Research Foundation, Inc.*

The biggest speculator of them all.

DEDICATION

—To the professional speculator. That hardy soul
who, in the face of hazards which drive lesser mortals
to disordered retreat, stands his ground, calculates
the risks and dares to welcome the dangers which
others can not bear—or will not accept.

—To the professional speculator. An uncommonly
valorous exception in the ranks of common men.

TABLE OF CONTENTS

FOREWORD

This book has been in research and preparation for more than twenty years.

It began with a first venture into the unknown waters of commodity speculation in February, 1946, which involved one contract of eggs. Surprisingly, this first trade produced nearly $300 in profit; and the three positions which followed it were also "winners". Flushed with four straight victories, the speculative road to riches seemed both short and straight!

Trade number five, involving two carloads of potatoes, wiped out all the accrued profits and took an additional $281 along with it. Making a "quick million" in the market suddenly seemed fraught with at least as many *problems* as *opportunities*—but the opportunities still looked too good to pass up.

It was at this point that the "paper trading" system which is explained in this book was developed. It provided a means of gaining experience in the market, but without paying the high prices charged for instruction in the real arena. Fourteen months later, I returned to my broker's office and sold 5,000 bushels of wheat "short". From March, 1948, until the present day, commodity speculation has continued to be both a topic of engaging intellectual interest—and a highly profitable economic pursuit.

In two decades of almost constant exposure to it, I have, at one time or another, made all of the mistakes possible in speculation. Each one of them has carried its own price tag, so the information between these covers has all been "bought and paid for".

Foreword

Speculation in commodities is an intriguing business, but it is also a vital economic function. We will never fully understand how important the commodity speculator is unless, through short-sighted legislation, free markets are destroyed in favor of price-making by electronic computer—or imposed by self-annointed "experts".

The existence of free markets as price-discovery mechanisms, and as "control valves" in the distribution supply-lines importantly depends on maintaining sufficient public speculative interest to accommodate the huge and growing commerce involved in provisioning our world-wide population. The task grows ever larger, and the supply of speculative capital must grow with it. If the need is to be met, the ranks of speculators must be swelled by newcomers who have the courage and the resources to take a hand in the herculean job. But they should not be invited into the market without being afforded a chance to begin with some reasonable opportunity for success. There are enough hazards always present in professional speculation without multiplying the inherent risks by ignorance of elemental market procedures and basic trading strategy.

A heartfelt word of appreciation is due the hundreds of traders, hedgers, brokers and market technicians who have, over the years, had a hand in my trading education. In an era when the only way to learn about commodity trading was by word-of-mouth and by doing it, most of the "old pro's" were surprisingly willing to share their hard-bought information with a young competitor. Although they had neither the time nor the patience to reduce their wisdom to printed form, they served as unpaid "professors", both in the pits and out of them; and they still do.

The suggestion which first kindled the idea of developing this work came out of a discussion with Paul F. McGuire, who prior to becoming a full-time speculator, distinguished himself in financial administration both in the United States and abroad. A great many of the ideas contained herein are his, gleaned from a long succession of conversations which have been spread over the past two years.

A complete roster of individuals who have had some part in shaping the ideas and framing the contents of this book would read like a roster of the Chicago Board of Trade. In the course of a long-standing business relationship with this organization, the world's largest commodity exchange, I have enjoyed the priceless opportunity of ready access to such market authorities as Robert L. Martin, Alfred H. Gruetzmacher, Bernard M. Carey, Joseph J. Kane, C. W. Schultz Jr., Warren W. Lebeck, and innumberable other floor traders, brokers and Exchange officials. Untold hours have been spent with these busy people, ferreting out information and answers which, in my considered opinion, reflect the best perspective and the highest degree of expertise on the subject to be found anywhere.

Additional assistance has also been freely given by people connected with commodity activities in several of the nation's outstanding brokerage firms. Indeed, it would have been impossible to complete this project without such help from those who conduct the mechanics of trade.

A special word of thanks is due to Roger W. Gray, distinguished Stanford professor and one of America's most knowledgable contemporary market authorities. Repeated exposures to his theoretical competence and practical understanding of market function added immeasurably to this final result.

The original manuscript was first read and criticized by William J. Mallers, himself a professional speculator and currently serving as a principal officer of the Board of Trade.

Having thus acknowledged the major sources of assistance, it must now be stated that there will surely be some greater or lesser disagreements with the contents of this volume. Unanimity is not to be found among traders; and the more expert they are, the more sharply defined are the gulfs which separate the individual opinions on mooted points. This should not be surprising, since the concept of a free market is necessarily based upon differences of opinion.

It has been my continuing objective to stay as close to *consensus* as possible, where consensus will strengthen the hand of the *public speculator*. Where persuasions differed too broadly to permit identification of any useful middle ground, *conservatism* has been the guideline. It's hard to imagine a situation in which caution can do the public speculator any lasting damage; and lack of caution can certainly destroy his speculative future.

Little space has been devoted in these pages to the huge winnings and equally monumental losses of the "big time operators". That fortunes are made and lost in the commodity market needs no underscoring, particularly when we see that total volume in this category of trade is approaching $100 billion per year. But our attention has been focused directly on the interests of the *novice* to the marketplace. Our objective is to keep *him* out of the clutch of disaster until he can acquire some experience and develop a settled trading technique. With sufficient capital resources to justify it, he will need no urging to undertake ever larger involvements in the business.

Neither this nor any book can guarantee success. Like a good road map, all it can do is show *directions,* point out major *obstacles* and draw attention to principal *points of interest.* The user is still going to have to keep his eyes open for hazards which may lurk around any turn.

Finally, whatever compliments this treatise elicits must be shared with a great many highly skilled and most gracious mentors. Its shortcomings must all be laid at the door of the author. Hopefully, this will prove to be another step along the road to better understanding and greater usefulness of the institutions which provide a dependable and increasingly efficient mechanism for collecting, standardizing and distributing the world's commodity wealth.

The repetitions which occur textually, it should be noted, are journalistically regrettable but editorially intentional. In the interest of making the volume optimally useful as a continuing reference source, each major section has been presented in as close to self-sufficient context as space and reader patience permits.

Thus, collateral points of demonstration, rules and key trading procedures are often set forth in more than one location. It is hoped that in so doing, the particular information sought will be findable with a minimum of reliance on cross-referencing and maximum economies of time to the reader.

L.D.B.

Wilmette, Illinois
August, 1967

INTRODUCTION

The title of this volume is "Commodity Speculation", but the subject is profit.

Protracted and inconclusive debate continues to surround the topic of speculation, as it has since time immemorial. There are otherwise astute individuals who claim to see no difference between speculation and gambling; damning both with equal vigor. It is to be hoped that some of these blind critics may find at least some small measure of enlightenment in the following pages. Speculation and gambling are two completely different kinds of activity. The distinction, moreover, doesn't depend on the *intention* of the participant so much as it does on the *classification of risk* involved in each.

The confusion doesn't end in trying to clarify *speculation* vs. *gambling.*

Distinguished members of the financial and economic community, including such an eminent personality as J. Paul Getty, the internationally celebrated billionaire, occasionally attempt to draw a clear line of distinction between *speculation* and *investment.* In so doing, they may reveal something of their own money-management inclinations; and often delude others—and perhaps even themselves—about the real nature of the activities concerned.

"Investment" as defined by economic purists involves the *placement of money in a property from which one intends to receive earnings.* "Speculation" is the acquisition of property without the hope of earnings in the form of dividends, interest, rent, etc,; but with hopes for profit pinned to an expectation of *price change.*

1

Introduction

The distinction is clear—and should be easily understood. It is often muddled, however, by the proponents of "investment", who credit investment with being more *noble* than speculation. Then they forge far beyond the ridiculous and unfounded moral distinction, in blanketly ascribing *investor interests* to virtually all buyers and sellers of common stocks. While true *investors* are present in substantial numbers among the stockholder class, there is another large, active and growing group of participants in the securities markets with influence—and holdings—far too large to be ignored. They are clearly stock *speculators,* by the definition set forth earlier.

A great deal of corporate equities listed on the major exchanges and sold over-the-counter are in "strong hands" including, but not limited to, the founding families of the companies involved, investment trusts, insurance companies, banks and the treasuries of the corporations that issued them in the first place. The balance of the shares outstanding in most securities classifications tend to change hands at an impressive velocity; and properly so.

A buyer of stock which is selling at thirty or forty times earnings must view his *earnings* of 3% or less as cheap "rent" for use of his money; unless he can see added returns coming from changes in price. Obviously, IBM, which at this writing is selling at $300 per share, and pays a $4.40 dividend on earnings of $10.00, has little "investment" attraction. Its buyers must be speculatively inclined, or they would buy higher return government bonds. Were it not for a speculative interest, many of the most popular securities wouldn't find buyers—or they would be exceedingly rare. Most profit-minded individuals would prefer insured savings accounts or alternative money-use opportunities which guarantee superior long-range "earnings" return.

In actuality, buyers of high price/earning ratio equities have both an investor and a speculator interest. They welcome the dividend (if any) and fervently hope for a price increase; price being the value measurement of their assets at any given time. Securities market participants who are interested in fixed-price investments obviously represent a small minority among investors of all classes—as evidenced by the meager public participation in ten- or twenty-year bonds, as compared with common stocks. In short, it is patent absurdity

2

to accept the view that buyer interest doesn't go beyond dividends or other promised *investment return*. To the extent that an "investor" hopes for price appreciaion (and who doesn't) he must stand identified, even in the definition of Mr. Getty, et al, as a "speculator".

Economic activity, however, rests on much firmer foundations than subtle definitions of terminology. The problems are real. The possessor of money resources faces a constant dilemma:

(1) Use his capital creatively and make it grow, or —

(2) Bury his capital in inactivity and watch it deteriorate in value.

History is replete with instances where inflation, devaluation, confiscation, and every intermediate kind of fiscal prodigality has sharply altered the value of money. Whether it be the pound sterling, franc, mark, dollar, lira, kopek, kronen, or peso, currency stands as only a relatively reliable long-term substitute for physical goods and services. Whatever its other virtues, that money deteriorates over time is too obvious to require documentation at this point. No one of voting age could be ignorant of the fact.

Local currency is theoretically convertible into the totality of things offered in the immediate economy. Hopefully, it is also acceptable in international commerce, at a fair rate of exchange, for an infinite variety of the world's tangible and intangible resources. Contemporary economics suggests that, since the supply of money and the supply of goods and services should maintain a measure of parity with each other (if monetary stability is to exist), ownership of corporate stock (which represents productive physical assets) should provide a useful hedge against inflationary pressures. Unfortunately, however, the axiom too often falls short of needs when put in practice, because the money/goods ratio is not constant.

The last decade in the United States has seen the purchasing power of the dollar impaired to the extent of some 18% by measurement standards generally accepted as valid. While some of the corporate stocks listed on the New York and American Exchanges have increased more than this, there are at least as many which have done infinitely worse. The individual investor is not privileged to buy 100 shares of Dow-Jones averages. His funds must be exchanged for selected corporate issues, from among the four or five thousand enter-

3

prises publicly owned. Whether the individual investor actually finds the protection against inflation he seeks depends directly on the caliber of judgment he brings to bear in choosing between literally thousands of uneasy alternatives.

In any case, even as the most orthodox "investor" comes to grips with the ever-present spectre of inflation and makes his decisions as to the most advantageous use for his free capital resources, he is *speculating* on the shape of things to come. His speculation concerns earnings, growth, inflation itself, and the relative attractiveness of the broad range of choices which beckon. Speculation, to repeat for emphasis, is inescapable.

Everything which has been said about investing in securities can be said with equal validity about entrepreneurship. The individual who has a million dollars to put to work may do so by purchasing shares in a going concern—or he may use his money to establish a new business. The course he chooses will likely be determined by his profit expectations from the capital being committed. Thousands of newly-established firms are victims of bankruptcy every year in the United States. Regardless of what occasions their demise, it can be said that each of them represents an unsuccessful speculation. The funds involved in these failures would have brought better results in other use situations.

However, speculation in new business enterprise is a vital and indispensable element in any dynamic business system. *Some* new business ventures succeed and become profitable. A *few* of them grow into impressive institutions. *Most* of them fail. Yet, without the speculative spirit in an economy, stagnation is the certain result. Doing business always involves the assumption of risks.

So, speculation is a word endlessly abused and misundertood. Regrettably, some of the greatest confusion is evidenced by people whose backgrounds and experience should enable them to reflect better insight into the matter. "Speculate" evolves from two Greek roots which mean literally to *foresee* and to *foretell* the future. There is another consideration also. Speculation concerns risks which exist in the nature of things. Unlike a "gamble", which is a risk situation contrived for purposes of entertainment or a hoped-for gain based on predicting the outcome, a speculation is coming to grips with a

4

natural hazard. In the words of an 18th century poet, it is "an open threat, held in the hand of God".

A house may burn; a person may die; a crop may be destroyed; prices may rise or fall; the value of money may increase or deteriorate. Each of these possibilities carries the seeds of disaster to those whose interests they affect. Some of these events may be assisted or precipitated by human action, but none of them is totally preventable by purely human means. As a consequence, the results of each of these events must be contemplated in the future plans of prudent individuals. Risk avoidance is a constant exercise for most of us.

In some situations, the institution of insurance offers a means of indemnification against the economic penalties imposed by the speculative hazard being considered. In other situations, the individual can only exercise caution and hope for the best. In still other risk situations, the possible outcome can be subjected to economic measurement; a dollar value can be assigned to the results of misfortune—should it occur—and the risk "exposure" passed on to someone else for a fixed monetary consideration—or for a flexible opportunity to profit. Such a "voluntary" *risk bearer* is accurately identified as a *professional speculator,* which brings us to the most useful definition of the personality being examined in these pages.

In the interest of a clear perspective, one further thought must be kept in mind in appraising professional risk bearing. It is the fact that everyone feels himself quite able to cope with all of the *good fortune* that might come his way. The risks offered to professional speculators are, at least in the minds of those who seek to pass them on, of such magnitude and likelihood that it is worthwhile to pay something—a *risk premium*—for escaping or lessening their impact. Consequently, the speculator must *always* choose between hazardous alternatives. There is only one way for him to upgrade his average safety factor: through selection of only the brighter opportunities; which are opportunities unseen or shunned by the *sellers* or *shifters* of risks—usually referred to as *hedgers.* If a situation promises profit, it would make no sense to hedge it—and surrender the profit. Therefore, the risk offerings made to professional speculators regularly entail clear-cut negative implications or, at best, are too problematical to permit reliable analysis by those who seek speculative protection.

Introduction

Speculation is invariably present in the *holding of property over time*. A speculator is one who assumes property *ownership risks over time* in the hope of realizing a profit from his accuracy in forecasting events to come. The function is real and valuable.

As implied earlier, an individual can meet the definition without being conscious of the fact that he is speculating. Thousands of farmers, for example, grow grain and hold their harvest in storage buildings, pending its sale and removal to a flour mill or a country elevator. Many, if not most of these producers would passively or actively resent being termed "speculators". They prefer being called "owners of grain". The fact still remains that the prices of farm products are constantly fluctuating; and each change in the market price of wheat alters the value of wheat stocks held on farms and elsewhere. The farmer who holds his wheat is certain to benefit or suffer—from higher prices or lower prices in the market—when the time arrives at which he elects to sell it.

From this brief statement, it should be apparent that every independent farmer must be a speculator. He has no choice! He must speculate to prepare a field, plant a crop and hold a product inventory for sale or use. Unless temperature and moisture relationships are benign, his labor and seed are wasted; his speculation that a crop could be raised in a given growing season may be unsuccessful. Conversely, nature may cooperate and help him produce a bumper yield; in which event his basic speculative risk has paid off.

With the crop raised, the producer is now interested in selling it and realizing cash-in-hand payment for his time, effort, investment, and risk in bringing it to harvest. Whoever elects to buy a large inventory of relatively perishable merchandise—especially during a period of great seasonal over-supply—has placed himself in a position of considerable risk. Obviously, he will not "buy the risk" unless he feels that demand for the product will, over a period of time, take it off his hands at a profit. Moreover, he must be confident that he can protect the merchandise from physical deterioration and other loss for the period he owns it.

The greatest area of speculative risk, and one to which no easy answer exists, is in the matter of price itself. If supplies prove to be excessive or if demand fails to come up to expectations, the owner

6

of a given commodity may do an optimum job with his maintenance and protection tasks and still suffer great loss through inventory devaluation. The price hazard is inherent in ownership and cannot be removed. Risk in changing values is the eternal concomitant of property ownership over a period of time.

To a greater or lesser extent, everyone who owns anything which is for sale—or could at any point in the future be offered for sale—is likewise speculating on future events. Some risks are "hidden", while others are clear—and are undertaken with full knowledge of the hazards present; but with the hope that the feared reversal will not occur and that a "risk margin" can be earned based on accurate analysis and sagacity in predicting future events.

It has been said that people only buy life insurance because they know they must die. The speculation always present is in whether each of us will die sooner, or later. Insurance companies undertake contracts which indemnify the heirs and estates of the deceased. In so doing, insurance companies stand preeminent among speculative institutions. Their "risk margin" is statistically determined from actuarial tables which reflect the years of life remaining on the *average* to people of good health at various ages (and policy-cancellation experience prior to death). So long as the mortality averages are maintained, the insurance underwriters make an average profit. Should widespread epidemics or proliferation of accidents occur to invalidate the acturial tables, the insurance companies concerned must lose money. If the opposite happens—an increase in average life span—the insurance companies' speculation will prove to be commensurately more profitable, for obvious reasons.

Two thoughts should be kept constantly in mind in evaluating both the methods and the morality of speculation. First, the speculative risk is ever-present; it cannot be avoided; it can often be evaluated; it can, in certain situations, be economically *shifted* from one risk bearer to another. Second, the objective of professional speculation is that of seeking profit. There is—there can be—no other economic justification for voluntary speculation.

Profit-seeking, whether through investment, entrepreneurship or speculation, is a thoroughly acceptable—even laudable—activity in an economic society; so long as the general tenets of legality, honesty, ethical responsibility and fair play are observed. To question the social propriety or economic rectitude of speculation in commodities is as absurd as an argument against the production of them. The latter inescapably gives rise to the former. Production and ownership both involve speculation, usually conducted by specialists in the given area of risk. Producers and subsequent owners of commodities presumably understand their hazards and weigh them against the opportunities for profit. From such an appraisal, each accepts or rejects a given proposition.

Economic quarrels which center on moral considerations can always be expected to contribute more heat than light to the topic being examined. This, since economics is not a moral field; it is functional—like mechanics.

Speculation deserves to be understood, but needs no special pleading. It exists as an ever-present element of human existence. If formalized speculation, as practiced on stock and commodity exchanges and in the money markets, did not exist, it would have to be invented for the valuable contribution it makes to the continuity and stability of a broad range of financial and productive activities. Future events lose a great deal of their terror when "discounted" by professionals who have the courage, the information, and the financial wherewithal to assume the risks of the unknown and "protect" those who are unwilling or unable to speculate on possibilities of events they fear.

Professional speculation must be viewed as the greatest single moderating influence available for apprehension and extremes of viewpoint. It brings a leveling influence between the present known situation and the future unknown possibility. It softens the blow of disaster when and if it does strike. It strikes a balance between the *best* that can be reasonably hoped for and the *worst* that can possibly happen, and reflects the composite result in price level.

Speculation brings a tempering influence into the marketplace. It is an activity which demands a cool head, a clear eye and adequate financial resources to underpin a fundamental equanimity. Without these things, a speculator will not succeed in gaining the profits he seeks. Without profits he will soon be rendered incapable of further speculation because he will lose out to more capable operators in the field.

8

The speculator who does succeed can expect excellent rewards. His prowess will be documented by financial gains which, in turn, permit him to take an ever larger role in the business activity of his choice.

In summation, to the extent that a speculator knowingly assumes hazards that he could avoid, he shows himself to be a person of courage, financial ability and possessing a commendable confidence in his own powers of evaluation. Add also, a large measure of faith in the future. To the extent that he succeeds, he stands as living proof that the "worst"—which is always expected by some—rarely if ever turns out quite that bad.

Were this not true, negative possibilities would be replaced by black certainties—and professional speculators, by professional crepe-hangers.

Plate 2

Courtesy, Chicago Board of Trade

The world's largest commodity exchange.

CHAPTER I

EVOLUTION OF TRADE

Before delving into the operational complexities of commodity trading, a brief review of trade evolution should be helpful in terms of overall perspective.

It is certain that man has been a trader since his earliest appearance on earth. Individual existence must have always depended on some measure of mutual cooperation, however rudimentary. It still does. Trade is the most basic and at the same time, the most vital communal activity imaginable.

Authorities seem agreed that earliest exchange of goods between individuals was probably accomplished by simple expropriation or theft. In the pre-historic jungle, devoid as it was of social amenities, the simplest, most expedient method of obtaining either a stone axe or a Stone Age bride was to steal the item in question. Since "survival of the fittest" means survival of the strongest or the wiliest, it also seems logical to suppose that where mere theft would not suffice to accomplish the transference of property, violence was a natural adjunct. Where it became necessary to crack the owner over the head before taking his possessions, our early ancestors probably had little hesitancy in adopting such strong-arm tactics.

Evolution of Trade

As the social climate in the Neanderthal jungle became somewhat better ordered, relationships between individuals and tribes improved. Alliances were formed between family groups which carried the three-fold benefit of strengthening their collective efforts in hunting food, better protecting themselves, and improving their harsh conditions of existence. As mutuality of endeavor developed, so did the social relationship we know as friendship. Gift giving came into being to serve the distributive requirement between friends; just as theft persisted as the transfer device between enemies.

Direct Exchange

Barter or direct exchange gradually evolved as a useful means of "impersonal" commerce between those who were neither close friends nor active antagonists. From earliest recorded history until about the twelfth century, barter remained as the essential method of commerce over most of the world. While it is true that much of the trading involved foodstuffs in exchange for gold or silver, the precious metals involved represented intrinsic rather than monetary values. The use of coins of designated values in buying and selling seems to have originated in the Orient or the Middle East, somewhere around 800 to 700 B.C. However, it remained for the Ceasars to "internationalize" coinage by spreading it throughout the continent of Europe.

Money Appears

The Roman legions carried money which bore Ceasar's likeness and, in the best tradition of invading conquerors, they forced the acceptance of Roman coins upon their reluctant victims. As time went by, however, it was learned that Roman specie could be trusted as reliable medium of exchange. The coins themselves were struck from gold and were, therefore, not as susceptible to counterfeiting as other local money devices. While the Roman soldiers initially forced the introduction of their currency in trade, they hastened its popular adoption by also accepting it back as a measurement of stable values. Use of Roman coinage grew apace and, as it did, the basic tool of modern commerce stood identified.

Money thus became an acceptable substitute for goods and services. It functioned as payment for a limitless range of both tangibles and intangibles, as well as providing a versatile measurement of values which had never existed within the more restrictive system of barter. It made it both easier and simpler to conduct trade.

Spot Markets

The earliest form of money/goods transaction involved what we recognize as a "spot" sale. The seller presented his goods to the buyer, a price was negotiated, and the exchange of money for the merchandise took place "on the spot". Both payment and physical transfer were immediate. A great deal of trade is still accomplished in this same fashion. Farmer's Markets and other "cash and carry" enterprises are spot markets in the truest sense of the word.

Efficient as spot markets were, compared to earlier trading methods, problems still existed which clamored for solution. Supply and demand imbalance in the spot situation was a major inconvenience then, as it is even now.

Whether the spot merchant is dealing in field-fresh strawberries or used automobiles, his constant challenge is to match market demands with equivalent supplies. Should he over-estimate the demand for his goods, it goes without saying, he will have excess unsold inventory on hand at the end of the market period. This is especially a problem when it concerns perishables. However, all products are at least theoretically perishable, since owning, protecting and maintaining inventory entails costs; to whatever extent applicable. Every inventory, whether it "spoils" or not, suffers somewhat from devaluation as it "ages" on the shelf.

The spot marketer also stands to lose if he under-estimates market demands. In this case he will offer his wares at a lower price than that which his customers would be willing to pay, with the result that his profits are needlessly reduced. The ideal situation, of course, (from the standpoint of seller profits) is to offer the precise amount of merchandise which the market will buy, at price levels which will generate the largest available net profit. Few spot marketers have either the ability—or the opportunity—to assess buyer response with sufficient accuracy as to make pinpointing such a return possible.

The situation ordinarily is one in which demand exceeds supply and the seller realizes less than he should from his inventory, or supply exceeds demand and the seller loses through inventory depreciation, spoilage or otherwise.

Trade Fairs

The hazards of spot marketing are likely to be less in a large market than in the small, remote one. This was as true in Renaissance Europe as it is in contemporary America. The fact played a vital part in what must be viewed as the most important commercial innovation of the 11th and 12th centuries: It was known as the Trade Fair. At more or less regular intervals, itinerant merchants would congregate in designated locations to display their wares and conduct business with the populace.

Pursuing a marketing program of this kind called for transporting a great deal of valuable merchandise long distances over rough and dangerous terrain. Bandits made a lucrative specialty of waylaying these merchant travelers, stealing their possessions and murdering them if the situation seemed to suggest it. Even if the bands of marauders were successfully avoided, ruling princes and territorial chieftans charged the merchants exorbitant fees for permission to travel through the country and conduct their trade. It is from this practice that the term "robber baron" first came into being.

In spite of the handicaps, however, the merchants prospered and so did their customers. Spices, fabrics, jewels, unguents, and a broad array of hard-goods were made available in the hinterlands only through the existence of the institution known as Trade Fairs. One of the largest of the fairs took place periodically, from the 12th century on, in the Champagne District of France. It should be noted that the Champagne Fair attracted hundreds of merchants, thousands of customers, and transacted an impressive volume of business, even by modern standards.

The more enlightened rulers finally came to recognize that commercial activity deserved to be encouraged rather than opposed through harrassment, excessive taxation, or both. Therefore, it developed that some of the medieval rulers actively undertook to attract Trade Fairs into their principalities. Merchants were issued valuable "Letters of Franchise" which authorized the holder to transact business and guaranteed the safety of his person and possessions "Under the King's Writ".

No longer fair game for looters and murderers, encouraged by the reigning personage and met by eager buyers, the itinerant merchants became more numerous and the volume of business they transacted grew apace. It was in this stage of development that a time dimension was first introduced into buying and selling. Precious metals and jewels were important elements of trade on the part of the Fair merchants. Transporting such valuable, highly saleable merchandise entailed risks that most owners preferred to avoid. As a result, a practice grew up whereby the only such goods actually presented at the Fair were samples. Buyers made their selection from the samples, then placed and paid for their orders. In return, the buyer received a "Fair Letter", which was actually a delivery order drawn against the merchant's warehouse and which entitled the holder to exchange the document for the designated quantity and quality of merchandise. The Fair Letter was, in fact, an early version of the item known in contemporary commerce as a "Bill of Exchange".

Once business could be conducted on the basis of deferred performance, it must be granted that a high order of trust had already entered the marketplace. It was said of many such early merchants that their "word was a good as the gold".

Concern for the morality of the marketplace also asserted itself in this period. Whereas "caveat emptor"—buyer beware—had been the rule in earlier times, merchants now organized among themselves and laid down broad rules of fair dealing which were calculated to prevent the unprincipled cheating of unsuspecting customers. Merchants who violated the rules of trade were summarily tried before the Merchants' Court and, if found guilty, were heavily punished. In some instances, the judgment went so far as to forever forbid the crooked merchant from doing business at future Fairs. Such a banishment amounted to depriving an individual of his means of making a livelihood. But harshness paid dividends and accomplished two major results: a vastly improved ethical atmosphere in commerce, and a previously unheard of measure of confidence among public customers. Then, as now, without mutual trust between buyer and seller, trade could hardly be conducted at all.

Evolution of Credit

A "sellers' market" is one in which *demands exceed supply* and the possessor of goods held for sale is clearly in the position of authority. It is only in quite recent times that some nations have developed productive capacities to equal or at times exceed their national demand. As a consequence, sellers' markets through history have, more often than not, prevailed.

The institution of credit is obviously an invention of the sellers rather than buyers. So long as a merchant can dispose of his inventory on a cash basis, this is certainly the way he would prefer doing it. However, conditions prevail, for greater or lesser periods of time, in which there is more goods offered for immediate sale than there is immediate market demand and immediate ability to pay for it. It is in situations of this sort that credit performs its most important function—and always has.

To use grain for purposes of demonstration once more, the prime owner of this foodstuff at the conclusion of harvest is the farmer himself. His supplies vastly exceed his own requirements and, in sum total, aggregate supplies may actually exceed a year's consumption requirements within the region where it is produced. The producers or "first owners" of commodities must have learned a long time ago that there were two alternatives available by which to dispose of excess crops: the first being to accept exceedingly low prices—or no prices; the second, to sell them under payment and/or delivery terms which permit users to anticipate future needs and buy or "contract" for larger than normal quantities, in advance of immediate requirements. Extension of credit makes deferred performance part of a transaction (and functions as a quasi-alternative to seller-storage).

Credit had become an important element of continental commerce by the early 1500's. A French writer commenting on social decadence during that period remarked that "the populace staggers tenuously between its current needs and its current indebtedness; present abilities are limited by old commitments, still undischarged. Present earnings are insufficient to meet accrued obligations and—day by day—keep body and soul together. Universal ruin is inescapable." Credit excesses, it appears, are no modern-day development. But, even though often subject to abuse, credit is indispensible in trade.

Earlier societies engaged in all manner of activities calculated to improve consumer credit risks. Defaulting debtors were, in ancient Oriental societies, tortured or executed. By medieval times, the penalty for failing to meet just obligations had been generally reduced to public whippings, a period on public display in pillory, or a term in debtors' prison, until the debt was paid off by the prisoner or his sympathetic relatives. It remained for the United States to constitutionally forbid imprisonment for mere inability to pay one's debts.

In addition to the familiar kind of "consumer credit" extended by a seller to his buyer, there is another form which amounts to "supplier credit", extended to the seller on the part of the buyer. In this situation, the purchaser of a given commodity commits himself to accept delivery of a specified amount of merchandise, at an established price, at some point in the future. Examples of this are to be found in examining trading practices in the jewelery trade during the 15th and 16th centuries. Fabricators of jewelry during that era were major artists, and the principal "consumers" of precious metals and gems.

The flow of gold followed a somewhat direct channel from the mine, through the smelter, to the manufacturing jeweler. It was not unusual for such a fabricator of rings and brooches to set up a firm arrangement with his supply source for delivery of a designated amount of precious metal at specified intervals of time. It was customary for the raw-material supplier to require prepayment of a portion of the total cost of the commitment as a "binder" on the deal. The practice is still encountered in contemporary business.

Cash-Forward Contracts

A flour miller, for example, may contract for a specified amount of wheat to be delivered during the first ten days of each month of the year. The contract price may be one firm price, or it may be flexible, depending on other considerations; particularly "going prices" in the cash market at the time each unit delivery of the total contract is made. A purchase arrangement of this kind in the grain market is called a "to-arrive" or "cash-forward" contract. The term denotes that it is "cash" or physical grain, which has been purchased, and its delivery is scheduled "forward" or at a later date. The arrangement involves *credit* extension *to the seller:* he has been given "time" in which to meet his delivery obligation.

Deferring performance often serves both the interests of the seller and the buyer. In the first instance, the seller is assured of a total volume of business, as represented in the aggregate order. By scheduling delivery segments at intervals, the seller is able to also schedule purchases, thereby saving the investment costs and inconvenience of owning and storing the commodity in his own facilities over the full period of time covered in the contract.

From the buyer's standpoint, the benefits are equally real. Assume his milling capacity to be 1,000,000 bushels of wheat per month. By scheduling arrival of this quantity of wheat at thirty-day intervals, he can be sure of uninterrupted production without ever needing to hold much more than this amount of grain in store. A cash-forward, or deferred delivery commitment involves bilateral obligations — credit — between seller and buyer. The seller *owes* wheat and delivery; the buyer *owes* delivery acceptance and money. Default on the part of either will seriously penalize the other. Unless the miller can depend on his constant supply of grain, his production schedule cannot be maintained. Interruptions can be very costly. By the same token, unless the supplier can be assured of his buyer's dependability in accepting each delivery and paying for it, he may be placed in the position of owning substantial amounts of grain for which he has no other buyers.

It was precisely this kind of consideration which led to the development of futures markets, the largest of which came into being in Chicago during the first half of the 19th century.

Development of the Chicago Grain Market

Authorities are unable to agree on the year in which grain was first traded on a deferred arrival basis in the city of Chicago. The practice, however, was well established as early as 1840. The mechanics of trade were really quite simple. A farmer would harvest his crop, load it on wagons or a river barge enroute to the midwest's grain capital. This done, the farmer would take the fastest transportation available, in order to arrive in Chicago well ahead of his shipment.

Grain brokers, merchants and processors congregated in Haine's Feed Store on the bank of the Chicago River. Here, for several hours each day, they negotiated with producers for grain stocks which flour milling and other activities required. The farmer with a harvest "on the way" offered his grain for sale "to-arrive" a few days or a few weeks later.

When the transaction was made, it involved a firm price. However, it was entirely possible that in the period pending arrival of the shipment, market prices could increase greatly, in which case it would be to the financial advantage of the seller to default on his end of the previous contract and sell the grain to someone else —at the higher price; or, the reverse could occur. Prices might fall to a level where the buyer no longer wanted to accept the expensive grain; preferring to default and obtain his needs at the now more attractive price level. Both buyers and sellers sought protection against default on the part of their opposite numbers.

Margin Deposits to Bind Performance

It was this consideration which gave rise to the practice of posting "margin" on grain trades. With a transaction completed, buyer and seller each deposited a mutually acceptable amount of cash with a disinterested third party. In the event of default on the part of either, the margin deposit was paid over to the other, to reimburse him for the inconvenience and direct financial loss occasioned by the other party's non-performance.

Margin deposit was never viewed as a down payment; it stood, rather, as a performance bond, binding the seller to deliver the specified merchandise — and binding the buyer to acceptance of the delivery and payment in full. Margin is no longer held by disinterested third parties, and is no longer negotiable between buyers and sellers on organized grain Exchanges. However, margin still constitutes an essential element in futures trading and affords the same stability in transactions presently as it did more than a hundred years ago.

Speculation Appears

Trading in "to arrives" entailed no immediate need for storage, since some of the deferred shipments were not scheduled for arrival for thirty, sixty, or ninety days. Still, a substantial risk was present, growing out of the possibilities of price change. Grain processors were primarily interested in obtaining their raw materials at stable prices, which would enable them to turn out their finished products uninterruptedly and at competitive price levels. A flour miller who bought wheat at $1.00 per bushel and saw the price go to $1.25 per bushel before the commodity reached his hands had made an impressive speculative profit. However, the opposite could also occur, resulting in a monumental loss. The risks from price fluctuation, however, were inescapable. The hazard had to be borne by the owner of grain — or passed on to someone who was willing to "speculate" on price, in the hope of making a profit from his "position".

Professional grain speculation thus grew out of the situation which naturally existed in a market which was vastly over-supplied with product during the post-harvest season and was, more often than not, confronted by real or relative scarcity throughout much of the balance of the year.

Early speculation took two forms. The "long" speculators would buy to-arrive offerings of the farmers, hoping that in the interim, between their purchases and the arrival of the physical merchandise, prices would increase and offer them an opportunity to sell out at a profit. Other speculators sold to-arrive grain "short", for thirty, sixty, or ninety day delivery, in the hope that during the interval, prices would fall, enabling them to obtain the cash grain required for their delivery commitment at a lesser price than their selling price. If this happened, they stood to make a profit.

Neither the "long" nor the "short" speculators claimed ownership of physical grain at the time they bought or sold it. They, and the grain trade generally, understood that in speculating, these individuals were merely *assuming the risks of price fluctuation* over a specified period of time — in the hope of profiting from subsequent price changes. Grain speculators were a welcome and most important element in grain trading, since the price risks present fifty or one hundred years ago were staggering, in terms of current grain price behavior.

Feast and Famine

Wheat at harvest time often sold as low as 15¢ per bushel. Barge loads of wheat and corn clogged the Chicago River, waiting for buyers at almost any price. Exposure to weather resulted in extensive damage to the merchandise. It was not unusual in peak harvest years for millions of bushels of grain to spoil at dockside and later be towed into Lake Michigan and dumped. Terminal storage facilities in those early days were woefully inadequate to needs, and transportation methods were unequal to the task of spreading the crop throughout the major markets and getting it all under cover against winter weather.

Spring and summer often presented an almost opposite situation. Wheat which sold in October for 15¢ per bushel might, in July, bring ten or twenty times that much; and with little to be found. Buyers, sellers, and consumers were *all* penalized by the gross inefficiencies of pricing, storage and distribution. Price fluctuations were fierce, but even the highest prices cannot recreate grain which has been lost or wasted six months before. It was truly a "feast or famine" as the Chicago grain market struggled valiantly to even out supply and demand and meet the ever larger food demands of a burgeoning national population.

It was against this background of alternating shortage and oversupply, high prices and low prices, that grain speculation came into being in the United States. One effect of speculation has been to reasonably ration available supplies and put a premium on storage of surplus during times of plenty. Speculation is not an economic contrivance. It is a practical outgrowth of risks inherent in highly unpredictable businesses. It has brought a leveling influence into the marketplace and has stood as perhaps the most effective counter-measure for the excesses which otherwise always develop in the face of unuseable surplus or inadequate supplies.

21

Speculation is often explained as a form of future "price insurance". The parallel is not well drawn, even though it has some usefulness in making the activity more understandable to newcomers to the field. The institution of speculation is a practice in evaluating risks and "discounting" present facts into future possibilities. Changing price level is a consideration which invites speculative evaluation — and seeks speculative protection. Futures markets accomplish both.

Professional speculation is a somewhat recent innovation, inasmuch as it is considered to have originated in Japan only a few hundred years ago. It has been raised to its highest level in the United States. It is at least noteworthy that the same nation which reflects the majority of all speculation conducted in the world also enjoys the highest standard of living the world has ever seen. It may be too much to infer that one thing grows directly out of the other. Still, there is every reason to think that speculation makes a far more significant contribution to both productive and distributive efficiencies than even its strongest supporters suspect.

CHAPTER II

THE BUSINESS OF
SPECULATIVE RISK BEARING

Life for everyone is a series of exposures to various orders of risk, chief among which is the matter of survival itself. Success or failure in meeting the problems of existence depends mainly on how well an individual and a society are able to forecast the future and make prudent plans for capitalizing on opportunities and tempering or escaping the impacts of various threats. Fortunately, the human race seems to be somewhat equally divided between optimists and pessimists or, to use the terminology of the marketplace, "bulls" and "bears". Thus, public opinion concerning the future always represents a composite of positive and negative attitudes.

Among the essential considerations in preparing to cope with the future is the matter of insuring an adequate supply of the things required to sustain and protect life. These may be, for purposes of simplification, covered in the all-inclusive term of *vital commodities*. Foodstuffs properly head the list in order of importance, since all must eat or die. Following closely, however, are a long list of things man cannot eat, but which he requires in order to fabricate tools, construct housing, produce clothing, and maintain a system of commerce. As a result, vital commodities denote such things as grain, meat, and fiber. Commodities also include metals, ranging from aluminum to zinc; including gold and silver, since they are the stuff upon which international monetary systems are very largely based.

Economy of Scarcity

All commodities usually share a common economic condition: relative scarcity. It is their scarcity which renders them valuable. Supplies, it seems are rarely if ever adequate to fill all existing demands, even though distinct over-supply of a usually scarce commodity may occasionally exist for a relatively short period of time. The most recent examples of this have been seen in the United States, where agricultural production for the past decade has tended to outstrip domestic demand, and has prompted the accumulation of government stockpiles to handle surplus, along with acreage restrictions calculated to suppress excessive output.

Scarcity is Usually Regional

Even in the face of such surpluses as have existed in the United States in recent years, however, a large portion of the earth's population has existed with malnutrition as a constant companion. Thus it must be said that the situation of over-supply existed only regionally (in the North American continent) and only existed by reason of the fact that *distribution methods* and *ability to buy* were insufficient to accomplish the economic leveling-out process.

Like individuals, few nations of the world have an *ability to buy* equal to their *propensity to consume*. Moreover, transport methods are not universally available to efficiently accomplish the task of physical distribution. If these two considerations were met, instead of approximately one-third of the earth's population existing on the bleak edge of real hunger, *all* would theoretically subsist in a condition of mere undernourishment. This, because world food supplies are not now, and probably never have been, fully adequate to meet *all* of the nutritional needs of all of the people, everywhere.

Assigning responsibility for this apparent impasse is basically simple. Virtually all foodstuffs are raised under some seasonal limitations. While wheat, the most widely grown cereal crop on earth, is being harvested somewhere on the face of the globe every month of the year, the wheat harvest in North America takes place mainly during July and August. It is harvested in Australia during November and December. Each regional harvest takes place in the span of a few weeks, while consumption of the crop is necessarily spread over twelve months. There is a period of time immediately following harvest when available local food supplies vastly exceed any current need for them, even in such chronic food short localities as India's interior. Whether food stuffs are available during periods between harvests depends on several factors, not the least of which is the ability and willingness of individuals to invest in, store, and protect excess supplies in anticipation of needs in periods of relative shortage, between crops.

Man has been described as a "planning animal". The compliment, to some limited extent, is deserved. In certain areas, however, human planning performance is less than impressive. Prodigality in a time of plenty is a common human failing. Some of the world's major catastrophes have been confidently predicted and could have been largely avoided, or their impact vastly reduced by countermeasures. Yet, precautionary steps are not always taken in the face of impending crisis, and the lapses stand as black marks against individuals, nations and the world as a whole.

Faced with a present problem, reason often succumbs to unreasoning fear and a situation which, appraised intelligently and with some deliberation could be solved, is multiplied by fright into totally unmanageable proportions.

Pessimists vs. Optimists

It is in a situation of this kind that the dyed-in-the-wool pessimist seriously contemplates and loudly forecasts "the end of the world". Optimistic voices may occasionally be heard, but the criers-of-doom usually occupy center-stage until overwhelming evidence appears to rebut their prediction of the worst.

In the area of food supplies, the pessimist operates on both ends

25

of the topic. During periods of over-supply, he insists that available commodities will never be consumed, hence, are relatively worthless. If his counsel is accepted, the result is seen in low prices, food waste, and the profligate utilization of high quality commodities in low priority activities; for example, the feeding of wheat to farm animals when the total supply is actually inadequate for all human needs.

In the opposite frame of reference, when serious scarcities do exist in food supplies, the pessimist compounds the problem with his opinion that starvation is inescapable. As such a position gains adherents, the actual shortage which exists can only be worsened, since the spectre of hunger is the stoutest possible argument in favor of food hoarding; and hoarding has probably starved as many as famine has. The best prescription in either situation is a measure of equanimity and a more balanced perspective.

Experience should remind us that future events will probably not equal the worst that can be feared nor the best that can be hoped for. Something between these two extremes usually represents a manageable situation which may require effort and sagacity to cope with, but given some industrious and intelligent attention, will likely prove to be somehow surmountable.

The counter-balancing influence for the pessimist is, of course, the optimist. His vision of things to come accentuates the positive factors and discounts some or all of the negative considerations. The optimist never seems to lose his abiding faith that, in the words of Mr. Micawber, "something will turn up." His unsinkable confidence at times eclipses good judgment, since he errs in one direction as much as the pessimist errs in the other.

These are the thrusts which comprise the essential inputs in any free market. The opposing economic camps wage a constant struggle to make their divergent viewpoints prevail. One may gain clear ascendancy over the other for a period of time but, if so, the tide is usually not long in turning. More often than not, "market psychology" is a quite closely balanced composite of bearish and bullish attitudes. "Bears" live with an ever-present feeling that prices are too high and will fall. They are always more-or-less ready sellers. The "bulls" invariably feel that prices are too low and will rise. They are usually ready buyers.

Cash/Futures Prices

The interplay between these forces which represent the "attitudes" of supply and demand, strike an equilibrium which the market translates as a price/value level for the given moment — and, through institution of future trading, projects for days, weeks and months to come. The "nearest" price is, of course, the "cash" price. The cash price may be taken as reflecting *things as they are* since, assuming a *free* and *informed* market, it is the one price above which the marginal buyer would not buy, and below which the marginal seller would not sell. We can largely ignore time dimension in a "cash" price.

The futures price must be viewed in a somewhat different light, since it represents a moving, progressive refinement in values over the life of the contract involved. It must be remembered that although a futures contract in commodities calls for ultimate delivery of merchandise, or offset, "delivery day" may be days, weeks or months away. So long as time still remains in which to resolve issues which bear on the matter of price, market attitudes will continue to change and futures prices will change also.

Once cash price is determined, and money and physical commodity change hands, reselling the "cash" is certain to involve some measure of inconvenience: elevation, loading, grading, etc.

In future markets, conversely, although each transaction is firm and conditions of the transaction are irrevocable within the requirements of the contract involved, buying and selling entails no physical handling. A speculator need never hold a pound of the cash item. There is a further difference between a cash transaction and a trade in futures. The buyer of a physical commodity invariably undertakes certain costs of storage, insurance, etc., along with possession of the inventory. There are attendant costs in connection with the buying or selling of cash merchandise which cannot be escaped or ignored.

This is not true in a futures contract, since the physical commodity is not involved, and will not be until delivery date. Costs which relate to storage and protection of the product are only theoretically involved in the futures pricing consideration. As will be seen later, the supply/demand situation will govern the amount of carrying charges, if any, in the price of the merchandise represented in the contract.

Where do Prices Come From?

Every student of commodity marketing quickly comes to grips with the question of price "leadership" in the marketplace. There are those who believe that cash prices enjoy ascendency over futures prices, in terms of establishing composite values. Their argument ordinarily is based on a contention that cash prices are the only "real" prices, inasmuch as they relate to "real merchandise". In pursuing this thesis, devotees of cash price leadership insist the market deals first with the present, and then projects future values — in the form of futures prices — based on expectations of improvement or deterioration from the present state of things. Reasonable as such a case might appear on the surface, it falls under close examination.

To begin with, futures prices *precede* cash prices by a considerable period of time. Trading in wheat futures for delivery in May, 1967 began in May, 1966. The price at which trading in this contract commenced represented the market's composite judgment of the available supplies likely to be on hand a year later, as compared with projected demand on the delivery date. Development of this "price" idea had to take into consideration such things as harvest expectations, projected usage, possible export requirements, and a host of lesser factors. As each day in the life of such a contract passes, new information comes to light which bears on all of these things. Each new bit of information refines and sharpens the traders' individual opinions — which all make up the market's perspective about the price of wheat in May. The price constantly fluctuates — it rises in response to larger than average consumption indications, or smaller than expected production. It falls in response to opposite influences. But, by the time delivery day on the contract arrives, the price of May wheat futures and cash wheat of contract grade will usually stand at practically the *same level;* since they are now interchangeable.

In view of the greater period of time over which futures prices are being examined and adjusted by commercial interests, speculators, and traders of all sorts, their ultimate consensus — as represented in the maturity price — must logically be viewed as more carefully developed; hence more substantive than the cash price. There is an additional and most important factor: the volume of trading in a given cash commodity represents but a small fraction of the trading volume in the same commodity's futures contracts. Since trading volume must reasonably be viewed as a direct reflection of supply/demand forces, there is little choice but to accept the futures prices as being a more reliable measurement of price equilibrium than cash trading activity; if for no other reason than that futures volume is so very much *larger*.

There is still a further point in support of the case that futures prices take the lead in determining cash prices, rather than vice-versa. Unexpected dislocations in supply and demand can and do bring sharp, short-duration price swings in the cash market. Immediate shortage of wheat must be immediately faced by the flour miller, since his survival as a processor depends on obtaining raw materials. Paying an exorbitantly high price for cash wheat over a short period of time is infinitely preferable to interruption of his production schedule. Part of the inflated wheat price can perhaps be passed on to end product users, but even if the miller is forced to absorb all of these added costs, he would still rather do so than close down his mill. In short, commercial processors must maintain some reasonable continuity of operation. In order to do this, they have no choice except to do business in the market; and at whatever price levels the market reflects.

The reverse is equally true when supplies vastly outstrip demand. At harvest time, for example, sellers of the cash commodity may be confronted by distressingly low prices, and for reasons which are perfectly obvious. Supply and demand balance out over time, but cash prices involve no time dimension; hence, offer no opportunity for the immediate situation to be "tempered" and "discounted" in the light of the mitigating probabilities. The individual who must sell "cash" today must accept "today's" cash bid, whatever it is.

The fluctuations which occur in futures prices may also be dramatic in both extent and suddenness. They are, for the most part, however, predicated on fundamental alterations of market conditions. A shipping strike which halts the flow of foodstuffs could be expected to exert a profound influence on cash prices in affected localities. The same strike would have a far lesser influence, if any at all, on the prices of a futures contract several months away from maturity.

All of the evidence, taken at face value, offers an eloquent argument that futures prices are usually in a position of relative leadership over cash prices.

Futures prices are refined and adjusted over a longer period of time and represent broader supply/demand forces than do cash prices. Except for technical market aberrations which will be dealt with in another place, futures prices are more deliberately determined and, therefore, deserve to be considered as more "rationally" determined. Clearly, they are less influenced by short-term problems of over- or under-supply than are prices for cash commodities.

Both "Cash" and "Futures" are Real

Finally, the contention of some that cash prices should enjoy preeminence in total pricing function because they refer to actual commodities, is specious at best. Both cash prices and futures prices relate to actual commodities; the only difference being that in one instance the merchandise is for immediate delivery and, in the other, delivery may be scheduled a year — or more — after transaction. The fact that a futures trade may be offset by an equal and opposite transaction at any time prior to maturity does not alter the situation, either, except to importantly mitigate the effect of market apprehension which can grow out of supply/demand dislocation in short-term situations.

The commodities speculator will quickly learn that the relationships between cash and futures prices offer an important indication of near-term supply/demand balance. This aspect must be given careful consideration in any trading decision, but the trader should never forget that cash prices are far more susceptible to short-term influences than are futures prices. If a choice must be made between the two as concerns market condition and directional trend, futures prices are almost invariably the ones to be trusted.

This brings us to the kernel of our topic:

A speculator in commodities is a dealer in *pricing risks*. He will hardly ever be a receiver of, or a deliverer of, the physical commodity. His concern with the facts which surround the cash product in the market is related to the continuing exercise in price forecasting, rather than any direct involvement with, or in, the "cash" commodity or the cash market.

The successful futures speculator will be a close observer of changing balances between supply and demand in "actuals", because this is part of the total equation which will determine prices at a later date. In the same manner, a speculator must also keep his appraisal up-to-date with regard to "market psychology". If the "bulls" have recently taken heavy losses in the form of a substantial price drop, they may be somewhat slow in coming back for another try — at least until the opportunity looks most inviting. In the meantime, the "bears" may have it all their way. Or vice-versa.

The speculator will keep a current notion about the level of export activity, weather patterns, transportation tie-ups which may be pending, interest rates and government farm policy practices and attitudes. Not all of these things will merit *equal weight* in making market judgments, but they all deserve *some weight*.

Speculative profits must be viewed as a "risk premium" which the trader *earns* for undertaking the hazards of property ownership for a period of time. Such profits are only earned on the basis of right judgments, and losses are the opposite side of profit.

Not only does it "*pay* to be right" — it *costs* to be wrong — in any business decision! And speculation is a business.

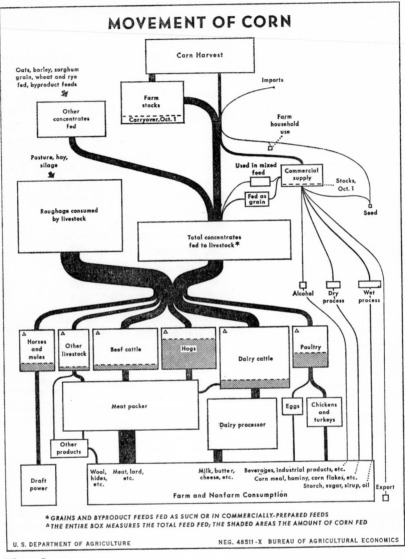

MOVEMENT OF CORN

Corn Harvest

Oats, barley, sorghum grain, wheat and rye fed, byproduct feeds

Farm stocks

Carryover, Oct. 1

Imports

Other concentrates fed

Farm household use

Pasture, hay, silage

Used in mixed feed

Commercial supply

Stocks, Oct. 1

Fed as grain

Roughage consumed by livestock

Seed

Total concentrates fed to livestock *

Alcohol

Dry process

Wet process

Horses and mules

Other livestock

Beef cattle

Hogs

Dairy cattle

Poultry

Meat packer

Dairy processor

Eggs

Chickens and turkeys

Other products

Draft power

Wool, hides, etc.

Meat, lard, etc.

Milk, butter, cheese, etc.

Beverages, industrial products, etc.
Corn meal, hominy, corn flakes, etc.
Starch, sugar, sirup, oil

Export

Farm and Nonfarm Consumption

*GRAINS AND BYPRODUCT FEEDS FED AS SUCH OR IN COMMERCIALLY-PREPARED FEEDS
△THE ENTIRE BOX MEASURES THE TOTAL FEED FED; THE SHADED AREAS THE AMOUNT OF CORN FED

U. S. DEPARTMENT OF AGRICULTURE   NEG. 48511-X BUREAU OF AGRICULTURAL ECONOMICS

Plate 3

Most commodities pass through a great many hands in the chain which
begins with production and ends with consumption.

32

CHAPTER III

THE NATURE AND FUNCTION
OF A FUTURES CONTRACT

In order to understand the characteristics which render a futures contract different from any other form of merchantable holding, one must begin by ridding himself of any stylized notions about similarities with other commercial documents.

A futures contract is thoroughly unique. While it is an actual contract binding both seller and buyer to specific performance obligations, a futures contract has only rarely existed in printed form. The terms of a futures contract are contained in the rules and regulations of the Exchange upon which it is traded. The bilateral commitments which it imposes are specific and completely enforceable — and have been declared so by no less an authority than the United States Supreme Court. However, it is unlikely that a speculator could obtain a copy of his futures contract even if he wanted to.

A futures transaction does not transfer ownership or constructive physical possession of anything. Execution of a futures trade only involves *firm commitments* on the part of the buyer and seller to mutually carry out their respective responsibilities, in a designated manner and within an established time table, set forth as conditions of their transaction.

1. A futures contract firmly binds the *seller* to *deliver* a fixed amount of a certain grade or grades of a designated commodity, within a given geographical area, on or before a specified date.

2. A futures contract firmly binds a *buyer* to *accept delivery* of the commodity and, upon delivery, to pay for it in full.

3. A futures contract affords *both* the buyer and the seller a continuing opportunity to avoid the making or taking of delivery, through execution of an *equal and opposite* transaction in the same commodity and futures month. Once having offset by an equal and opposite transaction, the buyer and/or seller have fully discharged pre-existing contract obligations and have no remaining responsibilities under it, either directly or collaterally.

No Limit to Futures Trade Volume

Newcomers to commodity trading oftentimes make the mistake of thinking there is some actual or theoretical relationship between the volume of trading in futures and the amounts of the physical commodity in existence — and which the futures contracts represent. This is absolutely incorrect. There is, for example, no limit — either theoretically or practically — to the number of futures contracts in soybeans which might be bought and sold in the course of a crop year.

The actual soybean harvest in the United States in the year 1965, somewhat exceeded 843 *million* bushels. Volume of trading in soybean futures in Chicago during that twelve month period totalled over 17 *billion* bushels — nearly twenty-times production. The statement appears to be a paradox, so let's review the considerations which validate the strange surrounding fact.

Everyone understands that automobile manufacturers currently produce some six or seven million automobiles per year. However, total car sales in a six-million car year may easily reach twenty million. This will happen because the automobile manufacturer first sells his car to a distributor, who re-sells the car to a retailer, who finally sells the car to the end user. Each new automobile in this example is involved in three separate transactions, as it passes through the distributive chain from producer to retail customer. Then, don't forget *used car sales.* The same succession of re-selling also exists in grain, metals, oil, and practically every other commodity in existence.

In tracing the movement of grain from farmers' fields to the consumer's dining table, we know that it passes through many hands — and in various forms — as it moves from producer, to wholesaler, to processor and product manufacturer, distributor, retailer, and ultimately to the customer. A bushel of oats may be bought and sold a dozen times before it finally is taken out of existence through consumption. To the extent that successive owners of this bushel of oats engage in *hedging,* its *equivalent* in oats futures will be both *bought and sold each time the commodity changes hands.* The farmer may hedge his crop by selling a quantity of oats futures equal to part or all of his anticipated harvest, several months before he plants the grain. The commodity merchant who buys the farmer's grain may simultaneously hedge his purchase of the cash product through a sale of equivalent oats futures. When the grain merchant later re-sells the cash oats to a processor, he will lift his hedge by buying back the oats futures he had previously sold. And so on, each step of the way.

Hedgers Have a Choice

When a hedger sells commodity futures, he may or may not intend to deliver the cash product in settlement of his contract at maturity. It really makes no difference what his delivery intentions are. The fact is that he *can* and *will* either offset by buying back futures, *or* he may choose to deliver the cash product. The course of action he chooses will depend on which best serves his operational and profit objectives.

Speculators Must Offset

The same thing may not be said, as concerns the speculator. When he buys or sells commodity futures, he does so purely as a means of assuming the positive or negative price risks of commodity ownership. He *owns none* of the product and he *wants none.* He rarely, if ever, has the slightest intention of either taking delivery or obtaining the physical commodity in order to deliver it against an open short position. Of course the opportunity always exists for him to do so if events urge it. Still, for the most part, the number of contracts, long or short, which a speculator has open can best be viewed as nothing more than a *measurement* of the ownership or risk he has taken on. His profits or losses will be computed on the basis of cents per bushel, per pound, per cwt., or per ton. But the speculator's position will almost invariably be offset prior to the date when trading ceases and delivery becomes mandatory.

To repeat for emphasis, speculative trading takes place in search of profit. The speculator *does not* want to *own* cash grain, minerals, or metals; he *does* want the opportunities for profit which are inherent in *changing prices*. His assumption of ownership risk is stated in terms of designated quantities of commodities, but doing so is only a communications convenience. The only thing the speculator really seeks is *risk*, as a means to profit.

Supply & Demand Governs

Newcomers to speculation are often puzzled by the question of what would happen if the wheat futures sold, for example, exceeded all available wheat supplies. How could the outstanding obligations possibly be met? The answer is that they could not be met if all of the longs in such a situation stayed long and insisted on delivery. Obviously a product which does not exist cannot be delivered. But the odds against this happening are overwhelming.

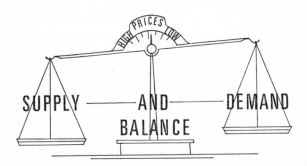

Plate 4

Price measures the balance between supply and demand.

To understand the reasoning behind this statement, we must remember that the balance between supply and demand in traded commodities usually maintains a close equilibrium. Market prices on commodities are established in trading, at levels which reflect supply/demand balance. Relative scarcity represents the normal state of things. When demand outstrips supply—prices rise, and the higher prices serve to ration the available product into areas of greatest usefulness. For example, when wheat is selling for $1 per bushel (and stocks are excessive) a great deal of cheap wheat will be fed to poultry and livestock. When wheat is selling for $2 per bushel, consumption of the expensive grain will be almost totally limited to conversion into food products for human consumption.

Price Rations Use

Thus it may be stated that so long as prices can fluctuate, relative price levels will ration whatever supplies exist into channels of use which justify their effective price. When prices are high, low-end, less valuable usage will dry up, and substitute stuffs obtainable at lower prices tend to take over the function either temporarily or permanently.

It is for these reasons that it is so vitally important that free markets exist and be able to establish commodity prices. Whenever the price on a given product is dictated by government edict or otherwise, the rationing influence of price fluctuation is frustrated and consumption proceeds without respect to the realities of supply/demand relationships. Dire results are to be expected.

Futures May Pass Through Many Hands

Now let's give our attention to the matter of futures trading, for the purpose of developing an understanding of how supply and demand in futures contracts also tends to be self-balancing throughout the life of a given contract. To begin with, there must be a seller for every buyer of a future; wheat futures, like cash wheat, must be bought from a seller.

Consider a contract in July wheat, which opens for trading in July of the year preceding harvest. On the first day of trading, we will imagine that only two traders are interested in transacting business in the maturity. Trader A offers to sell one contract—5,000 bushels—at $1.50 per bushel. Trader B considers the price attractive, and he buys the contract. The transaction is noted on their trading cards and the price is posted "on the board". Time passes, but no further trades are made. As the end of the session approaches, Trader A decides that he does not want to carry the short position overnight; so he offers to buy back one contract of July wheat—hopefully at a profit—so he bids for "five July at $1.49" per bushel. His bid attracts no sellers. He progressively raises his bid to $1.49¼, later to $1.49¾. He offers $1.50 per bushel, which is precisely what he sold the contract for earlier, but he still finds no seller. At last he raises his bid to $1.50¼ and Trader B, who previously purchased the contract at $1.50, accepts trader A's offer. The offsetting trade is made.

Now, let's recap these events. When the first transaction was made, the *opening price* was established at $1.50 per bushel on July wheat. With the first trade execution, *open interest* in the contract amounted to 5,000 bushels, since open interest reflects *one side* of all positions held. As the session wore on, bids on July maturity ranged from $1.49 per bushel up to $1.50 per bushel, but no transaction took place at these levels. Finally, a second transaction was executed at $1.50¼, and was consummated between the same two parties involved in the first execution. Having made the second trade, both Traders A and B have "offset," since their second transaction was "equal and opposite" to their first transaction: "A" initially sold 5,000 bushels of July wheat and later bought back the same amount in the same contract. "B" first bought 5,000 bushels and later sold 5,000 bushels in the July contract. *Volume* on this unlikely day's trading amounts to 10,000 bushels, which is the amount of futures which changed hands in the course of the session. The *trading range* was from a low of $1.50 per bushel to a high of $1.50¼ per bushel. Open-interest at the close of the day is zero, since all positions were offset by the closing bell.

Now let's involve a somewhat larger group of traders in the situation and consider the next day's trading in the same contract.

When the second session opens, Pit Broker X holds an order which was placed by a grain producer to sell 10,000 bushels (two contracts) of July wheat at $1.50¼ (which was the previous day's closing price). When the offering is called, Trader A buys it. As the session runs on, Trader A subsequently sells the 10,000 bushels to Trader B, who in turn sells it to C, after which it is in turn bought and sold by Traders D, E, F, and G. Trader G is interested in "accumulating" a larger position in the contract, in line with his conviction that the price is low and will go higher. He therefore keeps the 10,000 bushels of July wheat and devotes his attention to buying more of the same.

Time passes—some eleven months pass—and the July contract now approaches maturity. The First-Notice-Day on this contract falls in the last week of June preceding the delivery month. Trader G still holds the two contracts "long" which he purchased nearly a year before. The grain producer is still "short" the 10,000 bushels he sold a year earlier.

Oldest "Net Long" Usually Gets Delivery

The seller's crop has now been harvested and he wishes to make delivery. In order to do this, he has executed a *Notice of Intention to Deliver* and passed it to the Clearing House, which, in turn, passes it to trader G, who is the oldest "net long" in the contract. Trader G is a speculator. He has held the position in order to profit from price improvement. He does not, however, wish to take delivery of the physical commodity. When he receives the Delivery Notice, he immediately sells 10,000 bushels of July wheat futures in the pit. His buyer is Broker P, who represents a commercial processor. Having made the sale, Trader G has offset his position, and he "re-tenders" the delivery notice by returning it to the Clearing House along with the name of the buyer.

When the wheat is delivered, it will go directly to processor P. The interim holders of the contract (Traders A-B-C-D-E-F-G) are not concerned in any way. The futures passed through their hands, but they subsequently offset by an equal and opposite transaction—hence, they are out of the contract—and have been out of it since the moment of their earlier offsetting trades. The producer will make his delivery to processor P (through a "regular" warehouse) and receive a certified check for the total value of the shipment. The buyer's check is transmitted through the Clearing House and on to the seller. The following diagram should further clarify the various steps in this chain of events.

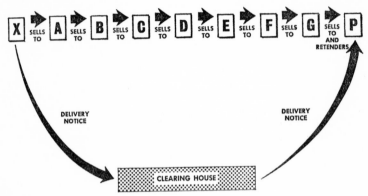

Plate 5

A single commodity contract may pass through many hands during its trading life, but only the **deliverer** and the **receiver** are involved in the transfer of cash merchandise.

Volume and Open Interest

As outlined above, this 10,000 bushels of July wheat changed hands eight times during the trading life of the contract. It accounted for 80,000 bushels of trading volume and 10,000 bushels of "open interest" throughout the life of the contract, since someone held the position at all times. It was "cleared" for the last time and disappeared from open interest at the point at which delivery was finally made.

All trading in futures contracts proceeds along these same lines. Trading rules and regulations vary, depending on the commodity involved and delivery requirements surrounding it. Each exchange reflects some slight variations in the particulars. In all futures contracts, however, for every buyer there must be a seller and, unless previously offset by an equal and opposite transaction, a short must make delivery and a long must accept delivery and make full payment for the merchandise.

Who Buys — Who Sells

The seller of a commodity contract has no way of knowing—and no interest in knowing—whether his offering is bought by a speculator, a commercial processor, or an exporter. He is only interested in two things: First; the price which he receives and, second; that he will have someone to accept delivery, *if he chooses to make delivery* upon maturity. During the trading interim, the contract "position" which came into being with the first transaction, between X and A, may change hands dozens or hundreds of times. Regardless of intervening events, however, the seller is always protected against default on the part of his initial buyer and all subsequent buyers who replace the first one through progressive transactions.

The same may be said for the purchaser. His interests are always insured. He can be confident that if he holds the contract to maturity, he will receive delivery. In the meantime, he can obtain his profits in cash whenever he offsets; from the original seller—or some other seller who has replaced him—on the short side of the trade. Protection for both the buyer and the seller is accomplished through the device of margin, which will now be examined in considerable detail.

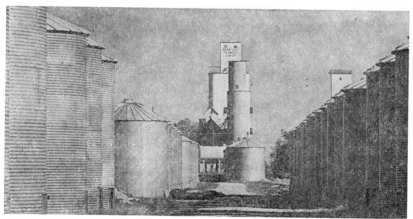

Plate 6

If futures have been sold "against" this stored grain, its holder is a hedger; otherwise, he is a speculator.

Commodity Margin

It was pointed out earlier in this text that margin is not a down payment on commodities represented in a futures contract but, rather, stands as a performance bond to indemnify both the buyer and the seller against possible default on the part of the interest on the opposite side of the position. In the early days of "to-arrive" trading, the amount of margin required on a given transaction was flexible and mutually determined by the parties involved. Depending on the financial reputations of the buyer and seller, margin required on an individual transaction might have ranged from 2% or 3% of the total value represented in the trade, to perhaps as much as 15% or 20%.

Now, as then, margin is equally required from both buyer and seller—since, if prices fall in the interim between execution of the trade and offset or delivery date, the purchaser or "long" loses; the seller or "short" requires protection from possible default on the part of the buyer. In the opposite frame of reference, if prices rise between the time of sale and the offset or delivery date, the seller or "short" loses; as a consequence, the long seeks, and is entitled to, protection against possible default on the part of his short seller.

In early days of commodity trading, margin deposits put up by the "long" and "short" in a given trade were turned over to a mutually acceptable third party; to be retained until the transaction was subsequently completed through delivery of the merchandise on the part of the seller and payment in full on the part of the buyer. In modern commodity futures markets, margin amounts are firmly established in the rules and regulations of the market, and margin deposits are held by the Clearing House organization which usually functions as a closely related but structurally separate organizational entity. The role of the Clearing House will be discussed more broadly later. For now, it is sufficient to say that the Clearing organization serves as "interlocutor" between all buyers and all sellers in futures contract trading. Once a transaction is made in the pits, it is turned over to the Clearing House which, in recording the trade, puts itself, by *substitution*, in the position of *seller to all buyers*—and *buyer to all sellers*.

Minimum Margin is Fixed

The minimum margin required from the principals in a futures transaction is set forth in the rules and regulations of the Exchange, but individual brokerage houses *may* require *greater* margin amounts from their customers if they wish. Ordinarily, margin levels represent something like 5% to 7% of the values of the commodities in trade. In soybeans, for instance, the *initial margin* required at this writing was 22¢ per bushel; *maintenance margin* of 15¢ per bushel. This is to say that, after a trade is accomplished, the price on the contract may fluctuate as much as 14¢ per bushel (7¢ per bushel to the disadvantage of the long or short) without requiring either of them to post additional margin money. However, should the soybean contract concerned *fall* 8¢ per bushel, the holder of the *long* side of the contract would immediately be required to post sufficient additional money to bring his margin back up to the *initial* margin level of 22¢ per bushel. If he fails to answer the call for additional margin, the broker may liquidate part or all of the position to keep the holding within established margin requirements.

Critics of commodity futures trading often base their criticism on the fact that buyers and sellers of contracts post a relatively small amount of cash. It is a recurrent contention of market critics that commodity traders have unrealistically small "investments" in futures positions and, as a consequence, the financial foundation of the trade is "shaky".

As a matter of fact, margin requirements in futures trading are based primarily on the consideration of *historic price fluctuation*. Commodity *price* is at best a secondary factor. Buyers and sellers of futures are dealing in fluctuative risks. They are not dealing in physical commodities. The cash commodities will not be involved in the trade until contract maturity makes delivery necessary. In the meantime, each contract may be bought and sold many times, with each holder of an open position responsible only for indemnifying his opposite number to the extent of the price change which occurred while he held the position.

For example, when corn is selling for $1.40 per bushel, there is an excellent possibility that the price may rise to $1.45 per bushel or fall to $1.35 per bushel. There is a smaller possibility that price will increase to $1.50 or fall to $1.30. The probabilities are heavily weighted against the chance that corn prices might increase to $1.60 per bushel or fall to $1.20.

Margin performs its full function when it is sufficient to cover the "risk end" of price. It would be absurd to require a commodity trader to post 50% margin on a position in corn. Doing so would be tantamount to saying that corn currently selling at $1.40 per bushel could be reasonably expected to suddenly increase to $2.10 per bushel; or suddenly fall to 70¢ per bushel. While such an eventuality could perhaps conceivably occur, such a huge price swing would certainly take place over a substantial period of time, during which disadvantaged traders could close out their losing positions by offset (sales or purchases) to other parties who were willing to undertake the risks of ownership at the new price levels. Even if a few hardy souls did not close out their positions in disappointment or despair as prices moved against them, *additional maintenance margin* would be required in order that they would constantly have a minimum deposit against their positions.

The foregoing should not be taken to mean that price moves in commodities are always of small scope or gentle occurrence. Cataclysmic events which may arrive in the form of unforeseen weather developments, a crop forecast which contains a big surprise for the trade, an outbreak of war, or events of similar impact, can reflect themselves in sudden and sharply precipitous price changes. When this happens, speculators may find themselves in a situation which involves great losses or great profits. But if so, it must be acknowledged that human illness, fire, flood, or theft can be even greater catastrophes; all of which must be occasionally faced up to as an inescapable hazard of being alive and/or undertaking ownership of property which is susceptible to devaluation, damage, or loss.

At least, the individual who speculates in commodity futures can draw quite reliable conclusions about the *probable* range of price fluctuation on his contract from readily available historical data. He can be certain that the price of his contract will not be doubled or halved in value, except as the result of an almost incredible event; and even then the change in value will almost certainly be spread over a considerable period of time. Due to the constant world-market which exists for commodities, they are always in demand at some price; and such time as there is will offer an opportunity for the speculator to "cut his losses" by closing out his position and transferring the risk to other hands.

How Much Margin is Needed

In view of the foregoing, we can categorically state that margin is adequate whenever it is sufficient to cover the *probable price-change* risks present, for whatever minimum period of time is involved in "getting out". The Clearing House has the prerogative of calling on its members for additional margin at any time—and requiring that the new funds be deposited within one hour. Since a variation margin call will be initiated by the Clearing House whenever the maintenance margin level is impaired, it goes without saying that considerable latitude still remains under the "call level" for further price fluctuation; without endangering the financial interests of the other party. If the call for additional margin is not met in the prescribed time, the broker and/or Clearing House has blanket authority to liquidate *part or all* of the position, freeing remaining margin funds to a point of adequacy in covering whatever portion of the member's position still remains open.

As a practical matter, it deserves to be noted that there is no recorded instance of a buyer or seller failing to receive his full settlement—either through delivery of the commodity or equivalent cash values—on any cleared position on the Chicago Board of Trade. When it is considered that volume on this huge Exchange exceeded $81 billion in 1966, it becomes clearly apparent that the margin requirement imposed on all classifications of market users *must* be adequate.

An added factor of protection is in the unique function of the Clearing House, in substituting itself as "the other party" in all transactions. The Clearing House, upon accepting each trade at the close of each session, stands as the seller to all buyers and as the buyer to all sellers. The individual seller is actually responsible to the Clearing House, rather than to the party who bought his contract. Likewise, the buyer can look to the Clearing House for either delivery of the commodity or payment of profits accrued while the position is held.

Nature & Function of a Futures Contract

Money/Credit Balance

The commodity market is somewhat like our total national economy in one respect: Aggregate obligations outstanding on the part of longs and shorts in commodity trading constantly exceed margin funds on deposit, by some fifteen or twenty times over. The same thing can be said of the American business system. Obligations to pay, as represented in accounts-receivable held by department stores, services stations, mortgage companies, and employees of operating firms, greatly exceed the total amount of money in circulation at any given time. There is, however, little restrictive relationship between obligations outstanding in the form of "total debt" and "total money" in circulation. So long as the money supply is sufficient to permit buyers and sellers to transact business uninterruptedly, the quality of any debt depends directly on the reliability of the person who owes it; and only incidentally to the fact that on the day it falls due there must be sufficient gold, silver, paper money, or acceptable substitute in existence to pay off the obligation.

Commodity trading merely creates a specialized form of debt which, on the part of the seller, involves a commitment to deliver the commodities—or offset the open position by an equal and opposite transaction. The case of the buyer is precisely the opposite: He must accept delivery of the commodity and pay for it in full or—prior to delivery date—offset his short position by purchase of an equal amount of the same futures.

Margin from each party to a trade must be adequate to insure that both will carry out their commitments. With performance insured, there is no conceivable justification for asking more. History provides the most inarguable evidence that margin levels have been and are sufficient. One-hundred-eighteen years of consistent settlement on the world's largest commodity exchange, without a single dollar's loss being sustained as a result of default, is the clearest proof that the commodity market is a sound and reliable institution. Moreover, that traders themselves can be expected to fully perform on their obligations undertaken in the marketplace.

CHAPTER IV

LEVERAGE THEORY IN SPECULATION

Profits can be considered the *primary objective* in all economic activity, although certain projects are undertaken by individuals, organizations, and governments, without a specific dollar profit goal in mind. Effort is almost always expected to result in accomplishment of something—which, from a standpoint of worth appraisal, should be at least theoretically reducible to stated values. Values, in turn, are usually translatable into monetary terms. Put another way, economic activities, in order to maintain analytical coherence, must be viewed as producing economic results: *positive results,* identified as a *profit*—and *negative results,* as a *loss.*

Any situation in which a dollar is able to undertake more than a dollar's worth of economic work is properly identified as a "leverage" situation. Leverage is a primary measurement of the earning potential of money in a given situation. Thus, leverage is a major speculative factor. As we shall see, it constitutes one of the prime considerations which encourages speculative risk bearing on the part of those who have the financial ability and the personal sagacity to undertake such a function in the marketplace.

At current margins, a buyer of securities (on margin) is only required to produce 70% of his purchase price in cash. Seventy dollars will thereby obtain possession of $100 of stock. The $30 deficit which remains constitutes a form of specialized credit extended by the broker to his customer. The $70 provided by the customer can be considered a "down payment" on the stock purchases, with the balance remaining outstanding over whatever period of time suits the mutual interest of the broker and the customer. Most stock purchases and sales are handled on margin, along with broker loans.

Stock, it should be noted, *changes hands* when it is bought on margin. Along with the physical asset, entitlement to dividends, etc., also passes to the new owner.

In commodities, margin also figures importantly; but as stated earlier, rather than constituting a "down payment", *commodity margin is a performance bond.* Unlike trading in stock, a commodity "futures" transaction does not result in the transfer of any physical property. All that is exchanged between buyer and seller is mutually bilateral commitments to do certain things in the future. The sole purpose of a commodity margin is to *indemnify* the parties to the trade against possible default on the part of the other.

Leverage in Commodities vs. Securities

Margin in commodities, therefore, is more properly viewed as a contract binder or performance bond, rather than "down payment", as is the case in securities. With the commodity margins usually set at 5% to 7% of the value of the trading unit involved, leverage on the commodity situation is about 95%, compared to 30% on stocks.

To demonstrate, consider a speculator who is considering two propositions:

(1) Buy 5,000 shares of ABC common stock at $3.00 per share; value of the block of stock is $15,000. Margin money required (70% of the price) $10,500. ($4,500 is a broker loan.)

(2) Buy a futures contract of 5,000 bushels of soybeans at $3.00 per bushel; contract value — $15,000. Initial margin deposit required (5% of the price) — $750. (No broker loan.)

The ABC stock pays no dividend; hence, a financial return from the stock, as with the soybeans, can only come from an increase in

48

the prices of the two holdings. *Both constitute speculations* on market value. One important difference exists, however, in the relative leverage available in each situation.

A 10% increase in the price of the stock would be worth 30¢ per share, or $1,500. However, a 10% increase represents a 200% return on the commodity margin, since the speculator was only required to post 5% of the contract value as a binder on the trade. (Margin requirements are subject to change as often as the exchange sees fit to do so.)

Here, in a nutshell, is one of the most practical and compelling reasons commodity speculators are willing and able to assume the risks of ownership through the holding of commodity futures contracts— either "long" or "short". There are few other financial situations in which a dollar can enjoy such leverage.

As a result, profits on working capital can be most impressive— and, by the same token, so also can losses. With $15,000 to work with, for example, a speculator can obtain some 12,000 shares of the ABC stock used in the example above. In so doing, he will have gained the opportunity to profit from increases in the price of the holding, and he will have to absorb the disadvantages which will come from a price decrease. The same $15,000 used to margin commodity trading will enable the speculator to hold twenty contracts—100,000 bushels—of $3.00 soybeans and profit or lose in accordance with the commodity's price fluctuations.

Financial leverage, to repeat, is of unparalleled importance in obtaining maximum return on risk funds, wherever they may be put to work in the business area. Everyone who uses credit in any form is recognizing the benefits of leverage, since their credit acquisitions— insofar as they result in acquisitions in excess of immediate capital on hand—are all obtained via the leverage route.

The "Risk Area" Concept

Arguments against speculation in commodities usually seek foundation in the fact that speculators ordinarily put up only a small proportion of the full price of the product represented in the contract. While the point is valid, it has little relationship to the real topic at issue. Earnest money, down payment, or binder in a credit purchase, performs the function of protecting the seller from subsequent default on the part of his buyer. Down payment on equipment, for example, is usually calculated to cover initial depreciation and bridge the gap from "new" to "used" in the event the item must be repossessed on default and re-sold. So long as the amount of the down payment is adequate to cover this eventuality (and repossession costs), the interests of the seller should be secure.

In buying or selling commodities, the extent of risk involved is not the full price of the commodity, but only the latitudes within which prices may be expected to fluctuate. This, because it may be assumed that wheat, for example, will always have buyers somewhere, at some price level. The only question which remains to be answered—and upon which the amount of margin required must therefore be predicated—is how far prices are likely to move up or down, to the disadvantage of the seller or buyer. As previously pointed out, commodity margins ordinarily represent approximately 5%—from each party to a contract. Past experience is the best evidence that 10% of total price is quite adequate in view of the scope of risk involved in medium-term price change.

Consider a situation in which, on February 1, Speculator A sells 5,000 bushels of July wheat futures to Speculator B at a price of $1.75 per bushel. Cash wheat of contract grade, at the time of the futures transaction, is selling at $1.65 per bushel with the 10¢ differential in price between immediate and July delivery representing payment for carrying charges on the grain for some five months.

Since the seller does not own an inventory of wheat when he sells the futures, he clearly expects he will be able to obtain the physical commodity (or equivalent futures) at a lower price than his selling price, sometime during the period between his sale and the delivery date. However, should events in the interim indicate otherwise—should prices move to his disadvantage—he has the constant prerogative of clearing his obligation by buying an equal amount of the futures that he previously sold. In so doing, he will have "offset" his short position and taken himself out of the market. His loss will be measurable in the differential between the price at which he sold the futures "short" and the higher price at which he bought the futures back.

From the point of view of the buyer, his commitment binds him to accept delivery of the physical goods on delivery day and pay for it, or prior thereto to sell an equal amount of wheat futures, off-setting his long position and taking himself out of the market. Should the price of wheat fall after the speculative "long" has purchased it, the latter alternative is very likely the course of action he will follow. As a speculator, his interest is not in obtaining the physical commodity. He only bought wheat futures in the hope of profiting on price appreciation during his period of ownership.

In the given situation, we have Speculator A who has sold "short" in the belief that prices will fall, enabling him to buy the commodity or its equivalent at a lower price in the future and thereby realize a profit. On the other side of the transaction, we have Speculator B, who considered the selling price a "bargain" and so he purchased the futures expecting that prices would rise, permitting him to sell out later and realize a profit.

In appraising buyer and seller risks, it is necessary to first consider the *worst* things that can happen to the interests of each, and later to consider the *probable* limits of disaster that might operate in the given situation. Clearly, the worst thing that could happen to the short seller would be for the prices to *rise* from the selling price of $1.75 per bushel to, let us say, $3.00 per bushel, which would represent an historic high price for contract grade wheat. In such a case, the short stands to lose $1.25 per bushel on his contract. In the opposite frame of reference, the speculative buyer would be equally disadvantaged if March wheat immediately fell to 50¢ per bushel, costing him $1.25 from his earlier purchase price.

Prices are Limited by Practicalities

While it cannot be said with certainty that such events are impossible, they are most unlikely for several reasons, the most important of which is that regional and world supply/demand equilibrium stands as a virtual bar to such dramatic price changes, except over an extended period of time. While it is conceivable that March wheat could, in a given situation, command a price of $3.00 per bushel, several months would likely be involved in reaching such a lofty plateau from a price of $1.75. Each trading session in the period would offer the "short" an oportunity to close out his position, take his loss, and protect the balance of his speculative capital.

The reverse is equally true—the value of a bushel of wheat in the market could conceivably deteriorate from $1.75 down to 50¢ per bushel. However, a protracted period of time would certainly be required for such a move, and the "long" who was suffering from the development would have a succession of opportunities to close out his position through offset and thereby shift the risk to someone else, at the lower price level.

Daily Price Fluctuation Limits

There is a further protective device for the speculator in commodities which is contained in the trading rules of most exchanges. Prices are only permitted to move a designated interval away from the closing price on the previous day's session. In wheat, for example, a 10¢ advance or decline from the previous day's close is the *maximum allowable fluctuation* on the Chicago Board of Trade. If March wheat closes at $1.75 today, it can go no higher than $1.85 tomorrow, and no lower than $1.65. In addition to installing an important safeguard against excessively wide price swings, fluctuation limits serve a further purpose. Rising prices in Chicago attract supplies from outlying areas and with the increase in wheat inventories (attracted by the high prices) fears of shortage are allayed and prices are moderated.

This is not to say that commodity prices hold within narrow ranges. They do not. The 1967 March wheat contract, for example, stood at $1.65 per bushel on April 4, 1966. On June 20, the contract closed at $1.99. This represents an increase of 34¢ per bushel, but fifty-seven trading sessions were required in the move up. The largest increase in the price of this contract took place on June 19 and amounted to about 8¢ per bushel. By dividing the total move, 34¢, by the fifty-seven day trading period involved, it will be seen that the *average* daily increment was about ¾¢ per bushel; hardly a disastrous amount.

Under rules in effect at this writing, both the buyer and seller of wheat futures were required to post margin deposits with their respective brokers, of 15¢ per bushel. They must maintain a margin of 10¢ per bushel in the contract throughout the period the position remains open. Should prices move against a trading position sufficiently to bring the trading margin below the required maintenance level, it will be remembered, the broker must call for more margin; and unless it is provided, the broker is authorized to liquidate part or all of the impaired position by either purchase or sale.

Thus it will be seen that, barring the most cataclysmic events, a trader's margin is always substantially more than the permissible daily trading range on his position. This, coupled with the fact that buyers and sellers are always present in the pits, thereby permitting quick offset of an impaired position—usually in a matter of seconds. The possibilities of contract default on the part of the buyer or seller are most unlikely, if not impossible.

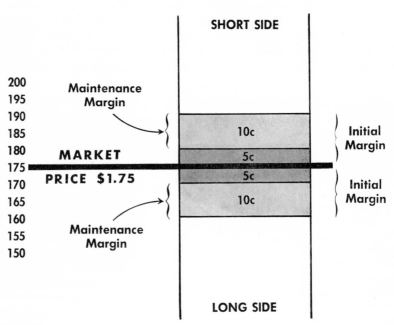

WHEAT FUTURES TRANSACTION

Plate 7

In posting equivalent margins on a given futures position, both buyer and seller have indemnified the other against default. Commodity margins cover the "risk end" of prices.

CHAPTER V

INTRODUCTION TO MARKET ANALYSIS

It should be noted at the outset that statistical projection affords a method of determining where you are likely to be going, by re-examining where you have been. The greatest weakness in most market analysis concepts is in placing too much reliance on events that are *past*, and failing to properly appraise *new factors* which will help shape the future.

Certainly there are cyclical patterns in commodity price behavior, as elsewhere, which repeat themselves with sufficient regularity as to make them valuable as possible projective clues. However, cyclical or seasonal price behavior, when it does develop "according to form", does so because fundamental forces of supply and demand, and related market influences, have materialized once more. The speculator must always remember that price levels, like temperature, are merely a measurement of forces operating in the marketplace. Prices, like temperature, rise in response to one set of circumstances and fall in the face of opposite forces.

Although market participants regularly speak of "forecasting price", a more accurate designation would be "forecasting conditions which *result* in price". To the extent that an individual succeeds in forecasting price, credit must be given to his more-or-less accurate appraisal of the forces exerting themselves in the market. Price, per se, is not susceptible to direct analysis. Price only takes on objective quality in the light of the market inputs which give rise to it.

In order to examine a price, the trader must always look behind it. He must seek out the positive factors which can be expected to *maintain or raise* the price; and array against these, the negative forces which can be expected to *maintain* the price or *lower* it. Prices, like physical bodies, have an inertial factor: in motion, they tend to keep moving; at rest, they tend to stay at rest. The balance is ordinarily a delicate one.

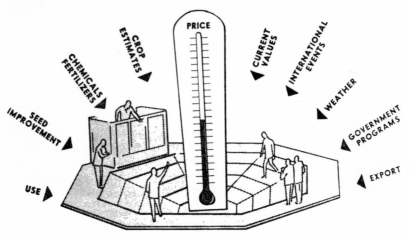

Plate 8

Price influences include a broad range of natural and human events; some of which are quickly "discounted," while others may persist.

Speculation is Economic Warfare

Market analysis calls for great care in dealing with a long list of pricing components, and requires appraisal of three distinctly different levels of inter-related concern. Speculation can be viewed as a form of economic warfare. In the prosecution of a war, the overall perspective is the so-called "big picture". Oftentimes this level of decision-making is designated as being the "policy" realm. A better term might be "grand strategy".

The second level of decision-making in warfare involves medium-range "field strategy", and permits wide latitudes for exercising initiative; providing doing so does not exceed overall policy restrictions or endanger the grand strategy which must govern all.

At the third level, warfare necessarily requires "short-range" tactics; maneuvering to exploit short-term opportunity—or avoid short-term loss. Tactical decisions are often made in the face of small advantages or small threats, and are often calculated to gain only limited objectives. In sum total, however, they are vital to the meeting of both strategic and over-all policy goals.

To demonstrate the simile in speculation, the policy or grand strategy level relates to the over-all market situation in the particular commodity of interest. There are few generalizations that can be applied at any time to several commodities. Strong markets and high prices may prevail in wheat and copper, accompanied by weak markets and low prices on corn and cocoa. Each commodity leads a life of its own. Each must be examined separately. The speculative policy or grand strategy which a trader adopts on a selected commodity should be founded on a firm opinion concerning the long-term expectations for the merchandise. This is only the beginning.

It is conceivable that the long-term outlook for a commodity might be overwhelmingly *bullish,* but with the medium-term and short-range prospects being either *bearish, bullish,* or *neutral.*

Take beef, for example: Red meat consumption has increased at a greater than proportional ratio to United States population expansion for the last twenty-five years. This, due to the fact that average beef consumption per-person tends to increase; a more prosperous America will consume more beef per capita than a less prosperouse one. Thus it can be said that if disposable income continues to increase and population also continues to increase, the increase in beef consumption will be a function of these combined factors—pointing to unusually strong demand in "good times" and less than arithmetic reductions in demand, even in periods of economic slow-down.

In the medium-range consideration, however, beef production and breeder stock may stand at levels which substantially exceed consumption capacity at a given price level. If so, lower prices may be predictable for one, two, or three years into the future. The period will depend on how long it takes for the surplus productive capacity to be brought back into economic correlation with demand. The *medium-range* prospects, therefore, could be for *lower prices*; notwithstanding the fact that the *long-range* trend clearly calls for *higher prices.*

Coming now to short-term considerations, and this is the frame of reference within which most commodity trading takes place, consider a beef situation involving futures contracts for delivery in January, with a position decision to be made the preceding September. It is well known that beef cattle are at less than top form during the winter months. Moreover, the various activities involved in preparing stock for market—penning them, shipping them and delivering them—presents difficulties during the winter time which are mitigated or non-existent during milder weather. As a result, stock raisers tend to reduce their beef shipments during the dead of winter.

With lighter offerings expected in January, the speculator might decide that higher prices would prevail at that contract maturity. If so, he might buy January live cattle futures in anticipation of a price rise prompted by smaller offerings some four months hence.

To recapitulate, we have developed a hypothesis in which the long-range cattle projection shows higher prices to come based on total population increase and larger per-capita consumption. The medium-range data points to lower prices based on beef inventories having temporarily outstripped demand at a given price level. The short-term condition is one in which higher prices may be expected to develop from reduced offerings in a specific period on the part of beef producers, in turn prompted by a most transitory consideration—weather.

Similar evaluations must be made in any commodity category before a speculator can hope to make the *right decision* at the *right time.* Prices rarely move in an orderly fashion from one level to another level over extended time intervals. Changes in supply/demand equilibrium—and erroneous decisions on the part of composite trader judgment—have the effect of "over-buying" or "over-selling" whatever implications are present. The result is seen in a price graph which, although reflecting a clear trend, upward or downward, or sideways, contains a great many sharp reversals of direction.

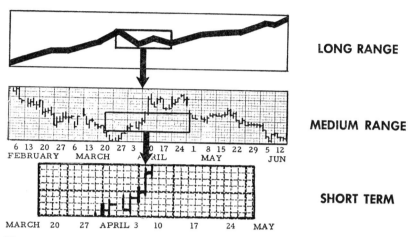

LONG RANGE

MEDIUM RANGE

SHORT TERM

Plate 9

Speculative Interval is Fixed

Futures contracts usually have a trading life of about one year. There is no way the fixed speculative interval on a given contract can be extended. Trading in December grain futures begins in December and terminates in December of the following year. A trader may buy or sell any time on or after the first trading day, but he must deliver in the month of maturity, or offset before. His calculation of profit or loss only relates to price change during the interval he held his position. The time consideration in a futures *can be shortened.* It can *never be extended.* (Contract "life" varies widely.)

This knowledge occasionally prompts otherwise astute individuals to the thought that they can ignore all except relatively short-term considerations. Provided a trader is able to critically develop valid opinions about events which will affect market equilibrium within the life of a given contract, it is fair to say that this is all of the information he will require. The problem is rarely this simple, however. Short-term considerations are closely bound up with the medium-range situation, and this in turn can almost never be viewed sensibly except in the light of a longer-range perspective.

Market Analysis

How Much Must You Know?

Summing up, there is no reliable substitute for doing one's "home-work" on the commodities in which he intends to be active. The more a speculator knows about soybeans, for example, the better the quality of his speculative decisions in soybean futures should be. Neither can the trader's information be limited to price behavior and product usage. He should understand something of the nature of the soy-bean plant, including its growth season, geographical distribution of the crop, optimum growing temperatures, and moisture require-ments, climatic extremes which will impede crop development, per-acre yields, and production costs. He should also know the end-uses to which the products—soybean oil and soybean meal—are put. He should also have some understanding of the other crops (cotton seeds, olives, ground nuts, etc.) that can compete directly with soybeans, as substitute sources of fat and protein for both humans and animals.

The price impact of an unusually small soybean crop will be im-portantly mitigated if, in the same year, groundnuts, sunflowers, olives or cotton seeds prove to be in super-abundant supply. Soybean oil often represents up to one-half of the processed bean in terms of relative value. However, oil is also extracted from the aforemen-tioned crops, and can very largely serve as a substitute for soybean oil in the broad spectrum of human usage. If high prices prevail on soybean oil and lower prices prevail on alternative oils, users will buy the lower priced supplies insofar as they are acceptable for their purposes. Consequently the speculator, if he takes a long position in soybean oil purely on the basis of a short bean crop, may have his profit plans upset by "outside" developments. Substitute crops al-ways deserve consideration in pricing forecasts; but an inexperienced speculator often overlooks these vital factors—in favor of giving all of his attention to figures on the single crop in which he intends to establish a position.

International Relationships

Similar risks should be understood in the medium-range also, especially as they grow out of the activities of governments, and exert profound influences on world trade conditions. The marked reduction of trade tariffs and embargoes, which has been a continuing pattern for the past thirty years, has freed up world commerce appreciably, but the situation still falls far short of being an unimpeded world market. The international trade situation merits close and continuing examination.

Relationships between nations tend to be stable over appreciable periods of time. Our enemies usually succeed in quite consistently staying in our bad graces; our friends tend to retain our good will, barring cataclysmic events. Small disagreements between nations usually result in small reprisals, chief among which is reduction in trade. Since the balance between supply and demand is so fine, a difference of two or three percentage points can create havoc in the marketplace. A relatively small adjustment in international trade activity can dislocate supply/demand balance enough to sharply distort price focus in our domestic market. Moreover, when such steps are taken on the part of governments, reversals in position ordinarily require several months or several years for the point at issue to be forgotten or adjusted through ponderous and slow-moving diplomacy.

Trade balances and competitive situations between nations do change, and each change alters the market equation somewhat. The astute trader must constantly keep an eye on government *policy*—and *practice*—as it bears on international trading. Failure to do so can make him victim of some terrible surprises.

Federal Involvement in Markets

Government machinations must be reckoned with in domestic areas as well. In the United States, certain commodities like silver and gold are produced under strict government regulations and enter the market at statutory prices. Other commodities, including grains, cotton, potatoes, etc., are subject to acreage limitations and covered by loan programs which are calculated to exert controlling influences on total production. Loan rates on regulated commodities are usually adjusted each year. Each adjustment prompts a careful re-appraisal in the marketplace in the light of what the new loan, or the new acreage allotments, can be expected to bring in the form of altered output. There is perhaps no more important medium-range influence on the prices of all major commodities than federal policy concerning production of them.

Price history firmly supports the case that the government loan rates provide a most effective "floor" under market prices. On the other end of the scale, stockpiles of regulated commodities held by the government exert a strong "ceiling" price influence. This latter effect grows out of the fact that sales from government commodity stockpiles are authorized by law when market prices exceed government accumulation prices by a *designated amount* or an *established percentage*. Additionally, the government may sell stockpile commodities in the marketplace at any time when, in the judgment of the appropriate federal agency, they have stocks which are in danger of *going out of saleable condition* for any reason.

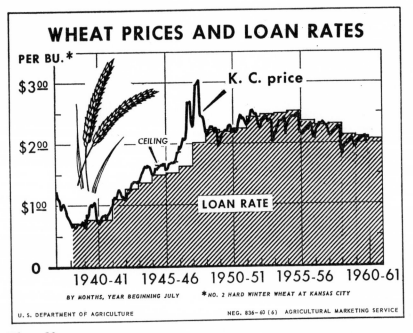

Plate 10

When supplies are ample, government loan rates and market prices present a "mirror effect" that can't be overlooked.

Past events are the clearest indication that decisions to hold or sell stocks held by the Commodity Credit Corporation are often made for the specific purpose of influencing prices, either up or down. Such a program, of course, can do either. In the first instance, the government acquires commodities and removes them from the market, which has the effect of raising prices. In the second instance, government reintroduces products into the market and thus forces prices downward.

While the thought of "administered farm prices" is anathema to most people, especially farmers, the end result accomplished via the

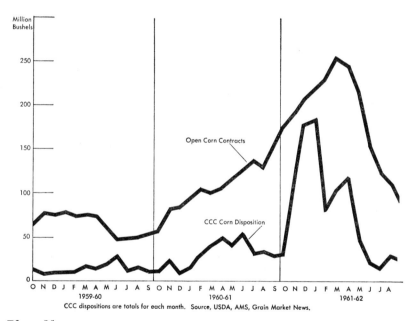

CCC dispositions are totals for each month. Source, USDA, AMS, Grain Market News.

Plate 11

Although officials in federal farm programs usually deny any intent to "manage" prices, sales out of government stockpiles exert tremendous influence in the marketplace. A speculator must be constantly aware of such possibilities.

63

regulated commodity route amounts to about the same thing. So long as our government remains an active participant in pricing, storing, and selling of commodities, the speculator has no choice except to try to "read Washington's mind" with regard to future plans. He must constantly weigh market decisions in light of federal price policies and degree of market interference discernible on the part of the government.

Scholars have developed innumerable theories, axioms, and more-or-less stylized explanations for price behavior. While it may be said that the main forces which constitute the price/value equation are quite well understood as separate entities, the interaction of these forces—which results in price—still presents an enigma of the first order. There is no substitute for extensive training in economics and statistics for the individual who hopes to become a professional market analyst. Price elasticity, price-value theory, marginal-return concepts and Thorstein Veblen's doctrine of "conspicuous consumption" all figure in the problem, along with ideas propounded by Adam Smith, Malthus, Keynes, and many others.

Expert Speculators Need Not Be Experts

Familiarity with the full range of economic dogma is not necessary for successful speculation, however. On the contrary it appears, embarrassingly enough, that the best economists are perhaps the worst speculators. The reason may lie in the fact that it is possible to have so much information about peripheral influences that a clear-cut decision cannot be made. In the short-term scheme of things, there is no opportunity to carefully appraise all the facts and conditions which bear on the issue, even if one were technically competent to do so.

Reduced to its lowest common denominator, a commodity market approximates a giant computer which accepts only two kinds of inputs: positive and negative. The *positive* input is a *buy order,* the *negative* input, a *sell order.* So long as positive and negative influences are equal, prices neither rise nor fall; they remain stable. When positive inputs exceed negative inputs, prices rise. In the reverse situation, they decline.

We may totally disregard the reasons which underlie orders to buy or sell a given commodity at a given time. Only the order itself has the slightest pertinence to the matter of price equilibrium. Some critics of the free market seize on this fact as proof that the establishment of prices through unfettered bids and offers results in "random price determination". The usual supportive argument hinges on the *quality* of trade decisions:

"Quality" of Trading Decisions

An order to buy 100,000 bushels of corn, when placed by a processor, is probably prompted by operating requirements. A corn processor must have corn in order to stay in business. Hence, his buying decision is founded on a *practical requirement*.

On the other side of the trade, we may find a speculator who is selling 100,000 bushels of corn purely out of a *profit motive,* and for no other reason except that he thinks prices are due to fall. In this example, the "practical" decision of a corn processor to buy is matched in the marketplace by the "speculative" decision of a trader to sell. It is the price case of those who argue along this line that the decision of the commercial processor deserves greater weight than the action of the speculator, because the processor's activity has a firmer foundation in reality.

Interesting though the hypothesis appears to be, the market is not equipped to deal with secondary considerations. One party elected to buy and one party elected to sell. One decision may be wise, the other foolish. The market does not qualitatively evaluate either motive or wisdom. It measures supply and demand pressures as represented in orders to acquire or dispose of specific property. The resulting balance is then translated into a price. The more desirable or necessary a commodity, and the greater its relative shortage, the higher the price it will bring from those who have none and want some, or who have some and want more. Over-abundance is measured in lower prices: The larger the surplus of a traded commodity one has, the lower the price he will accept for the first unit of the surplus. As his excess dwindles, his urge to unload diminishes and the price at which he is willing to sell correspondingly tends to increase.

These are the basic considerations present in price fluctuations, and while they may be set forth in far more extensive and more professional language, for our present purpose the foregoing will suffice. The more critical the buyer's need, the higher price he should be willing to pay. The more urgently a seller wants to dispose of property, the lower the price he will likely accept. The market accepts orders to sell or buy, weighs them against each other at a given point in time, and strikes a composite balance which is the "current quotation". Note that current quotation is not necessarily the same as "valid price".

"Valid Price" Theory

In order to be theoretically valid, a price must be one *below* which the seller would not sell, and *above* which the buyer would not buy. Commodity trading involves open outcry which is, in effect, an auction. The market accepts "market-orders" which authorize a broker to buy or sell at *whatever price* then prevails. It goes without saying that sellers who enter market-orders occasionally get *higher* prices than they expect. Buyers, it follows, occasionally acquire merchandise at prices *lower* than they expect to pay. Hence, pit prices in a commodity market cannot always be subjectively defended on the basis of their theoretical validity, but there is no gain-saying the fact that all buyers want to buy—and all sellers want to sell.

To some extent, both buyers and sellers may elect to accept the judgment of the market in establishing the price level at which their wishes are realized. From a practical point of view, composite market judgment as to relative values must be generally viewed as far more dependable than individual opinion on the part of any single trader.

CHAPTER VI

ANALYZING THE
LONG-TERM MARKET SITUATION

Developing a long-range opinion about a commodity calls for close appraisal of many fundamental factors which have direct or indirect influence on the adequacy of supplies. Long-term analysis of a selected commodity situation always seeks to discover which of the three following conditions prevails:

(1) Demand is tending to outstrip supply (and prices will therefore go *higher*).

(2) Demand and supply are in close balance (and prices may be expected to *fluctuate* in reasonably close ranges).

(3) Supply is tending to outgrow demand (and *lower prices* can be expected to result).

Only three possibilities exist concerning price behavior—that they will *increase, fluctuate* in a range, or *move lower*.

In the absence of statutory restrictions which may be imposed through price regulation or other governmental edict, prices will always fluctuate. The range of price movement may be wide or narrow, but some degree of change is a certainty.

For the purpose of demonstrating long-range commodity analysis techniques, we will confine our attention to wheat. The selection is made for several excellent reasons. First of all, this major grain crop is produced in some quantity over most of the world. While the quality of the crop varies from region to region, and the types of wheat grown in various localities represent a wide range of species, almost full interchangeability exists. Soft wheat is preferred for some uses, and hard wheat preferred for others, but if one type is not available the other can, to some degree of effectiveness, suffice. In addition to being almost universally produced, wheat is consumed throughout the world. Some civilizations rely more heavily on wheat than on any other cereal grain; still others put rice in the first order of importance. But man is, to some extent, a wheat eater—regardless of where you find him.

World trade in wheat is greater than in any other comparable foodstuff. Annual yields vary significantly from year to year in given localities, but world production of wheat presents a quite consistent picture over-all. The grand total of wheat harvested has been increasing throughout recorded history with only minor setbacks in the ascending graph.

Three principal areas must be given priority consideration as concerns wheat production. These are the North American continent, Europe, and Asia. The United States and Canada generally produce about 28% of the world's wheat crop in any given year. European countries produce about 40% of world supplies, and the Asian harvest, including Australia, accounts for some 25%

Like other agricultural crops, optimal harvests depend on ideal temperature and moisture conditions along with proper crop management, including fertilizers, pest controls, and harvest methods. The "western world" has developed a superior technology of wheat raising, but without the cooperation of nature, disappointing yields still occasionally occur. Thus it is that in any given year, relatively larger crops may be produced in so-called backward nations, and these may be accompanied by sub-normal crops in the more advanced nations. When this happens, a reduction in the volume of international wheat trading naturally occurs. In the first instance, the wheat deficit areas are better supplied by their own improved yield and therefore require less outside shipments. At the same time, the wheat surplus areas, due to a disappointing harvest, have less of the grain to offer in the world market.

World Prices

There is a further—and most important—consideration in the international trade analysis: A world wheat price is negotiated at intervals as situations require. The parties to the International Wheat Agreement include, but are not limited to, United States, Canada, the Common Market nations, Great Britain, Russia, Japan, Australia, New Zealand, some of the South American countries and several African governments. Discussions between these wheat-surplus and wheat-deficit nations give rise to a world price which is in practical effect, a "pegged price" for trading between the governments involved. At this writing, the world "hard red winter" wheat base price is $1.73 per bushel in so-called "hard currency". Other grades are priced from this "base". When United States market-prices exceed this world-price, in order for domestic wheat to move abroad, the Federal government must subsidize the export activity to the extent of whatever differential may be present. With the world price at $1.73 per bushel and the U. S. market price at $1.75 per bushel, for example, sale of wheat in the export market would involve a 2¢ federal subsidy to the selling interest—in order to put the foreign transaction on a par with domestic sales.

The reasoning behind export subsidies of this kind deserves to be at least generally understood. Treaty relationships with friendly nations oftentimes involve firm or implied commitments to augment foreign food supplies. In order to make grain move overseas, the seller must be able to realize at least as much for the product in export as he would in domestic trade. The only way this can be done is for the government to absorb a certain portion of the cost of the grain and charge it up to foreign aid, international assistance, Food for Peace, etc. To the extent that exports are subsidized, the process is one of maintaining an *artificial* world-price on the commodity in question.

In evaluating the overall world wheat situation, it is important to be aware of the world-wheat price and its relationship to probable

Long-Term Situation

effective free-market prices, in the United States and Canada particularly. Should domestic prices exceed the world price by too large a differential, the United States government might be reticent to absorb the heavy subsidy involved in moving large quantities of wheat into foreign channels. As pointed out previously, if export activity is curtailed appreciably as a result of price disparities or otherwise, the excess supplies which accrue can have great influence on free-market prices and can contribute to accumulation of surplus grain inventories that may take years to work off.

Crop Forecasts

Turning now to the domestic situation, the first order of business in analyzing our own market is that of forecasting production probabilities and projecting its rate of "disappearance". In January, 1965, for example, the United States Department of Agriculture forecast a total wheat crop of 1,342,000,000 bushels. This figure was revised on a monthly basis in the light of plantings, crop progress, and weather. In October, 1966, with the wheat harvest having been completed, this figure was seen to have fallen nearly 100,000,000 bushels short of first expectations. Statistically, the disparity amounted to about 6¾%.

If such a reduction had been announced all at once, it would have created a great price surge in the wheat market. However, the smaller crop prospects developed and became known only gradually. Reduction in the projected harvest grew out of unfortunate weather patterns, lack of moisture, and unusually low temperatures. The market was kept aware of these events as they unfolded and prices moved in quite an orderly fashion from a level of $1.40 per bushel to a high of $2.05 per bushel. Some of the trade foresaw the reduced crop prospects as early as May. They began to bid the price up, and by October their "price idea" had been validated in a scanty harvest.

There was a further factor in the 1965 wheat situation which related to a different crop completely. Asian dietary preference puts rice above wheat as the number one grain. When rice production is adequate, the Middle and Far East import modest amounts of wheat but rely mainly on their own domestic rice supply. Coincidentally with the disappointing wheat crop in the United States, the monsoon season failed to produce adequate moisture in the southeast Asia "Rice Bowl". This, in turn, generated unusual demands from those food-deficit countries. In the name of humanity — and urged by implicit and formal treaty obligations — the United States was constrained to make large shipments of grain to these under-nourished populations. Canada, Australia, Russia, and France also played important roles in saving millions of Asiatics from predictable starvation. But the United States stockpile of wheat which had stood at nearly one billion bushels on January 1 of the year under discussion, had been reduced to less than 600,000,000 bushels nine months later.

Canada produced a "bumper" wheat crop in 1965, which figured importantly in the world situation — but less than it might have. The Canadian wheat provinces include Manitoba, Saskatchewan, Alberta, and part of British Columbia. Export of Canadian wheat from these remote locations requires long-distance transportation over land and loading aboard ships either in the Great Lakes, at Montreal, or on Canada's Pacific seaboard. The difficulties involved in moving product through this kind of an export "pipeline" restricts the amount of grain that can be physically handled in export trade. In view of her land transportation problems and limited port facilities, Canada can raise far more grain than can be physically put aboard salt water transportation. Canada suffered from this export "bottleneck" in 1965.

Hence, the whole story is not contained in production figures alone. Unless supplies *can be moved* from surplus to deficit areas around the world, regional disparities will not be evened out, because they cannot be.

Crop Controls & Loans

From a purely domestic point of view, there is another area of function which can exert great influence on price viability. The United States has, through the Department of Agriculture, carried out a spate of programs of acreage control, price supports and commodity stockpiling, which exert important restrictions on the matter of supply. Through the so-called land-bank program, agricultural

71

acreage is taken out, or brought into production in light of projected needs for the affected crops. Price supports are extended through the vehicle of crop-loans which insure the participating producer of a minimum price for his output. Excess supplies which find no higher bids than "the loan" in the free market are accumulated by the Commodity Credit Corporation, and held in storage against future needs.

Attitudes vary as to what constitutes an adequate stockpile of wheat in the United States, but 500,000,000 bushels represents some kind of a useful consensus. When stockpiles exceed this amount, their existence may constitute a costly burden from the standpoint of both lending outlays and physical storage requirements. When stocks are less than this, the possibility exists that a disappointing harvest could face the nation with some real shortages in this vital food supply.

The impact on prices is clear: When excessive stocks are in CCC control, the possibility always exists that the administrators may release large quantities into the market and peremptorily drive prices down. When stockpiles are inadequate, the reverse effect is seen in rapidly rising prices and persistent fears as to the adequacy of supplies to historic needs. It can be noted that, so long as a loan rate is in force and a stockpile of wheat exists, the former tends to represent a "floor" under which prices are not likely to fall by very much. Stockpiles impose a ceiling of sorts, since the holdings can be used to depress prices, should they exceed the government opinion of what constitutes "reasonable levels".

Finally, it must be remembered that orderly pricing presumes an orderly flow of supplies. Any constriction in the distributive chain can produce temporary or protracted shortage in the first instance; and this condition will often be followed by a temporary or continuing surplus when the immobilized stocks finally begin to reach the market in volume.

Farmer Holding

Recent years have reflected a phenomenon that deserves particular attention. Whereas the historic pattern has been for the grain producers to raise their crop, harvest it, and sell it almost immediately, we have seen noteable departures from this pattern in recent years. Both in 1965 and 1966, a major holding-action on the part of farmers was discernible. Instead of selling their wheat in the period immediately following harvest, a considerable proportion of wheat growers placed their crop in storage — on the farm or elsewhere — and held out for higher prices which they confidently expected would result from meager offerings. Subsequent events validated their judgment. The producers who held their inventory did obtain better prices later on. With two successes to their credit, it must be expected that farmer holding may, in the future, be often encountered, at least to some degree. While the *first effect* of a farmer holding movement may likely result in *higher prices*, if their holding persists too long, the *second effect* may be *lower prices*.

The reason should be apparent. If wheat is held out of trade channels for a few months following harvest, export and other trade activities will be significantly reduced as a direct reflection of the contrived *shortage* — and proportionately *higher prices* on the commodity. When stocks are finally released by the holders, time may not remain — and the market situation may not permit — total recoupment of business which was lost during the preceding period. Optimal consumption of any commodity usually requires more-or-less *consistent flow*. If the material involved is unavailable for any reason over a period of time, substitutes must be found and, once found, will have irretrievably displaced a certain amount of the demand for the preferred product. People only eat fixed amounts, at designated intervals. Yesterday's meals were all eaten *yesterday!*

In a free market, price is expected to ration available supplies into areas of demand which represent the highest relative priorities; most urgent uses being filled first (at the higher prices) and less vital needs being filled later (at lower prices). *Holding* a commodity out of the market is a far different thing than *offering* the commodity at a *higher price*. When availability of a commodity is largely or totally denied to potential users of it, higher prices may be expected to result, but the quantity of trading to which the higher prices apply is reduced. Consumption or "disappearance" of the withheld product will inescapably be *reduced in total amount,* as well as within the period during which the contrived shortage or absence of the item persists. Thus, while buyers may be willing to pay a large premium for the product in the short-term, substitute merchandise and alternative sources for it will probably — over the long-term — effect a correction through market displacement.

The willingness and ability of primary producers to retain commodity stocks has already been noted in connection with wheat. Opinions vary as to whether such a practice will have the long-term effect of raising or lowering average prices for the products involved. Actually, results may be expected to vary from year to year, depending on other considerations. Withholding of wheat on the part of American producers might prove effective — from the farmer's point of view — if supplies in other parts of the world were only adequate, or less.

If other wheat producing nations have succeeded in raising bumper crops, however, the wheat deficit nations would probably exercise the buyer's prerogative of finding alternative sources — and lower prices — for the product they require. U. S. wheat producers would, in this situation, perhaps get a somewhat higher price for the portion of their output which they succeed in selling in domestic channels, but a sizeable proportion of the total crop would not be locally saleable, since we must rely on exports as an important factor in crop disappearance, year in and year out.

Thus, while receiving higher prices on the portion of the crop which found domestic purchasers, this initial benefit could be more than offset by inability to move the *entire* crop, bringing a lower total return for the aggregate harvest.

Nations May Contrive Shortages

Producers are not the only interests who may engage in withholding actions. Nations are often involved in attempts to contrive scarcities in commodities which represent important segments of their export trade. South American coffee offers an excellent case in point. In an attempt to maintain attractive producer prices on this popular beverage, Columbia, Nicaragua, Brazil and other western hemisphere coffee producing countries have created what amounts to an international cartel in the commodity. Through negotiative process they assign annual export quotas to each national participant in the group; establish minimum prices in world commerce, and impose other trading requirements. The same practices mark world trade in sugar, cocoa, cotton and spices.

Domestically, similar activities take place in connection with so-called "market orders". In citrus fruits, as a case in point, market orders are developed cooperatively by the U. S. Department of Agriculture and the citrus producers. An individual farmer may put his crop "under the order" or not, as he sees fit. If he accepts the market order conditions, however, he can expect to receive a certain minimum price for a fixed proportion of his crop. Prices, of course, may still range widely, depending on current and projected supplies and demand for the product. Moreover, if harvest yield is expected to exceed demand, the market order may require deliberate destruction of part of the fruit prior to picking. This is sometimes designated "frost drop".

If the market order calls for a 15% "frost-drop" on oranges, then the orange growers who put their production under the program must go into their groves and shake an estimated 15% of the fruit off of the trees. Failure to do so is a violation of the market order and such non-compliance deprives the orange grower of his guaranteed market price. He will, in effect, be left at the mercy of the free market. Depending on the price situation, he may either prosper of suffer from his refusal to conform.

Production controls are established by governments over a wide range of commodities. Since price is a function of supply and demand in a free market economy, and since both political and private manipulations affect price, the speculator must always make his appraisals in the light of whatever restrictions may be placed on output at the source. The results are the same, whether occasioned by actions in concert on the part of the producers, or through the device of government edict. The more volatile the overall situation is, the more difficult it may be to develop firm appraisals, and the greater the risk inherent in speculation in commodities which are actually or potentially susceptible to federal controls. It should be added that governments have a long, but not particularly brilliant record in their efforts to "manage" economic forces.

To sum up, whether a trader is attempting to develop a long-term opinion about the situation in grain, metals, or fiber, his first equation will probably have to be world-wide in scope. "No man is an island," and there are few places where Donne's statement is as valid as it is in commodity marketing.

Improvement in transport technology and ever-increasing recognition of the inter-dependence of nations in feeding their populations have brought almost incredible increases in the volume of world trade. There is no reason to expect that the trend will not continue, escalating at an even faster pace in the future.

Ideological alignments tend to segregate buyers and sellers to some degree. The United States, as a case in point, does not, at this writing, trade with Cuba nor with Red China. However, our allies do. It is by no means inconceivable that American agricultural products exported to Great Britain could, in some subsequent transaction, be physically included in food shipments which Britain makes to our avowed enemies. We could, therefore, be a supplier of commodities to these Communist nations — through the trade activities of a middleman.

General opinion seems to view trade in foodstuffs and other non-military commodities as meriting a different set of ground rules than business in steel, copper, uranium and related items, which constitute the raw-stuff of armaments. A long-term viewpoint must contemplate a steady, perhaps slow, but inexorable move toward free trading around this globe. The accomplishment may take a decade, a generation, or a century for total accomplishment, but once it arrives, speculation in commodities will be a much simpler thing; if for no other reason than the fact that price differentials will then theoretically grow directly and exclusively out of locational differences and the realities of original production costs, handling and transportation between points.

As it now stands, a good deal of speculator time must be devoted to the frustrating and well-nigh impossible task of trying to read administrative minds and translate official attitudes into pragmatic price inputs. In spite of the level of sophistication to which economics has come, the state of the art will probably always fall short of being able to fully meet this kind of challenge.

World Wheat Production, Average 1957–61

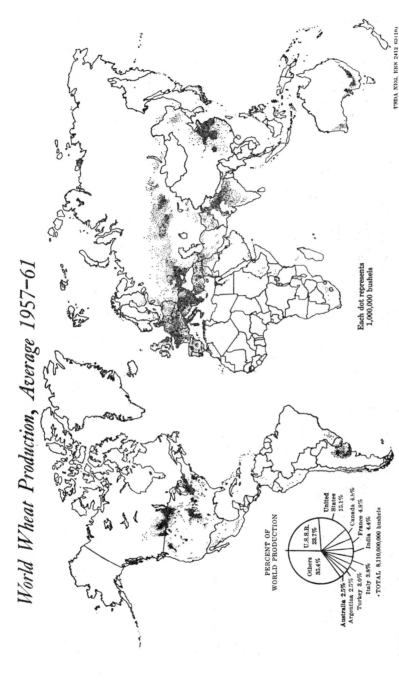

Each dot represents
1,000,000 bushels

USDA NEG. ERS 2412 63(10)

PERCENT OF
WORLD PRODUCTION

U.S.S.R.
23.7%

Others
35.4%

United
States
15.1%

Canada 4.8%

France 4.5%

India 4.4%

Italy 3.8%

Turkey 3.0%

Argentina 2.5%

Australia 2.5%

TOTAL 8,110,000,000 bushels

Plate 12

77

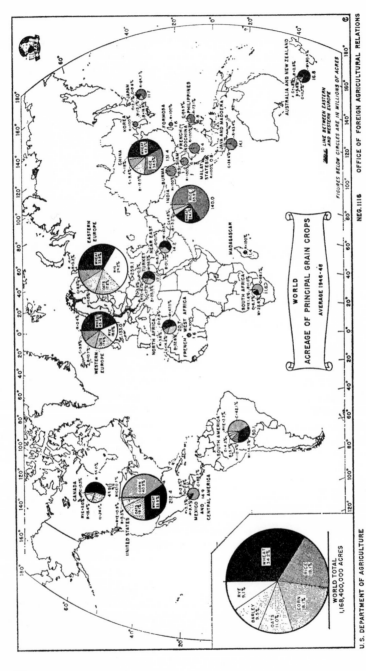

U.S. DEPARTMENT OF AGRICULTURE

NEG. 1116   OFFICE OF FOREIGN AGRICULTURAL RELATIONS

Plate 13   Although the advanced technology of the western hemisphere carries an advantage in per-acre productivity of the major grains, cultivation of these crops is world-wide.

CHAPTER VII

ANALYZING THE
MEDIUM-RANGE MARKET SITUATION

For purposes of this discussion, we will view the medium-range time segment as being one year or less. The reasons for doing so appear compelling. First and foremost, agricultural crops — which underpin the vast majority of all speculation in futures contracts — are produced seasonally, within a twelve-month period wherever they appear. Mining activities have greater overall continuity, but even here established practices in doing business, preparing reports, and scheduling market activities, suggest the use of a twelve month calendar for speculative appraisals.

Certain "crops" reflect longer periods of time from beginning to end, but these can most effectively be delt with as exceptions to the rule. Beef offers a case in point. The production cycle in this commodity usually extends over a period of some three years; this being the approximate time required to bring a calf to breeding maturity and produce an offspring for slaughter. As a consequence, fluctuations in breeder-stock populations tend to separate themselves statistically over something like a thirty-six month time span. Biological considerations impose the minimum limitation, although collateral activities on the part of stock raisers may lengthen the intervals between the peaks and valleys in the graph.

Medium-Range Situation

This second level of consideration in speculation has been identified previously as "strategy". It has also been pointed out that while the strategic, or medium-range appraisal, may be consistent — or in diametric conflict — with long-term projections, strategy must be cast in a frame of reference which gives proper consideration to the long-term trend of things. Failure to do so will put the entire speculative program in needless jeopardy. The reasons for this will become apparent as the topic is developed.

History Provides a Base

Strategic evaluation of a commodity market situation must begin somewhere. There seems to be no better foundation for developing a trading hypothesis than to take available figures from the past as the best available evidence of *how things have been*. With this data in hand, current information can be arrayed against the historic pattern, and a future projection developed.

For the purpose of this strategic discussion, soybeans have been selected for the following reasons: First, the crop is in a distinctly upward long-term trend, with respect to both production volume and consumption usage. In spite of this, the medium-range — year by year — soybean situation offers a complex and highly interesting study in balancing the changing forces of supply and demand. Soybeans are not extensively cultivated throughout the world. However, there are several substitute crops which are grown in quantity over broad areas of the earth, and which provide other sources for cooking oil and protein materials such as those obtained from soybeans.

In terms of our domestic situation, processing facilities do not appear to have quite kept pace with crop production. A billion-bushel soybean crop is a virtual certainty within the next year or two. However, while 472 million bushels of soybeans were crushed in American factories in 1962, the figure is not likely to be more than 530 million bushels in 1967.

Soybean exports are growing at a phenomenal pace. In 1954 — 60.6 million bushels of soybeans were exported. In 1964 — ten years later — the export total had reached 205.9 million. In terms of percentages, about 17% of the 1954 crop went to foreign buyers; in 1964,

Exporters took more than 26% of our total crop of 769.2 million bushels. Viewed in this light, the tremendous importance of foreign trade in this commodity classification becomes apparent. In appraising each crop year, the speculator must not only carefully weigh domestic demands for the products and available crushing capacity, but he must also develop a useful opinion as to probably out-movement to foreign shores. Unless both channels of usage maintain their past levels of performance and continue to grow proportionately to the increase in harvest yields, over-supply and depressed prices could be a suddenly-developing result.

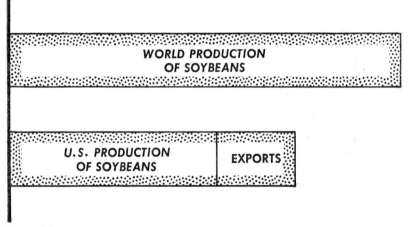

Plate 14

The world crop of soybeans in 1966-67 totalled 1.27 billion bushels, of which the U.S. raised 932 million and exported 251 million.

Crop Report Price Impact

As this material is being prepared, indications are that the 1967 soybean harvest will amount to about one billion bushels. In 1966, the harvest came to some 930 million bushels. The 1966 figure represented about 84 million bushels more than 1965 crop, and furthermore reflected approximately 69 million bushels increase over the U.S.D.A. estimate made on March 1, 1966. (According to official U.S.D.A. figures, 36 million acres of land were expected to be planted

81

to soybeans for harvest as beans in 1966. Applying an average yield of 24 bushels per acre, the figure of 864 million bushels arose.)

The initial impact of this projection was to send new crop soybean futures well over $3.00 per bushel, since the trade doubted seriously that the crop estimate would be adequate to meet historic needs. As the year progressed, dry weather added further pressure to already unusually high prices. The market clearly turned into an over-bought situation. Then, in the September 1, 1966 crop report, the U.S.D.A. revised its previous estimate upward by about 100 million bushels. The effect on prices was devastating. From a close of $3.27 on November soybean futures which was posted September 9, 1966, prices dropped 20¢ in the next two sessions and drifted on down to an intra-day low of $2.87½ on October 11.

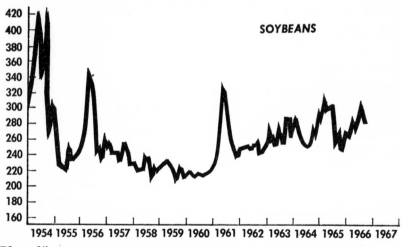

Plate 15

This price behavior is cited to demonstrate the fine balance which exists betwen supply and demand in a crop which demonstrates close historical equilibrium. Speculators who held short positions in anticipation of a dramatically increased harvest profited handsomely. Those who stayed long, expecting the more modest previous crop forecast to be confirmed in the September estimate, suffered monumental losses.

After release of the U.S.D.A. estimate, the market seethed with protests that the figure was unrealistically high; but valid or not, prices moved *in response to the new projection* — and profits or losses depend exclusively on price movements. All information which affects prices is not, and *need not be,* valid. A rapid-breaking and totally unfounded rumor can register its presence in the market-place and occasion broad swings in prices, until it is ultimately laid to rest by more substantial facts. In the meantime, however, the *price movements* are exceedingly *real,* whether or not the thing which occasions the move is subjectively true. Also, the less "news" there is in the market at any given point, the more responsive it is likely to be, to anything which appears to alter supply/demand perspective.

Considerations of the sort noted above have their primary impact in the short-range, or tactical scheme of things. However, they have a medium-range impact insofar as they help establish the over-all market tone of a given commodity, as being "bearish" or "bullish".

War & Peace

International relationships are another most important consideration in the medium-range price situation. The United States has deliberately or unwittingly taken the position of being the food warehouse for much of the world. Involvement in "cold war" and armed conflict has, for the past twenty-five years, involved us in furnishing vast amounts of commodities to friendly nations who align themselves with our policy positions. Cessation of hostilities has almost invariably brought peace arrangements which include feeding our erstwhile enemies. As a consequence it might be generally said that international tensions are bullish, with respect to food commodities; armed conflict even more so. Peace, regrettably enough, must be broadly viewed as bringing lower commodity prices in the first instance, and somewhat higher prices later on, as food exportation to the vanquished enemy gets underway.

Commodity "Glamour Girls"

"Glamour" is a word well understood in connection with girls and stocks, but it is less frequently heard in connection with commodities; still, there are glamour commodities. It is difficult to identify the forces which bring a particular commodity to the wide attention of the public, but once this has happened, the "fan club" demonstrates amazing loyalty. Wheat, cocoa, and pork bellies are currently enjoying widespread public interest and speculative participation. Corn shows some indications of dropping out of the group. Medium-term trading considerations must give careful attention to the amount of public interest in the commodity category. There are several characteristics which can be expected to arise from broad public speculation, which occur directly out of the fact that most of these buyers and sellers have little continuing market interest, or market information, and are only *occasional* speculators.

The Public Will Be "Long"

Of all of the behaviorisms which can be ascribed to the public, its tendency to be long rather than short is the most pronounced. The novice speculator always seems to prefer buying something to selling it. It may be that optimism about rising prices is a universal trait (or resignation to a recurrent fact). Whatever the underlying cause, large public interest in a commodity contract will usually show the public to be long — and the commercial hedgers and professional speculators to be short.

It is also demonstrable truth that the public is wrong in their market judgment most of the time. This is evidenced by the fact that about three fourths of all occasional speculators lose money rather than make it. Losing money grows out of occupying the wrong "position", or improperly "managing" the position; both arise from bad decisions. However, setting forth the *average* public speculator experience does not automatically guarantee that the public will *always* be wrong — nor wrong in a *given situation*.

In the soybean developments outlined earlier, the public was overwhelmingly short. They held the *right* position. Soybean prices advanced sharply in the session preceding release of the government's increased harvest figure. A great many public traders were "stopped out" of the market by the sudden price increase, which turned into a classical "short squeeze". However, those who had the funds and the courage to hold their short positions were richly rewarded when the crop figure was finally learned.

Weather Makes Prices

Of all of the strategic considerations in speculation, weather is perhaps one of the most important. In connection with growing crops, obtaining even an average harvest directly depends on the right combination of temperature and moisture, along with relative freedom from inserts and plant diseases, which can strike suddenly and with devastating results.

Each crop has its own climatic requirements and, generally speaking, the areas in which the crop is produced reflect the environmental conditions necessary to good production. It must be constantly borne in mind, however, that the weather characteristics in any given locality are usually stated in terms of statistical composites or averages. Averages, in turn, grow out of *all* pertinent data including extremes; and extremes ruin crops.

Too much moisture will delay planting, since farm equipment cannot be operated in wet fields; nor can harvesting be undertaken unless the ground is firm enough to support reaping machines. Likewise, excessively dry conditions make planting a crop futile since, unless moisture is adequate to produce germination, nothing will grow.

Plant characteristics vary widely, with respect to moisture and temperature conditions required during the growth period. Winter wheat, for example, produces maximum yields when the seed grain is planted in soil containing 15% to 18% moisture. Once the seed is germinated and stooled, lesser amounts of moisture will induce adequate growth so long as soil moisture does not drop below 9%. Once the crop has made its full structural growth, two or three weeks of temperatures in the 80° to 100° F. range aids in firming the kernels and maturing the crop. It is also helpful if the relative humidities which accompany such temperatures are below 50%, since this will reduce the moisture content in the maturing grain, and improve its grade characteristics. Excessively high temperatures will, of course, dehydrate the young, growing wheat plants and "burn up" the crop. Constant rain will retard wheat growth and support heavy infestations of weeds in the fields. Hail can knock a wheat stand down, making it impossible to harvest with conventional equipment. Abnormally high humidity accompanied by lower than average temperatures encourages infestations of wheat rust and other forms of disease.

Soybeans present quite a different picture as concerns crop hazards. It is said that if you are going to destroy a soybean crop, you must do it in August. Once soybean plants are established, they will survive wide extremes of unfavorable temperature and moisture, and still produce quite a good yield — provided the weather challenge is not too serious during the month of August. It is at this point in the growth cycle (in the Midwest) that soybeans are setting on blooms which will determine the number of pods per plant. If temperatures are high and moisture is inadequate, the bloom is correspondingly light and yields are reduced proportionately. Since soybeans are a "photoperiodic" plant with blossom development geared closely to a designated period in the life cycle, there is no "second chance". Unless the crop can set its blossoms in or around the August period, the subsequent harvest is doomed.

Similar restrictions exist to greater or lesser degrees for each of the agricultural commodities. It can be said that freezing weather or unrelieved drought will destroy any growing crop, but the recuperative powers of plants vary widely. While a given situation may result in irretrievable damage to one, the same condition may only delay the harvest for another. A serious speculator needs to have a fine understanding of the climatic limitations of the commodity in which he is trading. Without this information, he will more than likely render faulty judgments in appraising the aberrations of weather on the harvest potential of the crop. Here again, the speculative results can be disastrous.

Expect an Annual Weather-Market

A phenomenon of most agricultural commodity trading, during the spring and summer in particular, is what the business terms a "weather market". The designation is both accurate and useful. There is a saying in trade circles that "most crops are usually lost two or three times before they are harvested". The statement merely

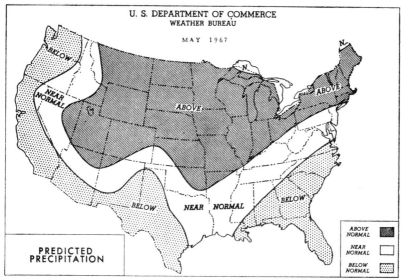

U. S. DEPARTMENT OF COMMERCE
WEATHER BUREAU

MAY 1967

PREDICTED
PRECIPITATION

ABOVE NORMAL
NEAR NORMAL
BELOW NORMAL

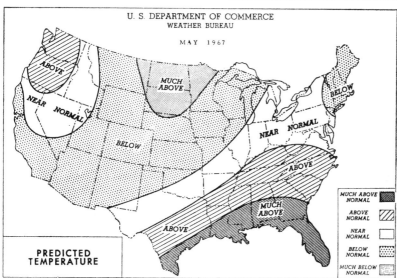

U. S. DEPARTMENT OF COMMERCE
WEATHER BUREAU

MAY 1967

PREDICTED
TEMPERATURE

MUCH ABOVE NORMAL
ABOVE NORMAL
NEAR NORMAL
BELOW NORMAL
MUCH BELOW NORMAL

Plate 16

The government's thirty-day forecasts are studied with keen interest by both producers and traders in commodities. During the growing season, weather is often the most important single factor in the pricing equation. It should be remembered that long-range forecasting is highly inexact.

underscores the fact that while a crop is growing, each change in weather outlook will be immediately reflected in price changes in the market, in terms of its possible impact on yield. Weather-market price fluctuations tend to be greatly magnified beyond the actual, measurable impact of transitory temperature/moisture changes on crop production.

A thirty-day forecast on the part of the U. S. Weather Bureau which calls for below-average moisture during the month of July may immediately be reflected in an increase of 2¢ or 3¢ per bushel in the price of corn. Each appreciable rain storm within the month (which is expected to be dry) will probably occasion a greater or lesser downward fluctuation in the price. Weather markets can be treacherous trading situations because of the suddenness with which summer storms occur, and the outsized impact which such a development may exert on prices.

1965 offers an excellent demonstration of weather market behavior. June had generally been a dry month and the thirty day forecast for July offered little hope for improvement. Agricultural commodity prices had responded to this situation, which seemed to indicate serious reductions in harvest expectations. On the day before the 4th of July week-end, both corn and soybean prices were sharply higher as longs established positions in what they considered to be drought-damaged crops. The holiday week-end had hardly begun when totally unforeseen weather changes took place and parched farmland was drenched with what the newspapers referred to as "a billion-dollar rain storm". At the opening of the first session following the three day holiday, soybean prices opened down 4¢ per bushel and corn opened down 2½¢ per bushel. Speculators who anticipated the billion-dollar rain storm realized great profits. But the traders who accepted the Weather Bureau's thirty-day outlook as the last word paid dearly for their unfounded confidence.

Suffice it to say that price changes which are occasioned by weather tend to be sudden in their development and wider than the facts justify; weather improvements trigger unrealistic price decreases and bad weather occasions excessive price increases. The fact is that, while the vagaries of weather do exert very real influences on harvest expectations, the impact of weather on trader psychology is infinitely greater than it is on the crops themselves. The successful speculator must learn to take such events in stride and maintain a measure of equanimity over all. When he considers that the market has "overbought" bad weather or "over-sold" good weather, he "sells the bulge" or "buys the dip" in expectation that when a balanced appraisal returns he will profit by having resisted over-reacting to short-term and limited news.

In summation, it must be said once more that medium-range trading strategy, to be effective, depends on keeping long-term considerations in background perspective, and dealing with more immediate probabilities as the first order of business. Long-range and medium-range conditions may not coincide. Whether they do or not, successful speculation requires that the trader keep "in step" with the *existing market*. Sometimes this may call for trading against the longer trend. But short-term events do not change trends — they often *extend* trends. "Trading against the trend" can be profitable, but it must be recognized as dangerous; and precautions must be taken which will permit quick escape from a too-hazardous exposure. Trading "against the trend" is always a *short-term tactic*, rather than medium-term strategy.

We are now ready to give our attention to short-range considerations.

Plate 17

Pit trading has been called "the fastest business in the world." In a busy market, some four-hundred traders and brokers buy and sell grain at a rate of $5 million per minute on the Board of Trade.

90

CHAPTER VIII

SHORT-TERM TRADING TACTICS

This subject should ideally begin with a firm definition of what constitutes "short-term" in commodity trading. Unfortunately, finding a usable definition is not as easy as noting the need for it.

The period of time involved in short-term trading depends greatly on individual perspective. It is not likely to be more than a week; it will oftentimes encompass only a session or two and, in fast moving, highly volatile market situations, ten minutes might cover a particular price move from beginning to end.

The minimum period one can effectively deal with in short-term trading activities is largely governed by the amount of time and concentration an individual trader is able to devote to the market. Most public traders rarely have any continuing awareness of intra-session price behavior. Each evening they check their newspaper to see where prices opened and closed, what the highs and lows for the session have been, trading volume, etc. On the basis of this brief data, they then decide whether to maintain their present market position, buy, or sell.

There are other public traders who maintain sufficiently close broker relationships as to be able to get prices a few times during each session, and appraise their daily activities in light of market behavior

at reasonably regular intervals. Still other short-term market participants have immediate and constant access to prices through "ticker"
equipment which reports each price change as soon as it occurs.

It is difficult to select any single group of market participants as
enjoying a distinct trading advantage. The "tape trader", unless he
exerts great self control, can be stampeded into unwise decisions by
exceedingly brief price aberrations which quickly fade and which, in
the final analysis, have little if any significance with respect to trends
in the near- or medium-range of things. It must, at the same time,
be acknowledged that the individual who limits his market contact
to checking opening prices, and intra-day highs and lows is in a position of considerable risk unless he establishes continuing safeguards
in the form of "resting orders".

Once a commodity position is taken, its holder is at the constant
mercy of market prices. Minute-by-minute throughout the trading
session, price quotations on the contract involved publicly declare its
value and measure profits and losses. Whether the going market price
evolves from solid information or the flimsiest kind of gossip, the
quoted price is still the only effective price.

Someone once asked J. P. Morgan, "What will the market do?"
The fabulously successful old speculator with the bulbous, purple nose
had a short reply: "The market will fluctuate." No one has ever
materially improved on Mr. Morgan's prognosis. Prices endlessly fluctuate — the only question to be resolved is whether they will fluctuate
narrowly or broadly and whether they will fluctuate in an upward,
downward, or a sideways trend — but fluctuate they will.

Three areas of consideration deserve analysis in attempting to
evaluate price movements. They are, in no particular order of
importance:

(1) Fundamental changes in balance between supply and demand
forces.

(2) Technical market conditions (which relate to over-bought or
over-sold imbalance).

(3) New information (which may be hard fact or groundless
rumor).

Only Two Market Inputs

The fundamental elements in a market are only two: demand, as measured by buying orders; and supply, as measured by selling orders. There are those who hold that all selling orders do not represent supply, and all buying orders do not represent demand, since speculators are selling and buying with no intention of ultimately making or accepting delivery. The point, even if true, is not pertinent. As already noted, a selling order from a speculator is given the same weight in the market's pricing function as a selling order from a producer or a commercial handler who has — or wants — a warehouse full of the commodity in question. Likewise, a buying order placed by a speculator — who has never taken delivery of any commodity, and never intends to do so — carries the same weight in the market as a buying order from a flour miller who needs the physical product desperately.

The market has no way of differentiating between the motives of buyers or sellers. Indeed, from a purely economic point of view, there is no difference. Both the speculator and the processor buy and sell commodities futures as necessary steps in their *search for profit.* Whether profit shall accrue from milling delivered wheat and selling flour, or holding a wheat futures contract and selling it later at a higher price, makes no particular difference. A search for profit (or avoidance of loss) prompts both interests to take their respective actions.

It is imperative that in considering the economic function and the operational methods of commodity markets, the examiner keep his viewpoint completely clear as concerns these basic inputs: The positive element in the market is the *order to buy.* It makes no difference who originates a buy order, or what his motives or justification may be. The buy order is definitively positive because the very act of buying reflects a *new demand* element which was not communicated in the market until the order arrived. Once known, a buy order urges prices upward.

The negative force in the market is the *order to sell.* Again, we need spend no time trying to qualitatively differentiate between the several classes of sellers. An order to sell represents *new supply* availability which was not in the market until the order arrived. Once entered, a sell order urges prices downward.

Plate 18

Don't Forget the Fundamentals — Even in the Short-Term

The market *fundamentalist* is usually a long-term trader who tends to limit his viewpoint to the adequacy of known or projected *supplies* in light of known or projected *demand*. To vastly oversimplify the situation, the fundamentalist would consider that a finite market which had historically consumed a fixed amount of wheat — say 600 million bushels in a year — would be adequately supplied by a crop which promised to be in the volume of 600 million bushels. He would, furthermore, take historic supply and demand and, from this, strike a balance at the historic price.

Now, assuming that demand remained constant, but supplies decreased by 5%, the fundamentalist would translate the imbalance into a higher price. How much higher would depend on price elasticity in the commodity category and other related economic considerations. If demand remains constant and supply increases 5% over the historic level, the fundamentalist would translate this imbalance into lower prices. His appraisal would hinge importantly on marginal demand for the 5% surplus.

The commodities in which organized trading takes place have been produced and consumed over long periods of time. While historical data leaves much to be desired, production and consumption statistics for the last twenty years or so are surprisingly good in most respects. The student of the topic can readily avail himself of information which will permit drawing some sound conclusions about the fundamental factors surrounding each of the traded commodities. Historical market behavior is less than a sterling criterion for future events, but it does provide an indispensable foundation for creating a projection of things to come. Certainly the speculator who undertakes to make decisions without an awareness of fundamentals is engaging in a most hazardous practice.

Changes in fundamentals can have long-range implications. For example, when the changes involve such things as increased planting intentions on the part of producers, a lifting or easing of a government imposed production restriction, a new use for the commodity in question, etc. Changes in the fundamental market balance, as previously noted, may also relate to medium-range considerations. A transportation strike, for example, while not altering the actual physical supply of a commodity, can temporarily limit its availability in localities of use or consumption. Natural or man-made events such as earthquakes or border hostilities may, likewise, impede the flow of a commodity until the situation returns to something approaching normal.

Fundamental Balances Can Make Short-Term Prices

Changes in the fundamental balance between supply and demand may also be seen in the short-range of things. Unexpectedly excessive arrivals from outlying points of supply may exceed storage capacities for the product in a terminal market location. The reverse may also occur; inadequate arrivals may result from supplier decisions or interference by the weather or other "natural" considerations, giving rise to sudden shotage. The possibilities are almost without limit and each event will create a price reaction which reflects the market's appraisal of the seriousness of the matter and the period of time over which it is likely to persist. Generally, it can be said that small problems result in small short-lived price fluctuations; large problems bring greater longer-lasting price swings.

It is most important that the speculator always look at price behavior in terms of attempting to define its underlying reason. A well-tried axiom is: "Never trust a price move you don't understand." Until some explanation for the market's re-appraisal of price is developed, the speculator has no way of knowing whether he agrees or disagrees with the consideration which is sparking the market's fluctuation. Establishing a position in a "blind" situation may prove profitable but, if so, the result must be attributed to good fortune rather than good judgment.

Technical Imbalances Can Make Short-Term Prices

"Technical" market conditions often occasion short-term price moves, with *no change* of consequence in *fundamentals*. Understanding the technical vulnerability and technical strength in a market can sometimes provide the key to quick and impressive profits. In attempting to analyze this facet of price behavior, it is well to begin with the thought that there are two kinds of market participants, both of which are to some extent continually involved in buying and selling futures contracts. For lack of better labels, we may call them "weak hands" and "strong hands". The distinction refers to their respective capital and other resources, rather than to the commercial motives or lack of them — which may be represented.

Weak-Hands and Strong-Hands

The public speculator tends to be a weak market participant for several reasons. First of all, he reflects an unfortunate tendency to over-trade, with the result that when prices move against him even moderately, he may have no choice except to liquidate his position. The public speculator is also likely to be a poor student of the commodity in which he is trading. His information, as often as not, consists of rumor, hunch, and market "tips" from others, who are probably no better informed than himself. Lacking solid confidence in the reasons which prompted him to establish a commodity position to begin with, at the first sign of a problem he may peremptorily liquidate his holdings as the only way to find protection against unanticipated and unforeseen developments. A further reason the public speculator tends to constitute "weak hands" in the market is his unending search for a "quick million". He is a *plunger*.

Commodity speculation, like other forms of economic activity, requires information, perspective, and above all, great patience. The public speculator who has had a few successes in the market wants to be constantly committed. To do so is to court certain disaster. The wise speculator only takes a position when he has strong reason to believe that "the trade is wrong" and will subsequently revise its price opinion. As long as prices are at levels which appear reasonable in the face of known facts, then it follows that there is no reason for price to change appreciably. Taking a position in a commodity ties up money. Until prices do move in the speculator's favor, he will merely succeed in inactivating a portion of his risk capital on the flimsy hope that something beneficial — but totally unforeseen — will happen to benefit him. Such a course of action is, at best, folly. It will certainly lead to eventual failure.

The "strong hands" in the market are strong for good reason. First, they represent well-financed professional speculators, along with commercial interests who use the market for hedging purposes. With adequate resources to underpin their judgment and absorb some reasonable "paper losses" while they wait for their expectations to be realized, they are much harder to "shake loose" from a good position. They have the financial ability and the speculative professionalism to take a loss and forget about it when events refute their earlier appraisal. But so long as their first judgment continues to appear valid, they will not be driven into liquidating a position for small or transitory reasons.

The "strong hands" in the marketplace are, for the most part, careful students of the topic. They have made it their business to acquire broad knowledge of each commodity in which they interest themselves; including its production, processing methods, trade channels and vulnerability to substitution by other materials. Finally, these "strong hands" are invariably pursuing an established speculative policy which includes firm *profit expectations* and *maximum limitations* on total *commitments* — and acceptable *losses* — at any given time. They do not mind occasionally being out of the market, having learned that the opportunities they seek are not always present. However, when an attractive situation presents itself they have both the capital and the courage to exploit it fully. In speaking of technical market conditions, we are referring in large measure to the behavior of "strong" and "weak" hands in establishing and managing commodity positions; and how they perform in the face of adversity. This, in turn, is greatly influenced by the respective objectives and expectations of the two classifications of market users.

Price is Secondary to a Hedger

It was previously pointed out that the strong hands in the marketplace include well financed professional speculators and *commercial interests*. The latter group is made up of merchants, processors, transporters, etc., who conduct business in the commodity involved. These interests use the market for the purpose of hedging and, as will be seen in the section devoted to this topic, are less concerned with "flat price" movement than they are with the *relationship* between prices in the different delivery months, different geographical locations, and between similar products. As a consequence, the commercials view price movement in a substantially different light than does the individual whose hopes for profit are exclusively pinned to a flat-price change in his favor.

The professional speculator, while usually at the mercy of flat-price movement in his search for profits, tends to establish a position with a well-developed frame of reference as concerns his profit expectations on the one hand, and the "paper loss" he is willing to accept in the interim, while waiting for his objective to be realized.

Weak-Hands Make Bad Matters Worse

Public speculators usually operate without the advantages of a firm opinion concerning either profit goal or loss limit, and further handicapped by a scarcity of solid information upon which to govern his decisions. When they "run for cover", the retreat is seldom an orderly one.

For example, in a market situation in which the public overwhelmingly occupies the long side, downward price movement which results in losses on the part of the "weak hands" may set off a rash of selling orders as the public speculators scramble to escape from their losing positions. The added selling volume, of course, merely adds downward pressure to the prices, accelerating and worsening the situation. The farther prices move downward, the more desperate the weak-handed longs become. The price slide may not be halted until all of these weak-holders are driven out of the market.

The same thing — in the opposite frame of reference — may occur when a large public interest is present on the short side of a contract. An increase in price represents losses to the shorts. Without either adequate financing to weather the storm or sufficient information to enable them to see a temporary price fluctuation for what it is, the public shorts, in their rush to offset their impaired positions, may send the prices sharply higher on the crest of a flood of orders to buy back and offset their previously established short positions.

It is precisely this kind of market phenomenon which can grow out of alternative situations that are usually described as "over-bought" or "over-sold" market conditions.

Over-Bought/Over-Sold

Let us consider an "over-bought" market in which there is a substantial long public interest. Obviously the longs want prices to move higher. Some rapidly developing piece of news may have bearish implications. Prices fluctuate downward slightly in response to the new information and, in doing so, they touch off resting "stop loss" orders, or precipitate defensive selling on the part of public longs who are keeping a close "eye" on the market. In the face of this increasing "bear" pressure, prices continue to move lower; much lower in fact, than the news which set off the initial fluctuation would conceivably call for.

The result is that what could have ordinarily — and should have logically — been a minor downward adjustment, is turned into a major price slide due to the general selling "chain reaction" which the bearish news *only started*.

When this happens, the "over-bought" condition may turn into an "over-sold" situation. Now we have the exact opposite frame of reference. The predictable tendency on the part of "weak hands" in the marketplace to abandon commodity positions quickly and in concert, tends to over-emphasize price fluctuations; price rises are carried higher than the facts indicate they should go, and price drops fall farther than reasonable appraisal of the news actually justifies.

Trading "Bulges" & "Dips"

Since this tendency to over-buy good news and over-sell bad news is so pronounced, it offers an excellent opportunity for seasoned and more sagacious traders to capitalize on the price extremes which are thus produced. A well-recognized trading technique among professionals consists of selling "price bulges" and buying "price dips". This merely pre-supposes that a price move downward in a contract with a large public interest will probably be driven further than it should go. Once the sell-off has run its course, the wise speculator can often turn a quick profit by taking a long position near the bot-

Plate 19

tom of the dip and riding it back up to the point of re-established market equilibrium.

In the opposite situation, once a price bulge has taken place as a result of "squeezing" public shorts, the more discerning speculator can profit by going short at the crest of the bulge and riding the position back down to the price balance point.

Commodity markets vary widely, but it is perfectly safe to say that the larger the public participation in any given market, the more susceptible it is to wide fluctuations precipitated by stop-loss orders triggered by news, rumor, or mere suspicion. Commodity exchanges invariably have rules prohibiting the spreading of rumors and yet, human nature being what it is, rumors endlessly float across the trading floor. Some of these tales later prove to be reliable. Many of them prove to be largely or completely false. But the impact of each new piece of information, whether valid or not, will probably be given credence by a few traders. If the story "catches on" it can, like a small rock tumbling from the top of a snow covered mountain, precipitate first a slide and then an avalanche. In the short-term scheme of things, sharply breaking news or gossip must be accorded an important place among all of the things which can affect prices.

The "position" trader must be constantly on guard against being stampeded into unwise action which grows out of this sort of transitory consideration. The public trader is rarely in any position to capitalize on these small price movements. Therefore, he has little choice except to steel himself against the urge to make longer-range judgments on the basis of exceedingly short-term considerations.

To sum up, analyzing a commodity market calls for three levels of evaluation:

(1) Long-range or "big picture" situation

(2) Medium-range trading strategy

(3) Short-term tactics.

The answers developed in connection with each of these time segments *may not coincide* at any particular point. However, unless all three intervals of concern are brought into focus, the speculator runs the risk of being misled in pursuit of his over-all objective. It takes perspective to keep from giving a short-term price development weight out of all proportion to its true value.

The experience of millions of traders is the best possible evidence that it is easier to establish a position than it is to close one out. This is all the more reason that the trader should have confidence in his *reasons* for placing an order to buy or sell any commodity; and that he have a loss limit firmly in mind; or formally entered with his broker—along with a solid profit expectation, *before establishing any position*.

Speculation is not an exercise in lucky guesses. It is an activity which depends on knowledge, courage, and financial ability. Only by keeping this operational trinity constantly before him can a speculator enter the market with reasonable hope of profit from his activities here.

CHAPTER IX

HOW HEDGERS USE THE MARKET

In order for the speculator to be able to render reliable judgments about market behavior, he must be at least generally aware of the interests and methods of his "competition". Among the several classifications of buyers and sellers, one of the most important groups can be broadly identified as "hedging interests". By and large, hedgers are commercial firms who deal directly in the various commodities. In grain, for example, hedgers include farmers who produce the crops, merchants who buy and then re-sell the cash grain, processors who convert the commodities from their natural form into various products, and wholesalers who put the finished products into their ultimate channels of consumption and use.

In order to explain hedging, it seems best to begin with the chronological events in a normal cash or spot sale. A grain merchant might buy 5,000 bushels of oats from a farmer and immediately resell it to a breakfast food manufacturer. Provided both the purchase "at wholesale" and the sale "at retail" could be made at about the same time, there would be slight, if any, risk to the merchant on the basis of price change on the commodity during the short interval between his acquisition and resale of the merchandise.

We might even consider a situation in which a grain merchant consummates the (short) cash sale to the breakfast food manufacturer *first* and then *later* makes the purchase of the grain required to fill his sales commitment. In either event, the grain merchant's profit would be the difference between his buying and selling price. (For purposes of this example, we have ignored handling and transportation costs.)

Trade Sequence Doesn't Affect Profit or Loss

It is important to keep in mind that trading *profit always and only accrues from selling at a price greater than the cost of acquisition.* It makes no difference whether the purchase comes first followed by the sale; or the sale is made first followed by the purchase. The chronology of events can be ignored. A profit arises from selling something for *more* than you paid for it. A loss results from selling something for *less* than you paid for it.

Returning now to our example of the grain merchant who acquires oats from the farmer and resells them to a manufacturer, it was noted that if both ends of this transaction could be accomplished without delay, there would be little opportunity for price changes to alter the profit position of the middle-man. Now let us add a longer time dimension to the hypothetical case.

Time Involves Risk

Let us assume that the grain merchant has purchased oats from the producing farmer in early October and must put them in storage because he has no immediate sale for the product. Let us furthermore assume that at the time of his purchase from the farmer, the market price on oats "in the country" is 70¢ per bushel. With the product now on hand, the owner of the grain must recognize that the price of oats will certainly fluctuate. He has purchased the commodity at 70¢ per bushel. If the market price increases beyond this level, he will profit in terms of an increase in inventory value. If the price falls from this level, he will sustain a loss on the value of his inventory. Certainly a profit is always welcome, but the opportunities for a loss should be avoided, if at all possible. Hedging provides a means for *reducing negative risks* while still leaving an *opportunity for a trading profit* on stored commodities.

The "Perfect" Hedge

Fundamentally, a hedge is a protective device. A simple example is that of the individual who makes a $5.00 bet on runner "A" in a two-man race a week in advance of the contest. At the time he places his wager, he is confident that his man will win. Two days before the event, however, track star "A" pulls a muscle, which changes the situation completely. The bettor is, at this point, virtually certain that his man will lose. However, he has already wagered that "A" will be victorious. He cannot nullify the original bet, but he can *hedge* his risk exposure. A "perfect" hedge can be placed, by taking an *equal and opposite position*. He now places a second $5.00 wager that "A" will *not win* the upcoming race. (A and B may run a tie, and the hedge is still "perfect".)

Having bet *with* runner "A" in the first instance and *against* him in the second instance, he can watch the contest with complete equanimity, knowing that whichever way the event turns out, he will win one $5.00 wager and lose the other. Profit and loss will offset

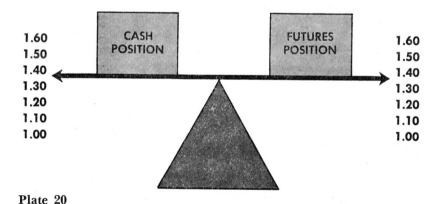

Plate 20

Theoretically "perfect" profit protection. Extremely rare!

exactly. He has a *perfect hedge* against the loss, which he obtained at the price of surrendering any opportunity to gain.

Commodity Hedges are Seldom "Perfect"

Commodity hedging is not this precise, for reasons which will be explored in detail later. However, although commodity hedges are something less than "perfect", they still provide a means of removing or minimizing possibilities for loss—while also offering opportunities for extra "hedging profit".

Reduced to its simplest terms, commodity futures markets permit a hedger to make *substitute purchases* and *substitute sales* which offer some measure of profit protection until such time as actual customer transactions in cash merchandise can be consummated.

Consider once more the grain merchant who buys 5,000 bushels of oats at 70¢ per bushel. On the October date when he purchases the commodity, July oats futures are selling on the Chicago Board of Trade at 79¢ per bushel. On the surface this would appear to present a clear opportunity for 9¢ profit, but this is not the case. The merchant purchased the oats "in the country". In order to get the 79¢ price, the product must be moved into the Chicago market, which involves transportation costs and handling fees. Also, the oats must be stored until July—some eight months away. It is therefore seen that, while the grain dealer has purchased oats at "9¢ under July", if he is to realize the 79¢ price the market promises him at the later date, he must first defray loading and transportation costs and carrying charges for the period involved.

Still, the fact remains that by *selling* the July oats *futures* against his *purchase* of the *cash* commodity, the market will offer a form of "profit insurance" during the period of time he holds the inventory— whether or not he elects to hold the oats until the following July and ultimately deliver it against a short futures position.

We might assume that the grain merchant would prefer buying from the farmer and immediately contracting its sale to a customer at an established mark-up and at a designated point in the future. However, purchase and sale of cash commodities cannot always be simultaneously arranged. Yet, in order to stay in business, the merchant must own and store a grain inventory. Although willing to hold huge stocks, commercial firms are usually reluctant to speculate on price behavior—and for excellent reason! With a million bushels of grain in storage, a price drop of 1¢ per bushel means a $10,000 loss in product value. In order to avoid this possibility, large holders of commodity stocks usually accumulate their supplies from producing sources and immediately hedge it by sale of an equivalent amount of commodity futures. The sales of futures contracts (against purchases of cash grain for physical inventory) are nothing more than substitutes for the sales of physical goods which will be made later.

After purchasing grain from the farmer and selling an equivalent amount of futures contracts, the grain merchant will later transact sales with customers for the cash product. As rapidly as cash sales are consummated, the "short hedges" in the futures market will be bought back—or offset—since there is no longer any purpose for maintaining the futures position. The hedge in futures has performed its function for the period of time the inventory needed profit protection.

Prices Move in "Concert"

Hedging is an effective means of minimizing risk exposure, because of the tendency of futures prices and cash prices to maintain *more or less stable relationships*. For purposes of demonstration, we shall consider three levels of values. Consider contract oats in the Chicago cash market as selling for 75¢ per bushel on September 1. The carrying charge on oats, which is comprised of insurance, storage costs, and interest on money represented in stock, will average about $1\frac{1}{2}$¢ per bushel per month. Consequently, if the spot price is 75¢, the *same grade* of commodity in the *same location* might be expected to reflect a price of $79\frac{1}{2}$¢ on the futures contract which calls for delivery *three months hence*. The $4\frac{1}{2}$¢ differential would be comprised of the carrying charges for the period of time involved: $1\frac{1}{2}$¢ per month multiplied by three months. The futures contract for delivery six months later will usually reflect a larger carrying charge, based on the longer storage time involved. This element in price relationship may be viewed as a *time differential*. There is also a differential based on geographic location.

Location Differences Affect Prices

The major grain market is in Chicago and prices in the Chicago market are predicated on location (or delivery) of the commodities within the market complex. "Out of position" products are worth proportionately less, since they must be moved to the market city in order to command the market price. If cash oats in Chicago is quoted at 75¢ per bushel, we might expect to see cash oats in Peoria, Illinois, quoted at 70¢, since freight rates indicate that it will cost about 5¢ per bushel to load and move oats by rail over the 200 miles or so involved. Oats in Lincoln, Nebraska would be worth proportionately less because freight costs would be greater. Oats in Wichita, Kansas could be worth even less than the same product in Omaha, because of the greater distance it would have to be hauled before it would be "in position" for delivery in the pricing market.

The price surface chart in Plate 62, although necessarily useful only as a rough gauge of locational price differences, will indicate the magnitude of transportation considerations in establishing values on grains in key production and market locations.

Discovery of price, as has been noted previously, takes place in the market in which the commodity is traded. Although central "market prices" and "country prices" differ, both with respect to geographical location and the period of time which the merchandise must be held pending delivery date, cash prices, futures prices, and country prices, all tend to move up and down together. As we will subsequently see, the differentials between these price levels may narrow or widen, depending on considerations of current *local* shortage or over-supply. But—with occasional exceptions—they *do move in concert*. An increase in the central market price will usually bring an increase of about the same magnitude—in all of the other commodity's categories, both locationally and time-wise.

Futures Price is the Cash Price Reference

Offers to buy or sell traded commodities are usually quoted in terms of a designated premium or discount "on" or "off" the nearby futures contract. Thus, if the nearby (December) oats futures contract is selling at 75¢ per bushel in Chicago, the Peoria offering for oats might be "3¢ off December", and the Wichita bid might be "6½¢ off December". In certain situations, the country bid might be a premium over the nearby futures market price; but, in any event, the *nearest futures price* quotation is the usual *basing point for cash bids.* An increase of 2¢ a bushel in the futures price will therefore bring an immediate 2¢ increase in the country bid, inasmuch as offers are not communicated in terms of established prices, but rather of *price relationship* "on" or "off" *the futures.*

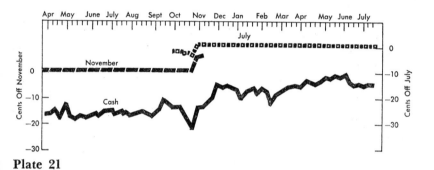

Plate 21

A "normal" market pays a premium for delivery at a later date.

To return now to the interest and the market activities of the hedger, let us again direct our attention to the basic purpose for which the commercial dealer in physical commodities uses the futures markets. We have stated previously that a hedge is an equal and opposite position in futures to the position held in the cash commodity. If a hedger is long—owns—cash coffee, he will be short coffee futures. Conversely, if the coffee merchant has contracted to deliver the cash product at some point in the future at a fixed price, his position is one of being *short the cash* commodity, and his risk will be hedged by holding a *long* position in *futures* contracts. In trade terminology, a "short hedge" consists of *selling futures* contracts; a "long hedge" involves *buying futures* contracts.

An unfortunate tendency exists on the part of most economic writers to demonstrate hedging with examples of perfect price correlation, where the market value of the cash product raises a prescribed amount and the price on its futures climbs in perfect step with it. Thus, the hedger who holds a cash inventory gains (or loses) a designated amount on his inventory and recaptures precisely the same amount on the value of his hedging position.

Ideal though this perfect hedge may appear to be, price behavior is seldom so closely attuned between the two markets. A hedge in actual practice is rarely "perfect". (It seldom results in a zero net outcome on the combined cash and futures situation.) In the world of reality, hedges, imperfect as they are—can be used to reduce risks, and in some cases, a well placed hedge can produce an impressive additional profit. It deserves to be emphasized that the *additional hedging profit* opportunity is an important, if not the principal, reason that commercial interests engage in hedging. A badly placed hedge may, on the other hand, actually *increase* risk exposure. It can be assumed that the highly skilled professionals who conduct this type of operation for their firms, earnestly attempt to place profitable hedges. They studiously avoid those situations which promise little, if any, mitigation of risk exposure and offer only limited opportunities for enhanced return from their combined cash/futures operations.

From a practical point of view, the speculator must recognize that the commercial hedger, more often than not, represents his "competition" for profits in the market. This, because when a commercial firm places a hedge, the public speculator is usually on the "other side" of the transaction, as either buyer or seller. If the hedger is to profit from his hedge, it follows that he must do so at the expense of "other parties" in the market. If the speculator profits, it must also come from a commensurate loss sustained by "other parties" who hold opposite positions.

Hedgers Select the Risks They "Pass" to the Market

It has been said before, but it cannot be over-emphasized—hedgers seek more than mere "profit insurance" from their market operations. While a great many firms pursue a consistent policy of hedging a large proportion of both their long and short positions in cash commodities, it must be understood that hedging is *not an automatic procedure.* Unless a given cash position presents substantial elements of risk from price change, a hedge may not be placed at all. Or, in another situation, where the futures market shows an attractive opportunity for trading profits, so-called "anticipatory hedging" may take place which, until the related cash transactions are consummated, represents speculation in futures.

It is not unusual for a commercial interest to describe his position as being "90% hedged" or "110% hedged". This merely indicates that people who deal in cash commodities also render subjective judgments about the *good risks* which they are willing to bear themselves and the *bad risks* which they prefer to pass along to the market. Hedging, as practiced in the commercial trade, is a highly selective kind of thing. This knowledge should serve to underscore the importance of the speculator also carefully selecting the risks he is willing to undertake; using equal, or—if possible—even greater caution than the hedger does. This, since the risks which hedgers—and other traders—offer to the market must *always* be viewed with some *suspicion*.

The speculator must make his choices between propositions which, in the appraisal of other traders or commercial hedging interest, are too negative, or fraught with too much uncertainty to permit their being carried directly. If this were not so, they would probably not be hedged in the first place.

"Basis" in Hedging Activities

The key consideration in commercial hedging is the price *relationship* between *cash* commodities and the *nearby futures* price. This price differential is ordinarily spoken of as the "basis". As pointed out earlier, futures prices in a "normal" market are higher than current "cash" prices by part or all of the costs of carrying the merchandise from the present date to the projected date of delivery. Bear in mind that this is nothing more than statement of the *average* condition. Depending on relative scarcity or over-supply, the basis may vary substantially. In understanding the differential between cash prices and the nearby futures prices, or the differential between the nearby futures price and prices on more deferred contracts, it is well to begin with a closer look at what carrying charges entail.

How Hedgers Use the Market

First and foremost is the matter of *storage* itself. Each commodity has its own storage requirements which are translatable into a storage cost, which must be absorbed by someone. The second element in carrying charges is *insurance* on the commodity in question. Depending on its susceptibility to spoilage or other deterioration in quality or quantity over time, and further depending on the kind of warehouse or other storage facility in which it is being held, insurance rates can differ widely. The third cost of carrying a commodity is *interest* on money, since if the commodity exists, *someone* owns it; and so long as it is in storage status, it represents *invested capital* to the extent of its full market value. An interest charge for use of the money tied up must be theoretically accepted, whether interest is actually paid to a bank or other financial institution, or not.

Carrying charges, therefore, are made up of three separate items; storage costs, insurance, and interest. In a market situation where supply and demand are in reasonable equilibrium, the market will reflect a carrying charge "premium" on products being held for later delivery. In a situation where an immediate scarcity exists, however, carrying charges on deferred contracts will narrow, disappear, or actually reflect an "inversion", which may be viewed as a *negative carrying charge.*

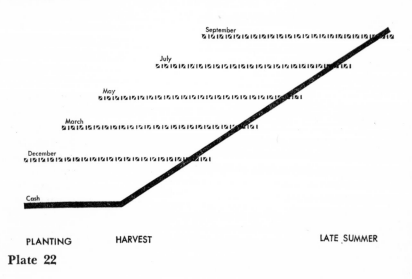

Plate 22

112

Inversion — "Negative Carrying Charge"

For example, in a situation where wheat is in relatively short supply and goal demand, the immediate crisis in this foodstuff would bring high prices in the cash market as well as into the nearby futures. The market gives priority attention to the immediate situation and tends to "discount the future". Therefore, in the situation outlined, we might find cash wheat selling at $2.00 per bushel, with the nearby futures at about the same level. The more deferred futures—six months or more off—may be selling at several cents per bushel *less* than either the cash price or the nearby futures contract.

In practical effect, the market is saying to the holder of wheat— "Your merchandise is needed *now*. Present it in the market, and we will pay you a premium for it. If you continue to hold it, we will not only refuse to pay you for your carrying costs, but you will likely realize an even lower price for the merchandise itself."

In a period of serious scarcity, current and nearby prices always rise more precipitously than deferred prices. It is in such a situation that steep inversions—negative carrying charges—are invariably encountered.

In the face of excessive supplies, the absolute opposite situation exists. Immediately following harvest, for example, the market is usually vastly over-supplied with grain. The post-harvest glut nearly always produces low prices for the cash and nearby deliveries, with relatively higher prices offered in the more distant contracts. Here, the message of the market is—"We have more grain than we can presently use. If you insist on selling your wheat now, you must accept a low price for it. However, if you will hold the product for a few months, we will pay you a carrying charge and may pay a higher price for the commodity itself."

In periods of over-supply, distant contracts usually reflect the greatest premiums. The phenomenon arises directly out of the fact that the market is attempting to discourage increases in the already excessive physical stocks on hand in the market. By offering premiums for later deliveries, it encourages holding stocks back until consumption has a chance to catch up with supplies.

Plate 23

In an adequately supplied market, **deferred** futures will reflect some carrying charge over **cash** and **nearby** prices. Shortage puts a "premium" on the **present,** and "discounts" the **future.** Over-supply may produce a differential between cash and futures prices which is equal to full carrying-charges for the period involved. The **premium** on futures will **never exceed** full carrying-charges, although "inversions" may reflect **any** extent of **discount.**

In view of the foregoing, it should not be surprising to learn that the *basis,* (which may refer to the price differential between *cash* and any *named futures*) fluctuates significantly throughout the year. Immediately following harvest, the basis tends to be at its widest point, reflecting high costs of insufficient storage. The result is produced by an excess of commodities seeking a home. In order to find storage, owners of cash comodities must be willing to pay a high price for it (or accept lower prices for their mechandise).

In periods of current scarcity, the basis reaches its smallest differential, since this condition produces an excess of available storage space and a shortage of commodities to occupy it. The price that storage—like other services—can command in an over-supplied market is reduced; may be nil. Or, if the situation is sufficiently extreme, the carrying charge may go below zero, producing a price inversion defined earlier as a "negative carying charge".

114

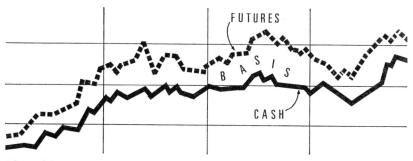

Plate 24

Even in "normal" markets, the price differential between cash and futures fluctuates widely, offering opportunities for profitable hedging and attracting a great deal of speculative "spreading" between multiple futures contracts.

Buy "Discounts" — Sell "Premiums"

Excessive supplies of cash commodities in the market produce *discounts* on cash commodities usually accomplished by *premiums* on futures. A shortage of cash supplies tends to put *premiums* on cash and the nearby futures prices, accomplished by *discounts* on more distant maturities. Hedgers and experienced speculators—if they can do so—prefer *buying discounts* and *selling premiums*. Therefore, it is logical to discover that at the end of a harvest season, commercial interests are large buyers of the discounted cash grain and equally large sellers of the premium priced futures. The price differential is the "basis" for their hedging.

As the season wears on, and the stock of cash commodities is reduced through distribution and consumption, commercial hedgers gradually become net buyers of futures. They must do so. As they transact cash business out of their inventories, they "lift" their previously placed hedges by buying them back in the market. With the previously-existing over-supply problem reduced or non-existent, the hedger may not be able to actually "buy discounts" in offsetting pre-

115

vious short "premium" sales in futures, but any narrowing of the "basis" can bring a good profit, as we shall see.

Theoretical price relationships *limit the amount a deferred futures contract can exceed a nearby, to the amount reflected in carrying charges* on the commodity. This is to say that if carrying charges on a given commodity amount to 3¢ per month per bushel, the July premium over May will not exceed 9¢ (Three months $\times$ 3¢ per month.) As a practical matter, it will probably never reach the full carrying charge. As it approaches the point, commercial interests will sell the distant full-carrying-change month, and buy back their hedges in the nearby—discounted—month, thereby assuring themselves a better return on their storage space and inventory investment.

In "moving" their short hedges "out", their buying activities will tend to raise the lower priced nearby contract, while their selling activities will lower the higher priced distant contract. The same consideration will also prompt speculators to simultaneously "buy the discount" and "sell the premium"—thereby taking a *spreading* position. As a result, the price differential between the two will be narrowed to *something less* than full carrying charges.

Similar evaluations can be made of price dislocations which may exist between markets. If the price of Minneapolis wheat goes out of line either negatively or positively with respect to Chicago prices, speculators will buy in the relatively under-priced market, and sell in the higher priced market. Their activities will re-establish something approaching a reasonable pricing equilibrium between the two, in light of transportation costs, etc.

Although the carrying charge theory limits the amount by which the price on a deferred futures may exceed a nearer futures to the carrying costs involved on the commodity, there is *no theoretical limit* to the amount of *inversion between futures prices.*

As this is being written, expiring November soybeans futures in the Chicago market are trading at $3.06 per bushel. January soybeans are trading at $2.98. Thus, an 8¢ per bushel premium is being currently offered for contract grade soybeans for immediate delivery. The owner of soybeans will not only fail to receive a carrying charge by holding onto his inventory for the next two months; he will receive 8¢ per bushel *less* for them two months hence, on the basis of today's prices! Of course, further price changes over the next sixty days may alter the January quotation significantly. As of today, however, a serious shortage of soybeans exists which has produced a steep price inversion. The market is saying, "Your soybeans are needed far more urgently now than they will be two months from now when new-crop supplies should be adequate. If you sell them today, we will pay you more for them than we will in January. If you hold them, you stand to lose both your costs of carrying them to the later date, as well as sustaining an appreciable reduction in their intrinsic value."

It is important that the speculator clearly understand the various factors which can create price inversions like the one set forth above. In the given soybean situation, there are ample stocks of the product in existence. However, the farmers, following harvest, elected to hold their beans rather than sell them. This concerted holding action on the part of producers created a shortage which can only be corrected by offering sufficiently higher prices to lure farm stocks out of their "first hands". The market is not concerned with the *reason* behind the shortage. It can only reflect the fact that demand for this product substantially exceeds offerings. Until such time as supply/demand forces resume a measure of balance, prices can confidently be expected to hold at this level or work higher. Should the holders of soybeans suddenly decide to bring their stocks to market, over-supply could quickly replace the current scarcity, forcing prices down; and re-establishing a carrying charge on more distant futures months.

As pointed out earlier, excessive holding on the part of producers or any other group of interests, or a "bottleneck" of any kind in the distributive chain, may be reflected in price increases in the first instance—and substantially lower prices later on. As concerns agricultural crops particularly, consumption must necessarily be spread somewhat evenly over the "crop year". If owners—or events—hold the product out of the market too long, the result can create a situation in which existing supplies cannot be physically consumed in the time remaining before the next crop. If such a condition develops, it could be expected to result in depressed prices on the "hoarded", hence excessive stocks.

In summation, it can be said that price relationships between nearby and more distant futures contracts are a measurement of shortage or over-supply. A "normal" market will reflect *some* premium for carrying an inventory. If supplies are excessive, the carrying charge may be a large one, covering most or all of the costs involved.

In a situation of under-supply, the carrying charge on the deferred futures will be reduced; may disappear entirely; or may come to an inversion. To repeat for emphasis, there is no limit to the extent of price inversion which may develop, depending on the market's appraisal of the crisis which exists. The private speculator should always bear in mind that commercial hedgers try to *buy discounts* and *sell premiums*. Whether establishing flat-price speculative positions or *spreading*, when a speculator departs from this practice, he should have strong reasons for doing so. Whenever he can be in the position of also buying discounts and selling premiums, he can usually count on hedging activity to assist in moving prices in his favor.

CHAPTER X

LAUNCHING A PROGRAM IN COMMODITY SPECULATION

There are few, if any, beginning flight students who would undertake to "solo" without first getting a good deal of ground training and "dual" instruction. It would be an equally rare individual who would go into a world series without pre-game preparation. Yet, strangely enough, the speculative plains are literally strewn with the bleached bones of courageous, inexperienced speculators who felt it completely unnecessary to develop their techniques and pre-test their abilities in the market through study and practice. Most of these speculative casualities enter the market with little more than a notion that "there is money to be made in commodities". They leave the market convinced that money can be both *made* and *lost* in commodities. Their own experience is grim documentation of the second fact.

A highly qualified agricultural economist who combines academic distinction with a firsthand knowledge of the commodity markets, is authority for the statement that most public speculators suffer two financial debacles before they leave the market for good. Perhaps it does take two disappointing experiences to convince the average newcomer to commodity speculation that he has neither the finances nor the nervous system to withstand its demands. Perhaps it takes three such catastrophes; or only one. The number of failures required to

Launching a Program in Speculation

accomplish the result is not so important as the fact that a high proportion of speculative failures could be turned into successes by some *common sense preparation in advance* of actual entry into the market. Commodity speculation should be learned *without risking money on one's untried judgment.*

Most people are less than satisfied with their first efforts in any demanding field. It should not surprise anyone to learn that unskilled speculators are prone to lose more money than they make in the beginning stages of their speculative careers. There is hardly a successful professional speculator alive who will not admit that his first speculative undertakings produced highly disappointing results. With experience comes ability, however, and provided one has the intelligence, tenacity, finances and strong nerves required to take the speculator's role in the marketplace, rich rewards await him.

There is no such thing as having a "natural talent" for commodity speculation. While the field is far less complex than speculation in stocks, real estate, or international currencies, it is, nevertheless, a most demanding business. Those who seriously apply themselves to it have a good chance for success. Those who approach it haphazardly—as a financial "fling"—will certainly lose their money sooner or later—and they deserve to lose it.

The first step in embarking on a speculative program is to equip yourself for efficient function. Ships of the U. S. Fleet, combat pilots and performing artists make innumerable "dry runs" or rehearsals to sharpen judgment and develop reflexes necessary to insure efficient operation when faced with the "real thing". This is precisely the way commodity speculation should be approached. Several weeks, or even a few months of practice, is *minimal preparation* before a beginning speculator should hazard his first dollar in the market.

The first question which requires answering involves selection of a single commodity in which to concentrate initial attention. Whether the choice be coffee, corn, pork bellies, or wool, an almost limitless amount of information is available from both private and official sources. Let's assume that an agricultural crop is selected for a beginning. The homework should follow a more-or-less firm outline:

    1. Using the facilities of a good library, familiarize yourself with

all of the pertinent information you can find about the crop itself; its geographic distribution, growing season, historical production and use patterns, federal support and acreage control program, if any; and other commodities which compete directly or indirectly with it in the marketplace.

2. Accumulate a background of price and trading information on the futures contracts, including historical high and lows, seasonal price behavior, open interest, hedging activity, crop disappearance, and trading volume. Any good brokerage office will be glad to help you locate this kind of material.

By seeking out such information and *digesting* it, the serious student of the subject will, in a surprisingly short period, have acquired well-above-average knowledge about the commodity. With his interest thus concentrated, he will discover that the daily newspaper, business press, weekly news magazines and trade publications, constantly add to his fund of knowledge about the crop and enhance his "feel" for the commodity and its market.

3. As soon as the commodity is selected, the speculator-in-training should begin immediately to follow daily price quotations on the exchange or exchanges where it is traded. Note particularly the price behavior of the selected commodity, *as compared with the market in general.* Attempt to develop an understanding of why the *general market* might be up, and prices on the *selected commodity* unchanged or lower; or why the selected commodity might out-perform all other agricultural commodities on a given day or week. Do not abandon interest in finding the answer to a question of this kind just because the event has passed. Market analysts are always experts in hind-sight. They can invariably explain why a particular price adjustment occurred—twenty-four hours later. The successful speculator must learn to *project* a given piece of news in terms of probable impact on prices. The primary function of the speculator is to forecast changes in value in the future. If he can do this, he has no other worries. Learning to do it takes both *knowledge* and *practice.*

4. While a professional charting service can be an important aid and a great time-saver for the individual who is unable to

maintain his own price behavior data, at the outset subscribe to only a weekly or monthly service—and mark your own *daily* price data. A daily newspaper, pencil and ruler are all that is required. After each day's trading range is known, enter the high, low, and closing price on the contracts in which you are interested. In addition to maintaining this simple bar chart on price ranges and closes, plot a ten- or twenty-day moving price average as well. Moving-price is arrived at by taking all daily *settlements* prices for the period involved, adding them together and dividing by the number of days in the control interval. Each day thereafter, the *oldest* settlement price is dropped, the *latest* settlement price is added, and the total figure is re-divided by the number of days being used. The result is plotted as a dot on the chart. A moving average will help you identify short-term aberrations— and *think in terms of trend.*

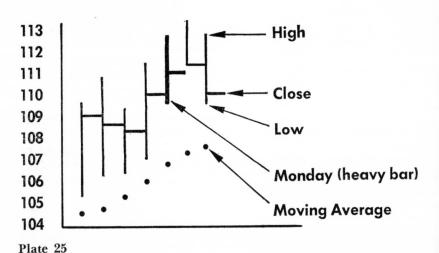

Plate 25

Launching a Program in Speculation

Charts & Chart Traders

Chart devotees are by no means agreed as to the best charting method. Nor, for that matter, do they concur as to the theoretical validity or practical usefulness of charts as price projection devices. This much can be said for the charts, however, and with no fear of contradiction:

There are sufficient traders in the market whose activities are influenced to *some* degree by chart patterns, that the individual trader—whether or not he is willing to pin his success exclusively to the chart concept—can ill afford to ignore the chart traders. Those who follow charts exclusively, or to some extent, are legion! They can "move" a market.

The mere exercise of maintaining a chart on daily prices and moving averages will force the newcomer to speculation to think critically about trading ranges and general movement of price levels—higher, sideways, or lower. While the beginning student of speculation is developing his own powers of analysis, chart patterns will materially assist him in developing a firm notion about new position

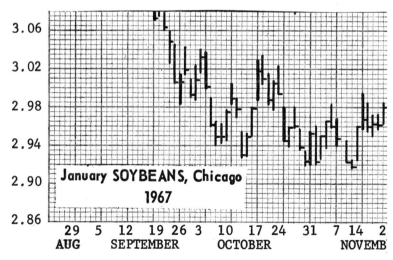

Plate 26

points—and profit expectations and loss limits in any particular position he might take.

In Plate No. 26, for example, a "long" position established at $2.96 in January soybeans has an obvious stop-loss point. If prices should break through the 2.91½ level, it would represent an important down-side penetration and would probably trigger heavy selling on the part of people who put important store in chart trading techniques. The stop-loss order should, therefore, be placed no lower than $2.91 to protect against such a possibility.

If the trader chooses to establish a "short" position at $2.96 per bushel in January soybeans, the chart again clarifies the point at which his stop-loss should be placed. If the price moves above $2.99½, it would constitute a new inetrim breakout on the top-side, with the next higher objective at about $3.04.

The stop-loss on such a short position, therefore, should be at the point at which the initial upside penetration is sufficiently obvious to prompt concerted buying on the part of chart traders.

Statistical price-projection techniques and chart analysis has been dealt with in great detail by other writers. For this work, suffice it to say that whether one agrees with the theory of price forecasting on the basis of past price behavior—and your author does not—there are enough market participants who do place some degree of store in this notion as to constitute a *significant force in the market*. While it may be argued most effectively that their reasons are not valid, the fact that chartists do tend to trade in concert produces price behaviorisms which attest to their collective "muscle" in the marketplace.

One need not unequivocally endorse the chartists' doctrine in order to recognize him as a force in price determination.

Experimental Trading

5. As soon as the beginning speculator has developed some reasonable background information on his chosen commodity field and has prepared his basic charts on the selected contracts in the commodity, he is ready to begin experimental trading. Plate No. 27 shows a trading card which the

COMMODITY ORDER

LONG
SHORT
OFFSET

Date _____

Order No. _____   Time of Day ____:____

Brokerage House _____

Solicitor Rep. _____

BUY   SELL   Amount _____   Contract _____

Price _____   Limits _____

Stop-Loss _____   Profit Obj. _____

Time-Limit DAY   OPEN   OTHER _____

Disposition EXECUTED   CANCELLED   EXPIRED

Confirmed by _____   Date _____   Time ____:____

Remarks _____

Plate 27

125

author employs regularly, and which will serve the beginning
speculator as effectively as the practicing professional.

Have a stencil cut in a letter shop and a supply of the
form run off on cards. Number each one of the forms in
advance to make sure that in days to come *every practice trade
is recorded.*

There is an overwhelming human tendency for us to remember
successes and forget failures. Speculation requires that *profits be
added* and *losses be subtracted,* with equal diligence. Unless this is
meticulously done, the student of speculation will have no reliable
score-card against which to check his progress in "out-performing the
general market".

6. In addition to the trading cards, a sheet like the one shown in
    Plate No. 28 should also be prepared. *Column 1* is for
    the entry of practice positions taken. *Column 2* carries the
    margin deposit which would be required. *Column 3* reflects
    the profit objective at the time the position is taken. *Column
    4* reflects the stop-loss level where—should prices move against
    you—the position will be automatically closed out by offset.
    Column 5 is for the gross profit or loss on each individual
    trade. *Column 6* carries the brokerage commission—which
    must always be *deducted* from profits, or *added* to losses.
    Column 7 will show net profit or loss on each trade.

    By documenting each position taken on a trading card
    and arraying the salient points of the trade on the recap
    sheet, the beginner in speculation will have an immediate
    check on his open positions, and a running recap of consoli-
    dated gains or losses to date. It is also urged that the losses
    be entered on the recap sheet in *red,* for added emphasis;
    and—hopefully—to prompt careful re-examination of the fac-
    tors which lured you into an unsuccessful speculative position
    in the first place.

POSITION							OFFSET			Gross Profit (Loss)	Brkr. Comm.	Net Profit (Loss)	Total Pos'n. Result	Risk Capital Balance
Date	Long (Short) Price	Amt.	Contract	Margin	Profit Obj.	Stop-Loss	Date	Buy (Sell) Price	Amt.					
6/23	$132\frac{1}{2}$	10	CZ	$800	140	$130\frac{5}{8}$	7/12	(142)	10	$950				2 500 00
2/8	$136\frac{1}{4}$	10	CZ	800	140	$133\frac{5}{8}$	7/12	(142)	10	575				
7/5	$139\frac{1}{2}$	10	CZ	800	147	$135\frac{1}{2}$	7/12	(142)	10	250	$132	$1,643	$1,643	1 643 00
														4 143 00
8/16	$(151\frac{1}{8})$	10	CZ	$800	145	$153\frac{3}{4}$	8/22	$153\frac{3}{4}$	10	$(2,125)$	$440	$(256 \frac{50}{})$	$(256 \frac{50}{})$	(256 50)
														3 886 50
9/1	$(146\frac{3}{4})$	10	CZ	$800	140	$147\frac{3}{8}$								

Plate 28

Each trade should be entered as soon as it is executed, and the data completed after it has been offset.

Launching a Program in Speculation

Practice Trading at a Realistic Level

A key consideration in this exercise is to begin your theoretical trading with a *fixed number of dollars* in the hypothetical margin account. The practice trading figure should be governed by the level at which the novice intends to conduct his *real* trading activity, later.

It makes no sense for a training program in speculation to be set up with the fictional million dollars, when the later entry into the real market will be made with a bankroll of a few thousand, or less. For maximum benefits from practice trading, it should be conducted within the *same practical limitations* that will apply to the real thing. Unless this is done, the exercise is little more than an intriguing game. Amusing though such an engagement might be, it won't have much direct connection with reality. More importantly, it won't contribute much to the search for speculative profits—which is the exclusive purpose of the project.

Establish your hypothetical margin account at the same amount you may expect to ultimately deposit with your broker. *Don't overextend yourself.* It often pays to settle for modest victories, in return for having to face only small defeats. *Patience, courage* and *conservatism* are the three keys to successful speculation.

In any event, an *initial* market position should never tie up more than *fifty percent of margin funds.* For example, the highest minimum margin requirement of any of the grains is that of soybeans which, at this writing, is 15¢ per bushel. The initial margin on one contract (5,000 bushels) of soybeans is therefore $750. In order to prudently undertake such a program, the practicing speculator should have a minimum of $1,500 of margin funds available. Moreover, until the soybean position is closed out and margin funds committed to it are freed, no further *initial* speculative positions should be taken, although a winning position *may later be added to.* This is a most important reason to always keep part of your speculative capital in reserve.

The thinking behind this method of capital management is exceedingly basic:

The overwhelming majority of speculative failures grow directly out of *over-trading.* Newcomers to the field fail to realize that the

128

only survival-insurance a speculator can have is additional cash resources to draw on. As will be demonstrated later, the commodity trader *need not be right even half of the time* in order to make a profit from his speculative endeavors. If four out of ten positions are "right", your survival as a speculator can be confidently predicted; if six out of ten positions taken prove profitable, the profits should be impressive, indeed.

The reason this is true is that throughout his speculative career and in every trading situation, without exception, the successful speculator rigidly adheres to rules which maximize profit opportunities and minimize loss exposures. In the language of the marketplace, he "cuts losses short and lets profits run".

As a result, the *average profit on all profitable positions will be appreciably larger* than the *average loss which will be taken on all losing positions.* Moreover, proven techniques for "pyramiding" can have the effect of multiplying returns from profitable positions. This multiplying factor *never operates in the loss realm,* because *additions are never made to a losing position*—regardless of the circumstances!

So, now, the beginning speculator is set:

1. He has selected his commodity area and informed himself about it.

2. He has obtained basic charts which graphically show short- and medium-range price movement patterns.

3. He has prepared numbered trading cards which will document every hypothetical position he takes and, later, assist in analyzing the components of success or failure in each trade.

4. A trading recap sheet constantly shows consolidated profits or losses to date, while red and black entries offer a realistic basis for evaluating his "batting average" as trading skills, market information and speculative judgment improve.

With his preliminary research done and the simple trading tools at hand, the beginner is ready to begin speculating "on paper".

The effectiveness of this method of study depends entirely on the consistency of the individual in maintaining *complete records* on his hypothetical operations. Each position should be most carefully appraised *before* it is taken. At the time it is taken, it *must be entered* on a numbered trading card, so that it cannot be later "forgotten", regardless of its outcome. The reason should be abundantly clear: Once *real* trading has commenced, every position involves a firm order placed with the broker, and commitment of margin funds to secure it. *Profits* and *losses* are the only two words that mean anything in the real world of speculation, because money is going to be made or money is lost on *every trade*.

The beginner who fails to apply the same hard-headed yardstick to his exploratory activities as the market will impose on him later is needlessly depriving himself of information and experience which will have to be gained somehow. The only pertinent question is whether the learning process will be carried out without jeopardizing funds, or whether speculative lessons will have to be learned later— in the expensive "school of hard knocks".

CHAPTER XI

SELECTING YOUR RISKS

For purposes of this discussion we will assume that the novice to speculation has selected soybeans as the commodity area in which he intends to concentrate attention. Soybeans have been, and continue to be, an exceedingly popular area for public speculation. There are several reasons for this, chief among which is the fact that soybean production in the United States is an expanding activity but one which does not yet appear to have succeeded in catching up with total demand for the product. In view of the continuing relative shortage, higher prices appear to be in prospect as the general trend—subject, of course, to the constant reminder that prices fluctuate in the short-term, regardless of what their longer-range trend may be.

Soybeans offer a good speculative exercise for the serious student for still another reason: There is essentially no use for soybeans in their natural state. The worth of the soybean depends on prices commanded by its two products: soybean meal and oil. Both meal and oil futures are also traded, thus providing the bean speculator with two additional and important points of reference. Soybean prices can be evaluated as being too low, too high, or about right, as *measured in product values.* The relationship between prices on beans vs. meal and oil will be explored in considerable detail later on. For now, we will restrict our attention exclusively to soybean futures, with a view to selecting a particular contract for trade.

Six Contracts From Which to Choose

Six different soybean maturities are usually open for trade at any given time. As this is being prepared, the Chicago Board of Trade has contracts in soybeans open for delivery in January, March, May, July, August and September. Some comment regarding this trading calendar may be in order. (Soybeans are also traded on the New York Produce Exchange.)

The crop year begins in October and runs to the following September. The first "new crop" contract therefore is November, followed by another contract maturity at two-month intervals, until July. The August contract was added to the market schedule to assist cleanup of "old crop" beans and preparation for storage and marketing of the new harvest.

In some years, depending on the weather patterns, a substantial amount of new-crop beans may reach the market in September. Consequently, the September contract has some quandaries in it that are not encountered in other months. If the harvest is late, September supplies may be scanty. If the harvest is early, September may turn out to be a "new-crop" month. As a result of this variable, the September maturity tends to be one of the most volatile in the entire soybean futures calendar.

To set the stage for the basic trading problem, we will use current conditions as they actually exist. The bean market closed yesterday (November 30, 1966) as follows:

Cash market price — $3.00 per bushel
January — $2.99½ per bushel
March — $2.95½ per bushel
May — $2.96 per bushel
July — $2.96¾ per bushel
August — $2.94½ per bushel
September — $2.87¾ per bushel

In analyzing the significance of the price differentials between these contracts, it must be remembered that if the value of the product is fixed and carrying charges are constant, price relationships between commodity months should ascend in a uniform stair-step fashion. Lack of uniformity reflects varying degrees of supply/demand imbalance, as appraised by the market and "discounted" in its assignment of price values.

For example, assuming that $3.00 per bushel represents the "right" cash price for soybeans on this date and further assuming carrying charges of 2½¢ per bushel per month, we could expect to see the several bean contracts reflecting prices as follows:

December 1 — $3.00 per bushel (cash price)
January   — $3.02½ per bushel
March   — $3.07½ per bushel
May   — $3.12½ per bushel
July   — $3.17½ per bushel
August   — $3.20   per bushel
September — $3.22½ per bushel (old crop)

These figures are based on the acceptance of $3.00 per bushel as the "right price" for contract quality soybeans in the cash market on December 1. The same product scheduled for delivery one month hence should theoretically carry a price of $3.02½, with the added 2½¢ representing storage costs, insurance, and interest over the period involved. The same quality product scheduled for delivery March 1 will have incurred 7½¢ in carrying charges over the three month interval involved, and so on.

Instead of finding this orderly state of affairs, however, we see that the current price on contract grade soybeans in the cash market stands at $3.00 per bushel, while the January futures is quoted at $2.99½; a ½¢ *premium* over the nearby futures is offered for "cash" beans for immediate delivery. The March maturity stands at $2.95½, a 7½¢ *discount* off cash. It is not until we compare July with May that we find a small ½¢ carrying premium offered for the later delivery. August, compared to July, returns to the pattern of discounts on more distant months, as does September.

Selecting Your Risks

In evaluating the trading opportunity in soybeans, the first decision is that of selecting the best contract for trade, in light of the personal desires and trading pattern of the speculator. In a *normal market,* often referred to as a "carrying-charge market", we will expect to find cash prices slightly under nearby futures contract, with more distant contracts reflecting carrying-charges in the form of somewhat higher values. Any time this pattern is reversed, it is a reflection of some degree of immediate—and perhaps urgent—scarcity. Whenever prices on the deferred futures show discounts rather than premiums over the nearby contracts, it is spoken of as an "inversion", indicating that the normal price relationships are inverted—"upside down".

In the situation being examined, the shortage of soybeans exists as a result of farmer holding. The 1966 harvest, recently completed, exceeded 931 million bushels, which is substantially greater than any United States bean harvest in the past. Export shipments are, to this point, running well behind the same period a year ago, and soybean "disappearance" as a result of processor crushing is also disappointing in comparison with statistics from earlier years. However, the holding action on the part of the farmers has deprived the market of the beans that it would *like to buy.* The shortage, although contrived, has forced prices up on the cash tables and in the nearby futures contracts.

The market has a consistent record of dealing with "first things first". Present shortage is the high priority problem. The market seeks to solve it by higher prices, which will lure soybeans out of the hands of producers and into the channels of distribution. At the same time, lower prices on more deferred deliveries indicates that the market feels that as time goes by, soybean supplies will be released in larger quantities, and that the larger releases will result in lower prices. The price pattern is a clear example of the market "discounting the future". It may be that in months to come, the present shortage will persist. If this happens, the price on March soybeans may very well move up to a par with present price on January, or may even go higher if the relative shortage becomes more acute. At this point, however, the "market doesn't think" this will happen. Lower price levels on deferred contracts are proof of the statement.

134

The overriding considerations in trading soybeans in the situation being examined are these:

1. Ample stocks of the product are available in the "country", but they have been held out of the market by producers as a means of obtaining higher prices.

2. Present stocks in commercial hands are well under stocks in the same hands a year ago, because farmers have not sold their harvest.

3. Crushing totals to date are running behind the same period a year ago; as are exports.

4. The prospects are that soybean acreage planted in the coming year will be appreciably larger than acreage devoted to this crop in the 1965-66 crop year, which should in turn bring a continuation of the trend to larger yields.

Two distinct possibilities exist for the soybean trader:

a. If he believes the holding movement on the part of farmers will continue beyond the first of the coming year, then the January (and perhaps March) contracts should appear inviting from the *long* side. Moreover, if the farmer holding movement is expected to continue through the first quarter of 1967, then both May and July should offer attractive *short* sales.

The reason is, quite simply, that 1966 beans which do not come to market in the year of their harvest must certainly come to market *prior to the 1967 harvest.* By withholding beans for several months and influencing prices upward, the producers will have obtained their high prices in the interim at the cost of disrupting orderly patterns of consumption through processing and export.

It is logical to assume that *concerted farm holding* will have to be followed by *concerted farm selling.* At some point in early spring or summer, 1967, unseasonally heavy arrivals—and resulting oversupply—will drive prices down, probably creating a "bear market" situation in soybeans for the last four or five months of the crop year.

b. The second possibility is that current premiums on nearby months will be eased by larger soybean arrivals immediately after January 1, 1967. It may be that current farmer holding grows out of a desire on their part to merely defer income on the 1966 crop until the new year, in order to avoid proportionately higher taxes on it. If this case proves to be correct, then the speculator might expect an easing of prices in the January maturity, and relatively higher prices on the deferred months as the contract returns to more "normal" relationships.

The only thing which can sustain premiums on the nearby months is a continuation of the shortage. At whatever point the shortage is broken, carrying charges may be expected to re-appear on later deliveries.

Trading Nearby vs. Deferred

In choosing a futures month in which to trade, it is imperative that the speculator remember that in the face of increasing shortage, prices on the near delivery will move *higher, faster* than on the more deferred maturities. In a situation of increasing over-supply, prices on nearby delivery will move *lower, faster* than on the later months. Generally speaking, trading in the *nearby* month calls for *closer attention* to price behavior, for the reasons stated earlier. Trading in a more deferred contract, while still requiring careful attention, does not call for day-by-day or hour-by-hour surveillance that the maturing contract does.

There is a further benefit in trading in the distant futures. A *long* position held in a commodity contract for *six months* or more offers an opportunity for long-term capital gains. This is to say that profit arising from a *long position* in commodities held *six months or longer* is taxable at about one-half the short-term capital gain rate. It should be pointed out that, for reasons understood only by the Internal Revenue Service, profits on a *short sale never* qualify as long-term capital gains, regardless of the period of time over which they were accumulated.

Entering the Order

With the foregoing information as a basis for judgment, let us now assume that on November 30, the speculator decides to "sell 10,000 bushels of May soybeans—market—on the opening" on December 1. He fills out the hypothetical "market order" on a card, to be transacted "on the opening", December 1. The following evening, his newspaper shows him that the opening gave him a price of $2.96¾ per bushel (a slightly higher opening than the previous day's close).

LONG
(SHORT)
OFFSET

COMMODITY ORDER

Date ___ *11-30-66* ___

Order No. ___ *1* ___   Time of Day ___ : ___

Brokerage House ___ *Practice Trade* ___

Solicitor Rep. _____

BUY (SELL) Amount _____ Contract *May Beans (SK)*

Price *296¾* Limits *Market - On Opening*

Stop-Loss *$3.00* Profit Obj. *$2.95*

Time-Limit (DAY) OPEN   OTHER _____

Disposition (EXECUTED) CANCELLED   EXPIRED

Confirmed by *Press* Date *12-1* Time ___ : *Opening*

Remarks *Opening Price - $2.96¾*

Plate 29

In addition to marking execution and price on the trading card, he enters the transaction on his recap sheet. Checking Plate No. 30, we note that the anticipated profit on the sale is only 1¾¢, indicated by the intra-day low recorded on November 28. Should prices break through this previous low, however, a second downside objective would then be identified as a "new contract low" of $2.86½. If attained, the total move would produce a 10¢ profit on the short position.

The risks on the up side have also been appraised and limited. The chart shows the most recent intra-day high on May beans, regis-

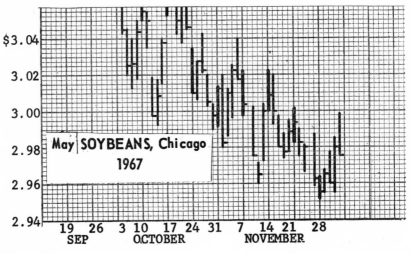

Plate 30

tered on November 21, at $3.00⅛. Should the price go above this, it could be expected to trigger some buying by chart-following longs, as well as producing stop-loss buying by the shorts. As a consequence, the stop-loss order on the short position in May beans has been placed at about $3.00⅜.

It is *never advisable* to place a stop-loss at the *even dollar, even dime, or even cent*. While these levels represent important "hurdles" in price movement, it is not uncommon for prices to move precisely to the even-money mark and then reverse directions. Experienced traders keep their stop-losses away from "even money" in all commodities which are traded in eighths of the cent; ⅝ to ⅜ above or below the even cent is a much safer "stop" point.

The initial short position is now established. It has been documented on a trading card and entered on the recap sheet. The initial profit objective is identified and the stop-loss order is established. The speculator knows that his potential loss is limited to about 4¢ which, on 10,000 bushels, will amount to $400. His initial profit objective is small, but a secondary objective which will return about of 9¼¢, after commissions. Unless new information comes to light which urges abandoning the position entirely, there is nothing to be done now except wait for one eventuality or the other to develop. If the reasoning was sound at the outset, lower prices can be expected eventually; *in the meantime, prices will fluctuate.*

138

Patience is a Virtue

So long as they move within the designated range, the speculator is still "right" and he must patiently wait for events to unfold. If he is wrong, he will know it when the price on his contract breaks $3.00 on the upside and triggers his stop-loss. One thing is certain, however; the speculator will *never* know whether he is *right or wrong* until the market *tells* him.

Inexperienced traders suffer as much from impatience as any other malady. This reflects itself in over-eagerness to take positions without sound reasons for doing so, and to later abandon positions because the hoped-for developments do not immediately occur. So long as a position is not "hurting", there is probably no reason to close it out. One of two things will certainly happen, if given time to do so: it will produce a profit or a loss!

No Trade is "Free"

On the other hand, a position closed out prematurely carries a sure penalty in the form of brokerage commission. It must be remembered that establishment of a position involving 10,000 bushels of soybeans costs $48. This is the price you must pay to have both sides of the transaction executed. Commission is fixed, regardless of whether the position involved stays "open" for ten minutes or ten months. Viewed in this light, the public speculator should recognize that the first ½¢ he makes on any grain contract is earmarked for the broker. It is only after this first ½¢ profit has been chalked up—and deducted—that the trader is adding to his own capital. All the more reason that good positions should be left alone and given an opportunity to produce their full return.

Don't Temporize With a Loser

If patience is a virtue in connection with "letting profits run", short temper is even more so in connection with positions which reach loss-limits. As previously pointed out, no position should be established without first having a firm expectation of the profit objective, and an inflexible limit on the loss you are willing to take before closing it out. There is no better way to determine profit objectives and loss limits than by use of a bar-chart. Other methods exist, which involve sophisticated application of price/value theory and equilibrium forces. Generally speaking, though, such an approach is too complex for all except highly trained practitioners of agricultural economics and statistics. Such a trading system is usually far too time-consuming to permit its regular application to trading problems, even if you can do the math involved.

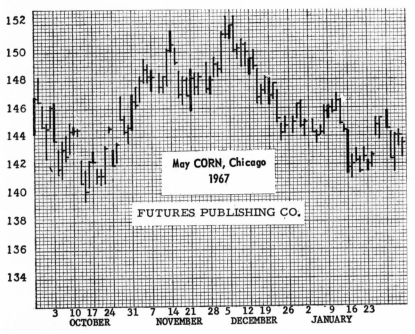

May CORN, Chicago
1967

FUTURES PUBLISHING CO.

Plate 31

Charts are admittedly less than perfect trading tools, but their strengths more than offset their weaknesses. With experience in their use, a speculator will find that relatively simple charts meet his need for a quick picture of price behavior, as well as providing strong clues as to the *probable behavior* of a large group of competitors in the market. To repeat for emphasis, charts are not infallible. Neither is any other system of trading, except the axiom of "cutting losses short and letting profits run". If this is done, the net outcome will produce *profits*. If the practice is not rigidly pursued, the result will be *losses*. All of the charts, statistics, and fundamental data in Christendom will not take the place of strict application of the basic speculative rule.

"Watched Pots Never Boil"

Once a commodity position has been taken, it is imperative that the trader steel himself to practice a high order of self-restraint. Prices which seemed to move most dramtically before you were in the contract now appear to have "gone to sleep". The price on your contract may trade inside the range between your initial profit objective and your stop-loss for days at a time. In another situation, prices may immediately move against you and flirt maddeningly with your stop-loss level; or they may move to within a small fraction of your first profit objective and then back away.

Impatience is the hall-mark of an inexperienced trader. With a small profit "on paper", his inclination, more often than not, is to close out the position and take the profit. When price on his contract fails to move decisively in either direction, the impulse is to close out the position and find another which promises more "action". It is only when prices move against him that the newcomer to specu-lation usually demonstrates real firmness. It has been said that all it takes is a drop in prices to make a long-term "investor" out of a short-term "speculator". Strangely enough, it's true. The beginning speculator regularly shows steadier nerves in the face of adversity than he does when confronted by success.

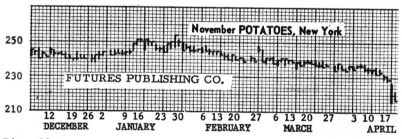

Plate 32

Selecting Your Risks

Once situated in a position which makes no really definitive move in either direction, it pays to "sit steady in the boat". Until something happens to demand a new decision and justify a specific action with respect to the position, *do nothing.* The speculative program for the trade was laid out before the position was ever undertaken; barring new information which invalidates the previous concept—or price movement which triggers the stop-loss or reaches the first profit objective—there is nothing to be done except wait.

Don't Move Stops "Away"

A losing position, however, should never present a quandary. If the price reaches the stop-loss level, *close it out* or let the stop-loss order do it. It's hard to envision a speculator *ever* making a mistake by such action. *Moving a stop-loss higher or lower to avoid being closed out* is, in the overwhelming majority of cases, a *serious mistake.* Adding to a losing position on the basis that in so doing you have "averaged" your buying price downward, or "averaged" your selling price upward, is also invariably a mistake—in spite of the fact that one may occasionally profit from such an atrocious trading practice.

Never Add To a Loser

A speculative position is always taken in the search for profit. Only the market can tell the speculator whether his judgment is right or wrong. Until price movement has given the speculator a profit in his initial trading position, enlarging the position simply increases risk exposure and imposes heavier demands on the available risk capital. *More money will never improve a bad trade!*

To sum up, then:
1. When prices move against you, do nothing; or close out part or all of the position in accordance with your stop-losses.
2. As long as the price on your position "waits", the trader must wait also.
3. When price moves in your favor and develops a "paper profit", a decision must be made concerning enlargement of the position or close-out to convert the paper profit into a cash profit.

Fledgling speculators tend to understand the first half of the trading admonition, "cut losses short and let profits run", but they have great difficulty in putting the second part of the rule into application.

Persistence in Price Movement

Prices, like weather, demonstrate a well recognized "persistence factor". This is to say that when prices are moving higher, their tendency is to continue in an upward trend. When prices are moving lower, they tend to maintain their downward path. When prices are moving in a sideways channel, they tend to stay in a recognizable trading range, with neither decisive upward or downward movement.

The laws of momentum seem to apply to price behavior, as they do to physical bodies at rest or in motion. Prices moving in a given direction will maintain their direction until diverted or reversed by a *new* and *stronger* force. Prices at rest tend to stay at rest until "shoved" by some new consideration.

Beware of Trying to Pick Reversal Points

Countless speculative careers have been brought to an untimely halt by efforts to "pick tops and bottoms". This is to say that when prices are moving downward, the brave but misguided speculator may, at some particular point, decide that prices have dropped "far enough". He takes a long position in the face of a clear-cut downtrend. All too often, prices continue to move lower, to the dismay and the financial damage of the trader who thought he had "seen the bottom of the move".

There is no measurement which can be effectively applied to the market and which will subjectively prove that a given price is right or wrong. The *right price* for anything is that price which represents the composite market level at which *buyers will buy it*, and *sellers will sell it*. Influences from the supply and demand sectors will alter prices upward or downward, and occasionally such a change in market value appraisal will be highly predictable. But the market is the *only authority* on price. The trader who undertakes to "argue" with

143

the market had better base his case firmly on all available facts. This warning should be especially heeded as concerns speculative positions which are producing profits.

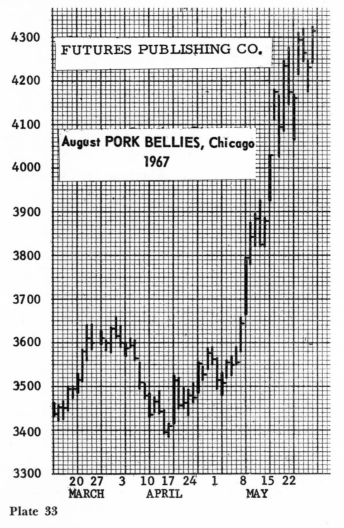

FUTURES PUBLISHING CO.

August PORK BELLIES, Chicago
1967

Plate 33

May 1st demonstrates a "trap" that caught a lot of short-selling "bears".

Adding to a Winner — "Pyramiding"

In the short soybean position previously discussed, the trader has sold the May contract at $2.96¾ per bushel, in anticipation of a 10¢ profit on the down-side. When prices move to $2.90½, for example, the trader may feel a strong urging to offset and take his profit. If he does so, he ignores the rule of "letting profits run". In moving down 6¼¢, the market has confirmed the speculator's forecast of lower prices. It has rewarded all of the short-sellers and it has penalized all of the holders of long positions. If the price goes through the previous contract-life-low to 2.86½, the move can be expected to bring increased selling on the part of disenchanted longs, who previously placed their stop-loss sell orders around this point on the chart. Their added selling will send prices lower still, further increasing the speculative shorts' profit. Should the price of May soybeans reach this important interim chart point, two courses of action are available to the speculative short; and only two:

1. *Hold the position* as it is and wait for the lower price which might materialize from sheer downward price momentum, or —

2. *Add to the position* by selling an additional quantity of soybean futures, which will enlarge profits on any further price deterioration. Doing this will also add some new downward pressure — aiding the shorts' quest for lower prices.

Pyramiding Increases Leverage

There is a further argument in favor of enlarging a profitable position: Whereas sale of the first 10,000 bushels called for posting margin in the amount of $1,500 out of the trader's risk capital, the second sale of 10,000 bushels, (at $2.86½) while requiring another $1,500 in margin, will only reduce remaining speculative risk funds by $500. The balance of the margin requirement is available from the $1,000 "paper profit" already realized on the position. Hence, the speculator is in the position of "trading on profits" and from a vastly improved leverage situation, as concerns his own risk dollars.

145

Selecting Your Risks

Picking Initial Risks

There is no single criterion which will separate a speculation which should be taken from one which should not be taken. This, in spite of the "voice from the tomb", and similar successes that one may occasionally hear about; in which a given trader *"always* buys May corn in November and sells it the last week in January — and *always* makes a profit". The market is full of such ready-made time-tables. As a rule, they have some basis in price trends on a given contract at a particular point in the crop year. If accepted at all, such formulas should only be viewed as *suggestions* based on *historic* price patterns. If infallibility could be ascribed to any such trading timetable, speculation would cease to involve risk; traders would need only to adhere to the rule to make a fortune. You can be sure that *everyone* would soon know the formula.

Initial risk selection is the most demanding part of speculation. Once a position is established, a given chain of events may call for its being closed out when losses reach allowable limits. Or, in the opposite frame of reference, a contrary series of events will suggest that the position be held, added to, or closed out to protect the profits it has produced. But there is no established formula for picking a risk which a reasonably conservative speculator should undertake, although there are a few guides to the matter which can be helpful.

In order to properly understand risk evaluation, we first need to recognize that the future always holds three major classifications of events to come:

1. Under the first heading must be placed all of those possibili-ties which, although confidently expected, *are not susceptible to any rational analysis:*

    For example, the color of the next automobile which will turn a particular corner. A proposition of this kind is *random* — it is devoid of a statistical continuity or a cause-effect relationship which can be evaluated or pre-examined. As such, it is unpredictable and, if one attempts to guess such an event, he is trying to make a selective forecast in an area which must be statistically viewed as *chaos.*

2. At the extreme other end of the scale, we have the *solidly predictable* event. Although it may be absolutely dark at midnight, we can predict sunrise a few hours away and precisely estimate the time at which it will occur; the solar cycle is stable, recurrent, and known. We are dealing with *certainty*.

3. Somewhere between absolute chaos and complete predictability, we have an area for qualitative evaluation which can be called *risk;* and which might be viewed as comprised of some elements of *predictability* and other elements of *unpredictability*. Qualitatively, greater risk relates to a reduction in predictability and an increase in "chaos".

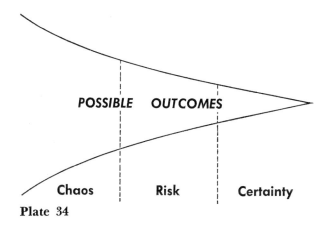

POSSIBLE   OUTCOMES

Chaos   **Risk**   **Certainty**

Plate 34

Speculation centers itself on values as measured by price. While we may not be able to firmly fix the "right price" on corn as of this moment, it should not be hard to gain agreement with the notion that deliverable grade corn in the present market would command a price within a "range" of 10¢ above or below $1.30 per bushel. Accepting this, $1.20 per bushel is viewed as something like the lower margin of price movement probability; $1.40 per bushel is identified as the upper limit of probable price value in the current state of things which affect the selected commodity. The *price range* spelled out stands as a *qualification of the degree of risk* involved in buying or selling corn at $1.30 per bushel.

147

Selecting Your Risks

As an extreme demonstration of the above hypothesis, consider a seller who wishes to dispose of commodity "X", the character and usefulness of which is unknown, both to his market and to himself. Being unfamiliar with the nature of "X" commodity, there is no theoretical limit to its maximum value; and its lowest possible price is only found at zero — since worthlessness in the market sense represents the bottom of the value scale.

Dealing in commodity X involves dealing in randomness; an exercise in attempting to forecast in an area of total unpredictability.

Now let us consider trade in a commodity like copper, which, under a wartime emergency, is rationed and governed by price control. So long as these strictures are imposed, there can only be one "effective price", except at the hazard of breaking the law. The price on the commodity must remain at the *administered price*.

Now let us consider these three market situations in the light of a speculator's interest and function:

1. Trading in commodity "X" is not a speculation; it is a *gamble*, since no criteria exists by which price/value judgment can be developed. *Any outcome of a trade in commodity "X" would be based purely on chance*, not speculation.

2. Trading in a commodity in which price is fixed by law — and in which fluctuation is not permitted — offers no opportunity for profit. Speculation is always directed to predicting *price change* in a search for profit or an effort to minimize loss. Hence, there is *no speculative opportunity* here.

3. Trading in corn which has a price value in a range from $1.20 per bushel to $1.40 per bushel offers a 20¢ *price fluctuation opportunity*, within which a speculator can be rewarded for being "right" in his price analysis — or penalized for his error in price judgment. *This is the essence of speculation.*

Of the three situations outlined, neither commodity X nor the fixed-price commodity offers the slightest attraction to the speculator. Trading in either of these classifications of merchandise would represent something other than speculation: In the first instance by reason of *no opportunity to make an appraisal of value*, and in the second, by reason of *no opportunity to make a profit*. It is only in trading situations where prices can move, and intelligent *appraisals can be made,* that speculation is feasible.

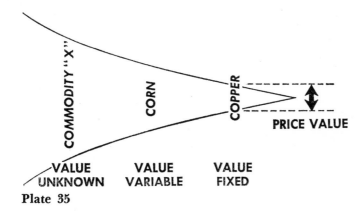

Plate 35

The commodity market offers a full range of risks from which a speculator must pick and choose those which appeal to him. Obviously, a *long* position should be established in a contract in which price behavior and fundamental market considerations lead one to believe that down-side hazards are minimal; or at least somewhat less than the probability of up-side movement. A *short* position should be established in a contract in which the reverse is true: Where the current price level appears to be higher than the facts justify, and where the prospects for down-side movement outweigh the probability of further price escalation.

Speculation is concerned with risk assumption. The successful speculator will never forget that *all* of the propositions offered to him represent risks that others are *unwilling* or *unable* to carry. This knowledge in itself should keep him eternally on guard. Although risk is his "stock in trade", a prudent commodity speculator will give every potential position the benefit of closest scrutiny. Unless he can find a risk he *likes,* he will keep to the sidelines and bide his time.

The speculator can also be comforted by the knowledge that if he is right only half of the time — but manages the "losers" and "winners" properly — he is certain to emerge with average profits that are larger than average losses. Success in speculation requires nothing more than this.

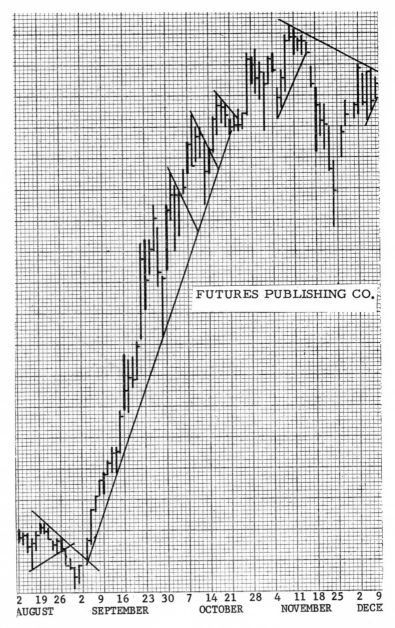

FUTURES PUBLISHING CO.

2 19 26   2   9 16 23 30   7 14 21 28   4 11 18 25   2   9
AUGUST   SEPTEMBER   OCTOBER   NOVEMBER   DECE

Plate 36

150

CHAPTER XII

USE OF CHARTS
IN TRADING DECISIONS

There is no end to the strange and wonderful devices which have, from time to time, been siezed upon by frustrated traders who seek a "fool-proof" key to market price behavior. Theories which have been seriously advanced run the gamut from measuring lunar attraction — as evidenced in high- and low-tides, to correlation of price levels with the relative elevation of the ladies' hemlines. Even the spirit world is consulted regularly by some who incline to put more faith in seances than in scholarly research.

A spate of trading "schedules" circulate through the market, each with its own band of devotees. The most famous of these is the so-called "Voice From The Tomb". The story is told that an old and highly successful speculator lay on his deathbed. As he neared the end, he called his family to him and told them that they would find their most valuable inheritance in a strongbox which contained his personal papers.

The old tycoon went to his reward and, understandably, the heirs went for the strongbox — expecting to find some kind of king's ransom in it. Instead of gold or jewels, they discovered a scrap of paper on which the old trader had written:

Using Charts in Trade

"Voice From the Tomb"

Buy Wheat	Sell Wheat
	January 10th
February 22nd	
	May 10th
July 1st	
	September 10th
November 28th	

Buy Corn	Sell Corn
March 1st	
	May 20th
June 25th	
	August 10th

The story fails to include any enlightenment concerning the outcome. We don't know whether the heirs were able to turn the instructions into additional millions or not. We do know, however, that there are a lot of present-day traders who still consider these dates to be highly significant, as key points of reference in wheat and corn futures prices. An examination of historical price behavior in the two commodities will suffice to shake one's confidence in blind application of the advice conveyed by the "voice from the tomb" — but it does conform to "seasonal" price behavior in both wheat and corn often enough to deserve consideration.

Perhaps the most valuable instruction the "voice" gives to speculators is not even related to price levels. It will be seen that *both commodities* are traded alternately "long" and "short". If a trader can learn to be as "comfortable" in one position as the other, he will be well along the road to real professionalism in his market activities.

Charts Can Help Decision-Making

The best capsulized appraisal of chart usefulness your author has ever heard came from a physician, who mixes some serious commodity speculation with his primary engagements as a chest surgeon. "Whether I'm trying to make a diagnosis of a patient or a market," he once said, "a good chart goes a long way toward *settling my attention on the things that are probably important.*" The parallel between medical charts and commodity charts is not as far-fetched as might appear at first glance. The three basic indicators of human health are temperature, pulse and respiration. In the market, three indicators are also present for those who take time to consult them. They are *price level, trading volume,* and *open-interest.* In combination, they offer some critical insights to current market condition; and permit the trader to draw some highly useful conclusions about possible future developments.

Like so many aspects of market activity, it is futile to try to evaluate these measurements subjectively. Price level means nothing, unless it is viewed as part of the continuum which measures supply/demand balance over time. Trading volume tells us nothing, until it is considered in light of the events which prompt it. Open-interest clarifies nothing until it is arrayed against the background of time sequence and trader motivation.

However, when we put these three market "dimensions" together, they provide some of the best clues we can find for both present conditions and future probabilities:

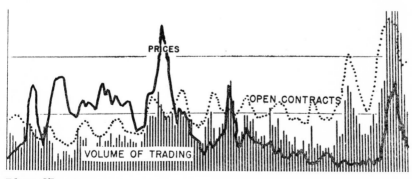

Plate 37

Price/Volume/Open-Interest Signals

When open-interest goes up, as:	(prices go up — new buying is present; "bulls" are in command
	(prices go down — new selling is present; "bears" are in command

When open-interest goes down, as:	(prices go up — shorts are offsetting, indicating technical weakness
	(prices go down — longs are offsetting, indicating technical strength

When trading volume goes up, and:	(prices go up — increased buying pressure; either shorts off-setting, or new demand — or both
	(prices go down — increased selling pressure; either longs liquidating, or new offerings — or both

When trading volume goes down, and:	(prices go up — reduced buying pressure; down-side reaction likely
	(prices go down — reduced selling pressure; up-side reaction likely

Behavior of prices, along with open-interest *or* trading volume can usually be taken as good indicators of both *direction* and *dependability* of a particular price move. When *all three* market factors are *in agreement,* there is usually little room for argument about price prognosis.

When: Prices go up, along with   )
) Extremely "bullish"—
    Increase in open-interest   ) may signal the
) beginning of a major
    Increase in trading volume) price move upward

When: Prices go down, along with   )
) Extremely "bearish"—
    Increase in open-interest   ) may signal the
) beginning of a major
    Increase in trading volume) price move downward

In order to better understand the relative significance of the market trinity, each should be looked at in terms of the reflection it offers of trade attitude and behavior.

Price Level

Price change, whether up or down, can never be trusted by itself. New buying pressure can send prices higher, certainly, and this kind of development calls for constructive appraisal. But "squeezed" shorts can also send prices higher and, once they have succeeded in buying back their untenable positions, lower prices can *nearly* always be expected.

The opposite is also true. *New* short-selling pressure can send prices lower in a hurry, but not nearly so fast as concerted liquidation on the part of disenchanted longs who have all decided to get out at about the same time. Once the wave of long-liquidation has run its course, higher prices are a *near-certainty*.

Futures Prices

Wednesday, May 31, 1967

	Open	High	Low	Close
CHICAGO–WHEAT				
July	166¾	168½	166¾	168⅛-¼
Sept	170	172	170	171½-⅝
Dec	175¾	177¾	175¾	177⅜-½
Mar	180	181⅜	180	181¼
CORN				
July	135	135⅞	134¾	135⅝-½
Sept	136⅛	137	136	136¾
Dec	134⅝	135⅝	134⅝	135⅜-½
Mar	139⅜	140	139⅛	139⅞-140
OATS				
July	71⅞	72	71⅝	72
Sept	73	73½	72⅞	73½
Dec	75½	75¾	75⅜	75¾
RYE				
July	125	125½	124⅞	125⅜
Sept	128	128¼	127⅞	128
Dec	131¾	132½	131¾	132⅜
Mar	135	135¼	135	135
SOYBEANS				
July	285¼	287	285¼	286⅝-½
Aug	285⅜	286⅝	285⅛	286¼-⅛
Sept	282½	284⅛	282½	284
Nov	280¾	282¾	280¾	282½
Jan	284⅞	286¼	284¾	286¼
Mar	288	289½	288	289½
SOYBEAN OIL				
July	10.19	10.23	10.15	10.16-.15u
Aug	10.24	10.26	10.20	10.20-.21u
Sept	10.25	10.27	10.20	10.20
Oct	10.13	10.13	10.10	10.09b
Dec	10.10	10.11	10.07	10.10-.09
Jan	10.10	10.10	10.08	10.09
Mar	10.10	10.12	10.09	10.09-.10
SOYBEAN MEAL				
July	73.10	74.55	73.10	74.45
Aug	73.05	73.85	73.05	73.75-.70
Sept	72.60	73.10	72.60	73.05-73.
Oct	72.15	72.50	72.15	72.35
Dec	72.00	72.40	72.00	72.40
Jan	72.15	72.45	72.15	72.40b
Mar	72.55	72.75	72.55	72.60b
CATTLE (CHICAGO BOARD OF				
June	26.20	26.30	26.15	26.27
Aug	27.32	27.37	27.25	27.37
Oct	27.77	27.77	27.65	27.67
Dec	27.92	27.92	27.85	27.90
Feb	28.20	28.20	28.15	28.20
Apr	28.35	28.40	28.35	28.30
June	28.55	28.57	28.50	28.55
Aug	28.60	28.60	28.55	28.60
KANSAS CITY–WHEAT				
July	172¼	174	172¼	173¾-⅝
Sept	175¼	176	175¼	175⅝
Dec	178¾	179¾	178½	179½
Mar	181¾	182⅝	181¾	182¼
GRAIN SORGHUMS				
July	210¼	210½	210¼	210½
Sept	210½	210½	210	210
MINNEAPOLIS–WHEAT				

	Open	High	Low	Close	Change	Season's High	Season's Low
Mar	38.00	38.55	37.75	38.55	+ .40	39.85	34.95
Sales: 6.045 contracts.							
LIVE HOGS							
June	24.35	24.60	24.35	24.60	+ .15	25.60	20.95
July	24.30	25.00	24.25	24.85	+ .35	25.45	22.00
Aug	24.40	25.00	24.40	25.00	+ .45	25.50	22.07
Sept	23.00	23.00	23.00	23.00	....	24.00	21.40
Oct	22.50	22.50	22.50	22.50	....	22.75	20.50
Dec	22.40	22.40	22.40	22.40	....	23.00	19.85
Sales: 68 contracts.							
NEW YORK–POTATOES (MAINE CONTRACT)							
Nov	2.38	2.45	2.36	2.45	+ .06	2.54	2.16
Mar	2.66	2.75	2.65	2.75	+ .07	2.75	2.43
Apr	2.85	2.95	2.84	2.95	+ .08	2.95	2.59
May	3.15	3.30	3.15	3.30	+ .13	3.30	2.96
Sales: 1,374 contracts.							
COPPER							
July'67	44.80b	45.45	45.00	45.35	+ .65	61.80	40.90
Sept	44.85	45.30	44.85	45.20	+ .65	57.45	40.55
Oct	44.55	44.90	44.55	44.75b	+ .55	55.95	40.55
Dec	43.80	44.25	43.80	44.00b	+ .55	55.00	40.05
Jan'68	43.20b	43.65	43.45	43.40b	+ .45	52.30	39.70
Mar	42.75b	43.15	42.90	42.90b	+ .35	49.10	39.50
May	42.30b	42.60	42.50	42.40b	+ .25	43.40	38.80
July	41.85b	42.20	42.20	42.00n	+ .20	42.20	41.75
Sales: 132 contracts.							
SILVER							
June'67	155.20	160.75	155.20	160.75	+5.55	160.75	130.10
July	156.10	161.10	156.10	161.10b	+5.00	161.10	130.60
Aug	157.50	162.35	157.40	162.35b	+5.00	162.35	131.10
Sept	158.25b	162.80	162.50	162.80b	+5.00	162.80	131.75
Oct	159.00	163.35	159.00	163.35b	+5.00	163.35	132.50
Nov	160.00	163.90	160.00	163.90b	+5.00	163.90	133.30
Dec	160.50	164.30	160.50	164.30b	+5.00	164.30	134.00
Jan'68	161.00	164.50	161.00	164.50b	+5.00	164.50	134.00
Mar	153.00	165.00	162.85	165.00b	+5.00	165.00	136.00
May	163.90	166.00	163.70	166.00b	+5.00	166.00	137.50
Sales: 523 contracts.							
HIDES							
July'67	16.00	16.23	15.65	15.65b	− .25	21.75	13.45
Oct	16.45b	16.50	16.05	16.10b	− .20	20.80	13.90
Jan'68	16.80	16.80	16.35	16.40b	− .20	19.45	14.38
Apr	17.00	17.00	17.00	16.70b	− .15	17.00	14.60
July	17.10b	16.80	16.80	17.05b	− .05	17.00	15.55
Sales: 35 contracts.							
SUGAR (WORLD CONTRACT)							
July'67	2.85	2.96	2.84	2.95-.96	+ .13to.14	3.18	1.34
Sept	2.95	3.08	2.93	3.06-.08	+ .15to.17	3.16	1.40
Oct	2.95	3.10	2.94	3.08-.10	+ .14to.16	3.20	1.43
Nov	2.96	3.11	2.96	3.10	+ .15	3.20	1.47
Mar'68	3.11	3.28	3.11	3.27-.28	+ .19to.20	3.38	1.61
May	3.15	3.30	3.15	3.29-.30	+ .19to.20	3.45	1.66
July	3.18b	3.34	3.18	3.34	+ .19	3.45	2.14
Sept	3.21	3.37	3.21	3.35-.36	+ .16to.17	3.44	2.52
Oct	3.23b	3.39	3.30	3.39	+ .18	3.39	3.07
Sales: 4,474 contracts. Spot: 2.80n.							
SUGAR (DOMESTIC CONTRACT)							
July'67	7.24b	7.27	7.27	7.26b	+ .01	7.27	[illegible]
Sept	7.25b	7.28	7.28	7.28b	+ [illegible]		
Nov	[illegible]						

Plate 38 *Courtesy Wall Street Journal*

A good commodity section is vital. Few papers have it.

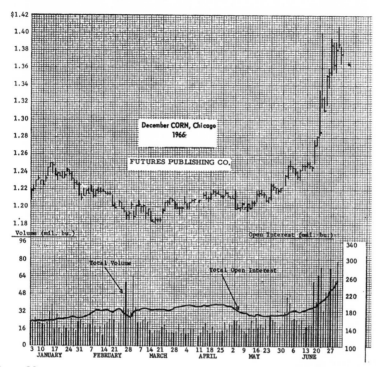

Plate 39

Open Interest

Open-interest changes are only slightly less of an enigma when standing alone. This figure only indicates the willingness of all classifications of market participants to hold positions in a given contract or commodity. An *increase* in long-interest on the part of "strong handed" commercial interests and professional speculators must usually be taken as constructive for prices; but if the rise in long-holdings is largely attributable to the "weak hands" of the public, the *opposite* interpretation must be at least considered.

A *decrease* in open-interest may be either a cause for rejoicing or alarm, depending on "who is leaving" and why. If "strong hands" are withdrawing from their market positions, the side they are abandoning is probably in for trouble. But if the departing holders are "weak hands", the cause of the "strong hands" may be actually improved after the temporary set-back.

BOARD OF TRADE FUTURES

Monday, July 10, 1967

Grains, dollars per bushel; soybean oil, dollars per 100 lbs.; soybean meal, dollars per ton

	Open	High	Low	Close	Prev. close	Yr. ago	Season's Range High	Season's Range Low
				WHEAT				
July	1.50¾	1.52¾	1.50⅜	1.50¾				
Sept.	1.54½-1.54¼	1.55⅞	1.53¾	1.53¾				
Dec.	1.61 -1.61¼	1.62¼	1.60⅜	1.60½				
Mar.	1.66⅛-1.66¼	1.67¼	1.65¼	1.65¼				
May	1.67⅜	1.68⅝	1.66¾	1.66¾				
				C				
July	1.31¼-1.31	1.31¼	1.29⅞	1.30				
Sept.	1.30¾-1.30½	1.30¾	1.29	1.29				
Dec.	1.28⅞-1.29⅛	1.29¼	1.27¾	1.27¾				
Mar.	1.33½-1.33⅜	1.33¾	1.32¼	1.32¼				
May	1.36¼-1.36⅜	1.36½	1.35¼	1.35¼				
				.O				
July	.71⅜	.71½	.71¼	.71¼				
Sept.	.69	.79¼	.68½	.68⅝				
Dec.	.70½	.71⅜	.70⅜	.70⅞				
Mar.	.73½	.73½	.72⅞	.72⅞				
May	.73	.73	.73	z.73				
July	1.22	1.22	1.21½	1.21½				
Sept.	1.26	126	1.24¾	1.24¾				
Dec.	1.30¼-1.30½	1.30½	1.29¾	1.29¾				
Mar.	1.34 -1.34¼	1.34½	1.33¼	1.33¼				
May	1.36	1.36½	1.35¾	1.35¾				
				SOY				
July	2.83⅜-2.83½	2.84⅛	2.82¾	2.83½				
Aug.	2.78½-1.78¼	2.79	2.77¼	2.77¾				
Sept.	2.72½	2.72½	2.70¾	2.71				
Nov.	2.70⅜	2.70⅝	2.69¼	2.69½				
Jan.	2.74¼-2.74½	2.74½	2.73¼	2.73½				
Mar.	2.77½	2.77½	2.76¼	2.76¾				
May	2.79¾	2.80	2.78¾	2.78⅞				
				SOYB				
July	9.05	9.12	8.96	8.9				
Aug.	9.14- 9.15	9.22	9.05	9.0				
Sep.	9.20- 9.21	9.29	9.11	9.1				
Oct.	9.18	9.28	9.10	*9.1				
Dec.	9.20	9.28	9.16	9.2				
Jan.	9.30	9.31	9.19	9.2				
Mar.	9.33	9.39	9.26	9.2				
May	9.44	9.44	9.36	9.3				
				SOYBE				
July	75.80	76.20	75.20	z75.2				
Aug.	74.05-74.10	74.40	73.30	73.3				
Sep.	71.40-71.50	72.10	71.40	z71.4				
Oct.	70.75	71.10	70.50	70.5				
Dec.	70.45-70.50	70.80	70.15	70.2				
Jan.	70.50-70.60	70.85	70.80	70.4				
Mar.	71.00	71.30	70.95	71.0				
May	71.60	71.70	71.50	71.6				
				CHOIC				
Aug.	27.37	27.40	27.25	27.2				
Oct.	27.87	27.90	27.72	27.7				
Dec.	28.05	28.05	27.90	27.9				
Feb.	28.22	28.22	28.02	28.0				
Apr.	28.40	28.40	28.20	28.2				
June	28.50	28.50	28.35	28.3				
Aug.	....	....	....	z28.4				

z-Bid.

Volume and Open Interest

The Commodity Exchange Authority reports grain futures trading on the Chicago Board of Trade as of the close of business Thursday, July 6 (in thousands of bushels):

	July	Sept.	Dec.	March	May	Total
Wheat ...	6,005	11,155	12,850	4,200	2,155	36,365
Corn	10,750	6,415	14,245	2,990	1,595	35,995
Oats	275	480	255	25	....	1,035
Rye	95	315	445	215	130	1,200

Soybeans: July, 6,130; August, 6,870; September, 1,965; November, 7,525; January, 1,690; March, 1,110; May, 490; Total, 25,780.

Soybean oil trading (in tank cars of 60,000 pounds) totaled 1,718. Soybean meal trading (in hundreds of tons) totaled 1,629.

Open interest (in thousands of bushels):

	Wheat	Corn	Oats	Rye
July	19,770	39,610	1,575	400
September	48,950	55,970	3,520	3,305
December	58,710	65,685	2,660	2,655
March		24,545	615	888
May		8,240	129	323
Total	175,565	196,350	7,975	7,505

	Soybeans	r-Soybean Meal	s-Soybean Oil
July	14,805	1,419	440
August	26,465	3,175	2,951
September	13,835	901	1,568
October	....	1,526	1,295
November	43,980		
December	...	1,934	1,429
January	25,060	891	1,228
March	8,240	129	2 888
May	8,240	129	325
Total	156,930	10,590	10,122

r-In hundreds of tons. s-In tank cars of 60,000 pounds.

Open contracts for Thursday and changes from Wednesday: Copper (50,000 pounds each), July 131, Sept. 419, Oct. 110, Dec. 306, Jan. 59, March 60, May 210, July 85. Total, 1,380, down 26. World Sugar (112,000 pounds each), Sept. 3,035, Oct. 2,987, Nov. 1,530, Jan. 17, March 7,044, May 3,819, July 2,190, Sept. 1,673, Oct. 430, Nov. 5. Total, 22,730, up 33. Cocoa (30,000 pounds each), July 37. Sept. 7,259, Dec. 6,594, Jan. 102, March 4,179, May 2,427. July 1,250, Sept. 901. Total, 22,749, down 451. Frozen Pork Bellies (30,000 pounds each), July 3,708, Aug. 5,536, Feb. 2,145, March 655, May 137. Total, 13,181, down 93. Fresh Eggs (600 cases each), Sept. 421, Oct. 220, Nov. 125, Dec. 32. Total, 798, up 38. Maine Potatoes (50,000 pounds each), Nov. 2,214, March 2,701, April 2,243, May 4,626. Total, 11,784, up 198.

Plate 40 *Courtesy Chicago Tribune*

Open-interest is compiled and reported daily by the Commodity Exchange Authority (on regulated commodities). A few papers print the figures, and some of the charting services include the data along with prices and volume.

Trading Volume

Trading volume can be no less difficult to analyze objectively, unless appraised with respect to the stimulus which prompts it. Volume often *explodes* in the face of new demand from those who see a new price level developing, and scramble to get aboard for the move. The same thing can happen to volume when large numbers of longs or shorts are caught in a price move that triggers concerted stop-loss selling.

Trading volume can *dry up* as a result of either *insufficient interest* in the contract to sustain market activity; or as a result of sheer *unwillingness* of present and potential position-holders to do business *at the given price level.*

Whether appraising prospects for an already-existing position or weighing the wisdom of establishing a new position, price-level, trading volume, and open-interest are always fundamental elements in the equation. It should be hastily added that there are traders who succeed without using these indices to market condition. There are also some race-car drivers who ply their trade without crash helmets, but the practice shouldn't be encouraged. Anything that can reduce risk exposure deserves to be considered.

How Reliable Are Charts?

The question can not be answered without narrowing it down a bit further. The usual bar-chart which most traders employ is nothing more than a means of creating a picture with statistical data. In terms of efficiency, as a communications tool, a chart is vastly preferable to columns of figures. A glance is sufficient to gain a useful impression of trading range, general trend, and notable exceptions to either. To this extent, a chart is the best means available for reminding oneself of what the market response was to a *given set of circumstances in the past.* The major fallacy in chart trading procedure lies in placing *too much* confidence in the *past,* as a guide to the *future.*

Charting techniques can be usefully employed as a projective method; but in order to do so, the chart must reflect *future data esti-*

mates. Usually, bar-chartists do not do this. They consider only that which has passed—and, by looking *backward*, they attempt to determine where things are *going*. If we operated automobiles and airplanes in the same fashion, population control would never be a problem.

Suffice it to say that, from this writer's experience, charts are an almost indispensable *trading tool*—even though they are only slightly better than *random determination* as a method of long- and medium-range price *forecasting*. Their *accuracy*, quite naturally, improves in direct proportion to the number of people using them in given areas of endeavor; and as their *accuracy improves, profitability decreases*. This is to say that if *everyone* traded December corn futures from a chart, and meticulously followed the same buy and sell "signals", *everyone* would be "right" about the direction of prices on the contract. Unanimity of action would insure the result. The only abberations would be predicated on time differences in executing trades, since *everyone* would *always* have to be in agreement about price *direction*. But, by being endlessly in agreement (and therefore always "right"), no one could be wrong. Unless someone can be "wrong", there is no theoretical loss possible; and without a *loss,* there can't possibly be a *profit.*

Under the above hypothesis, trade would not necessarily cease. It just wouldn't amount to much. When prices were headed down, "everybody" would want to sell, but there would be no buyers; and vice-versa. Fortunately, such a possibility is quite remote. Difference of opinion is the essence of trade. For each buyer there must be a seller and, at some price level, there always is.

Charts Offer Clues to the Past

The foregoing statements should not be taken as a blanket indictment of charts in trading—nor a diatribe against the intelligence of those who use them. The tools for success in speculation are sufficiently scarce and inexact as to urge a trader to use *anything* that helps him render better judgements. A less-than-perfect tool is far better than no tool at all. Charts fall into this category.

Examination of any commodity price bar-chart will disclose sev-

Cash Prices

Courtesy Wall Street Journal

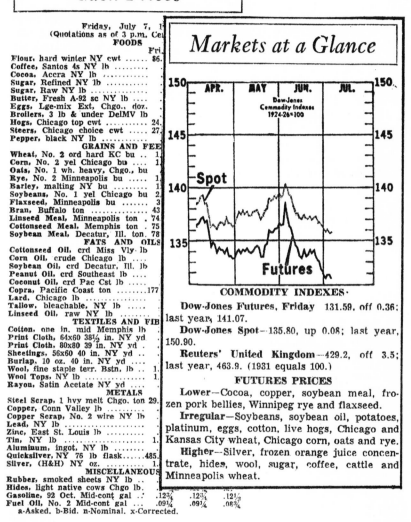

Friday, July 7, 1
(Quotations as of 3 p.m. Cel
FOODS

Fri.

Flour, hard winter NY cwt ..... $6.
Coffee, Santos 4s NY lb ....
Cocoa, Accra NY lb ....
Sugar, Refined NY lb ....
Sugar, Raw NY lb ....
Butter, Fresh A-92 sc NY lb ....
Eggs, Lge-mix Ext, Chgo., doz. .
Broilers, 3 lb & under DelMV lb .
Hogs, Chicago top cwt .... 24.
Steers, Chicago choice cwt ..... 27.
Pepper, black NY lb ....
GRAINS AND FEE
Wheat, No. 2 ord hard KC bu .. 1.
Corn, No. 2 yel Chicago bu .... 1.
Oats, No. 1 wh. heavy, Chgo., bu
Rye, No. 2 Minneapolis bu ..... 1.
Barley, malting NY bu 1
Soybeans, No. 1 yel Chicago bu 2.
Flaxseed, Minneapolis bu 3
Bran, Buffalo ton 43
Linseed Meal, Minneapolis ton . 74
Cottonseed Meal, Memphis ton . 75
Soybean Meal, Decatur, Ill. ton. 78
FATS AND OILS
Cottonseed Oil, crd Miss Vly lb
Corn Oil, crude Chicago lb ....
Soybean Oil, crd Decatur, Ill. lb
Peanut Oil, crd Southeast lb ....
Coconut Oil, crd Pac Cst lb ....
Copra, Pacific Coast ton 177
Lard, Chicago lb ....
Tallow, bleachable, NY lb .....
Linseed Oil, raw NY lb ....
TEXTILES AND FIB
Cotton, one in. mid Memphis lb .
Print Cloth, 64x60 38½ in. NY yd .
Print Cloth, 80x80 39 in. NY yd .
Sheetings, 56x60 40 in. NY yd ..
Burlap, 10 oz. 40 in. NY yd ....
Wool, fine staple terr. Bstn. lb .. 1.
Wool Tops, NY lb .... 1.
Rayon, Satin Acetate NY yd ....
METALS
Steel Scrap, 1 hvy melt Chgo. ton 29.
Copper, Conn Valley lb ....
Copper Scrap, No. 2 wire NY lb .
Lead, NY lb ....
Zinc, East St. Louis lb ....
Tin, NY lb .... 1.
Aluminum, ingot, NY lb ....
Quicksilver, NY 76 lb flask.....485.
Silver, (H&H) NY oz. .... 1.
MISCELLANEOUS
Rubber, smoked sheets NY lb ..
Hides, light native cows Chgo lb. .
Gasoline, 92 Oct. Mid-cont gal ..`   .12¾   .12¾   .12½
Fuel Oil, No. 2 Mid-cont gal ...   .09¼   .09¼   .08¾
a-Asked. b-Bid. n-Nominal. x-Corrected.

Markets at a Glance

COMMODITY INDEXES·

Dow-Jones Futures, Friday 131.59, off 0.36;
last year, 141.07.

Dow-Jones Spot—135.80, up 0.08; last year,
150.90.

Reuters' United Kingdom—429.2, off 3.5;
last year, 463.9. (1931 equals 100.)

FUTURES PRICES

Lower—Cocoa, copper, soybean meal, frozen pork bellies, Winnipeg rye and flaxseed.

Irregular—Soybeans, soybean oil, potatoes, platinum, eggs, cotton, live hogs, Chicago and Kansas City wheat, Chicago corn, oats and rye.

Higher—Silver, frozen orange juice concentrate, hides, wool, sugar, coffee, cattle and Minneapolis wheat.

Plate 41

Courtesy Wall Street Journal

By comparing cash prices, futures prices and the overall commodity Index, a good notion of market "tone" can be had.

eral areas of useful trading information. The tracings document past actions of all the traders—not just chart followers—in the contract as they pursued their composite "price idea". Each daily bar covers the trading range for one session; and the close is marked by a cross-bar. Thus, one quite simple structure visually presents daily high, daily low, and closing price. In combination, the individual bars offer a graphic picture of price development, movement, and congestive pressures at various levels.

Do Prices Agree?

By arraying open-interest data and trading volume in chronological sequence with prices, the experienced trader will be able to better identify the speculative opportunities he seeks. He will also become increasingly expert in spotting those situations that can only be labeled "traps". The majority of all bad trades are the result of putting too much confidence in a single aspect of market behavior, usually price. The prudent speculator will always look for *confirmation* of price reliability in *technical* and *fundamental* considerations. Unless it can be found, he will view the move as being suspect and perhaps of no more than short-term significance.

For example, when a strong case exists for higher wheat prices, *most* wheat contracts in the given crop year should reflect it to *some* degree. Nearby prices can be expected to reflect the situation to a greater extent than more deferred maturities, since the market "discounts" the future. But if a real shortage is developing, the condition is not likely to be restricted to a single contract, *except* at the extreme end of the crop year. When excessive supplies are on hand, either in private hands or held by the government, it usually takes an extended period of time to work off the surplus through increased domestic consumption, or export, or both. The revised price attitudes *may or may not* carry through into "new crop" contracts, depending on whether the projected harvest is calculated to aggravate, relieve or merely prolong the situation.

Based on this thinking, a trader will not put much confidence in a bulge or a dip in a given maturity which generates no corresponding activity in other contracts in the *same crop year*. Moreover, even if the price move does apply generally, he will still check *open-interest* fig-

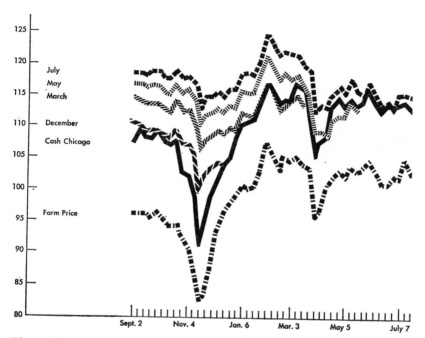

125
120
July
May
115
March
110
December
Cash Chicago
105
100
95
Farm Price
90
85
80

Sept. 2   Nov. 4   Jan. 6   Mar. 3   May 5   July 7

Plate 42

While it can be said that cash and futures prices always tend to move "in concert," this should not be taken to mean that they maintain stable price differentials. As the above chart shows, the "country basis" keeps in much closer step with market cash prices, than futures prices maintain with each other.

The two major price dips in these 1961 corn prices reflect heavy marketings immediately following harvest, and another period of heavy selling shortly after the first of the year. Most years do reflect a winter sell-off in corn; hence, the phenomenon is an important factor in the commodity's "seasonal" price pattern.

ures—as reported by the Commodity Exchange Authority each day—to see whether it is probably a result of people "getting in" or "getting out" of the situation. He will take a hard look at *trading volume,* to see how willing the market participants are to "go along" with the change and continue to buy and sell at the new price level.

The experienced speculator soon learns that every *substantial price change* offers a major *trading opportunity,* but before either buying or selling, he has to answer the crucial question of whether or not the move *can be trusted.* Short-term price action alone is not sufficient evidence upon which to make the judgment.

Picking New Position Spots

Examination of any commodity price chart will show that the path of existence for values on any traded futures is truly a series of ups and downs. Ignoring smaller interim fluctuations which occur constantly, there are distinct levels which clearly stand as the top and bottom limits within which traders will—during a period of time—trade in the product. To use the December, 1966 corn futures for demonstration, $1.25 and $1.18 per bushel represented the full trading spectrum for nearly six months of the contract life. Volume and open-interest remained at unimpressive levels, and the narrow daily ranges contained little to attract widespread speculative interest.

Then suddenly, on June 16, a "weather scare" triggered an upsurge which took the contract over $1.53 in 90 days. Untold thousands of traders who wanted no corn at $1.20 were eager buyers twenty-five cents higher. Short-sellers who had shunned the weak market offered billions of bushels as prices soared. The market's "price idea" on December corn as seen in data following was revised upward and widened to a maximum of $1.33. Toward the end of contract life, the range narrowed progressively, and it went "off the board" at $1.41.

By trading this contract on the basis of about a 4¢ maximum daily range, accepting the market's "word" as a reliable guide to *trend* at all times, and conservatively pyramiding profitable positions, one trader's records show what can be done in such a situation. The details are shown in Plates 44 thru 48. It should be noted that the prices reflected in the recapitulation are the levels at which the orders were *placed*. Actual executions varied slightly from order levels, depending on the type of order involved and market conditions. Also worth mentioning, the quantities reflected here are not the trading volumes of the speculator whose records we are examining. On October 26, for instance, he was short more than 400,000 bushels. The total December contract trade activity produced a net profit to the trader, after broker commissions, in excess of $41,000.

Plate 43

Cash grain brokers occupy the small tables in the foreground. Futures contracts are traded in special pits or rings, beyond.

165

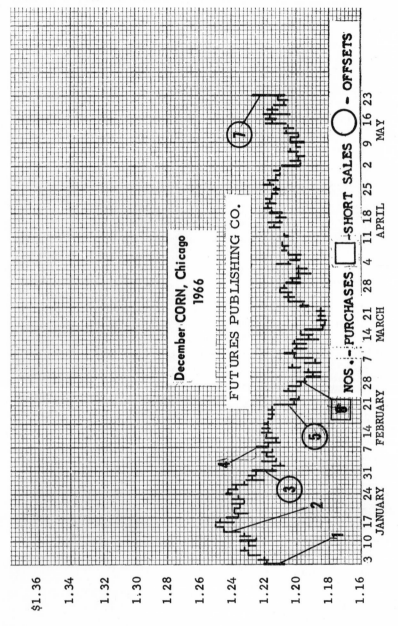

December CORN, Chicago
1966

FUTURES PUBLISHING CO.

NOS. — PURCHASES ☐ — SHORT SALES ◯ — OFFSETS

$1.36

1.34

1.32

1.30

1.28

1.26

1.24

1.22

1.20

1.18

1.16

3 10 17 24 31 7 14 21 28 7 14 21 28 4 11 18 25 2 9 16 23
JANUARY   FEBRUARY   MARCH   APRIL   MAY

Plate 44

166

Trade No.	Date	Trades in December 1966 Corn	Bought	Sold	P/L ¢ per bu.	P/L Dollars
1	1/3/66	*Buy:* 15M @ 121⅜; stop-loss @ 119⅝	15M @ 121⅜		¼	37.50
2	1/12	*Move stop-loss up to 121⅝* *Buy:* 10M @ 124⅜	10M @ 124⅜		(2¾)	(275.00)
3	1/31	Stop-loss hit @ 121⅝; total position offset		25M @ 121⅝		
				Position Result		(237.50)
				P/L to Date		(237.50)
4	2/7	*Buy:* 15M @ 122⅜; stop-loss @ 120½	15M @ 122⅜			
5	2/18	Stop-loss hit @ 120½; total position offset		15M @ 120½	(1⅞)	(256.25)
				Position Result		(256.25)
				P/L to Date		(493.75)
6	2/25	*Sell:* 15M @ 119⅝; stop-loss @ 122⅜		15M @ 119⅝		
7	5/23	Stop-loss hit @ 122⅜; total position offset	15M @ 122⅜		(2¾)	(412.50)
				Position Result		(412.50)
				P/L to Date		(906.25)

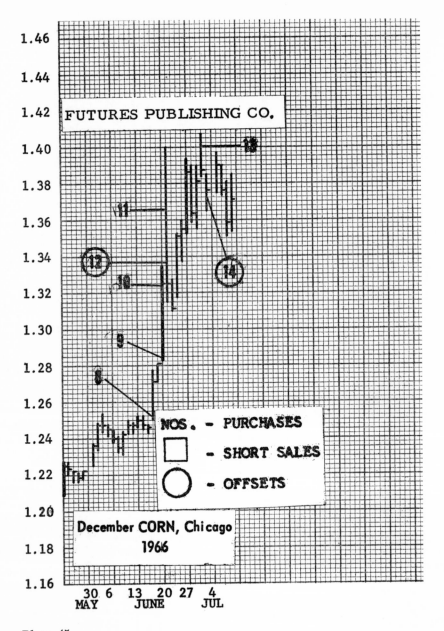

FUTURES PUBLISHING CO.

NOS. – PURCHASES

☐ – SHORT SALES

◯ – OFFSETS

December CORN, Chicago
1966

Plate 45

Trade No.	Date	Trades in December 1966 Corn	Bought	Sold	P/L ¢ per bu.	P/L Dollars
8	6/16	Buy: 15M @ 124⅝; stop-loss @ 121⅝	15M @ 124⅝		9	1350.00
9	6/20	Move stop-loss up to 124⅜ Buy: 10M @ 128⅜	10M @ 128⅜		5¼	525.00
10		Move stop-loss up to 129⅝ Buy: 5M @ 132⅜	5M @ 132⅜		1¼	62.50
11	6/21	Move stop-loss up to 133⅝ Buy: 5M @ 136⅝	5M @ 136⅝		(3)	(150.00)
12		Stop-loss hit @ 133⅝; total position offset		35M @ 133⅝	Position Result	1787.50
					P/L to Date	881.25
13	6/30	Buy: 15M @ 140⅜; stop-loss @ 137⅝	15M @ 140⅜			
14	7/1	Stop-loss hit @ 137⅝; total position offset		15M @ 137⅝	(2¾)	(412.50)
					Position Result	(412.50)
					P/L to Date	468.75

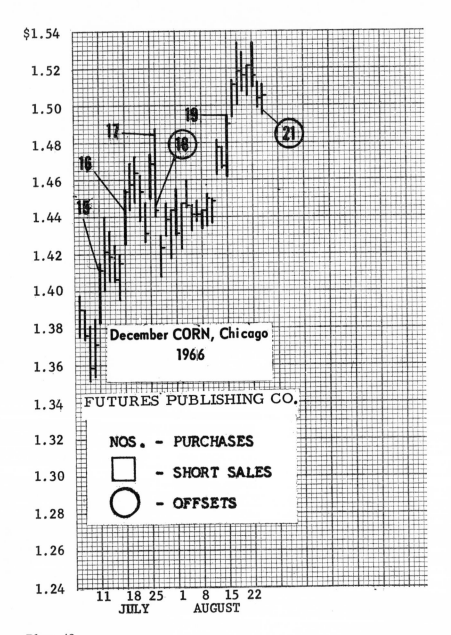

Plate 46

170

Trade No.	Date	Trades in December 1966 Corn	Bought	Sold	P/L ¢ per bu.	P/L Dollars
15	7/11	Buy: 15M @ 141⅜; stop-loss @ 137⅝	15M @ 141⅜		3¼	487.50
16	7/18	Move stop-loss to 141⅝ / Buy: 10M @ 144⅜	10M @ 144⅜		¼	25.00
17	7/26	Move stop-loss to 144⅝ / Buy: 5M @ 148⅜	5M @ 148⅜		(3¾)	(187.50)
18		Stop-loss hit @ 144⅝; total position offset		30M @ 144⅝		
				Position Result		325.00
				P/L to Date		793.75
19	8/16	Buy: 15M @ 149⅜; stop-loss @ 145⅝	15M @ 149⅝		¼	37.50
20	8/18	Move stop-loss to 149⅝				
21	8/24	Stop-loss hit @ 149⅝; total position offset		15M @ 149⅝		
				Position Result		37.50
				P/L to Date		831.25

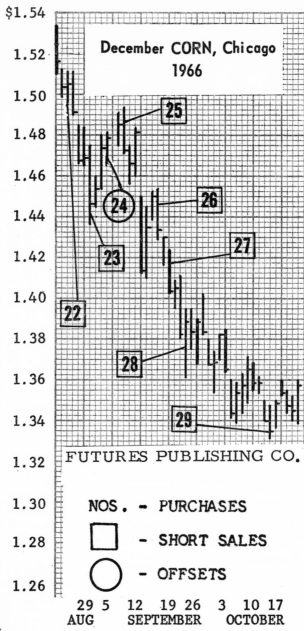

December CORN, Chicago
1966

25

26

27

24

23

22

28

29

FUTURES PUBLISHING CO.

NOS. — PURCHASES

☐ — SHORT SALES

○ — OFFSETS

29 5   12 19 26   3 10 17
AUG   SEPTEMBER   OCTOBER

Plate 47

172

Trade No.	Date	Trades in December 1966 Corn	Bought	Sold	P/L ¢ per bu.	P/L Dollars
22	8/24	*Sell:* 15M @ 149⅝; stop-loss @ 153⅜		15M @ 149⅝	3	450.00
23	8/30	*Move stop-loss down to 146⅝* *Sell:* 10M @ 144⅝		10M @ 144⅝	(2)	200.00
24	9/1	Stop-loss hit @ 146⅝; total position offset	25M @ 146⅝			
			Position Result		250.00	
			P/L to Date			1081.25
25	9/7	*Sell:* 15M @ 148⅝; stop-loss @ 150⅜		15M @ 148⅝	11	1650.00
26	9/15	*Move stop-loss to 146⅜* *Sell:* 10M @ 144⅝		10M @ 144⅝	7	700.00
27	9/19	*Move stop-loss to 143⅜* *Sell:* 5M @ 141⅝		5M @ 141⅝	4	200.00
28	9/22	*Move stop-loss to 141⅜* *Sell:* 5M @ 137⅝		5M @ 137⅝	even	—
29	10/13	*Move stop-loss to 137⅝* *Sell:* 5M @ 133⅝		5M @ 133⅝	(4)	(200.00)

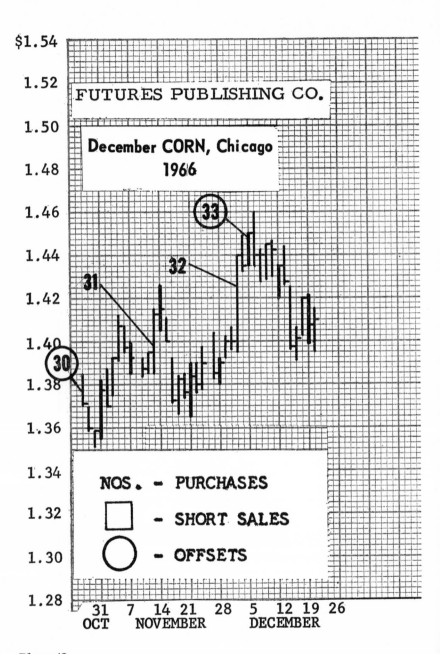

FUTURES PUBLISHING CO.

December CORN, Chicago
1966

NOS. - PURCHASES

☐ - SHORT SALES

○ - OFFSETS

Plate 48

174

Trade No.	Date	Trades in December 1966 Corn	Bought	Sold	P/L ¢ per bu.	P/L Dollars
30	10/26	Stop-loss hit; total position offset	40M @ 137⅝		Position Result P/L to Date	2350.00 3431.25
31	11/5	Buy: 15M @ 139⅜; stop-loss @ 135⅝	15M @ 139⅜		5¼	787.50
32	12/1	Move stop-loss to 139⅝ Buy: 10M @ 142⅝	10M @ 142⅝		2	200.00
33	12/5	Closed out in advance of "First Notice Day" @ 144⅝		25M @ 144⅝	Position Result P/L to Date	987.50 4418.75
		Less Broker Commission on 48 Contracts @ 22.00				1056.00
					Net Proceeds	3362.75

Using Charts in Trade

At the risk of undertaking to argue with success, there are a few points which deserve to be made with respect to the trading program which is reflected here. Ordinarily, the first few days of contract life after the futures opens is a *high risk* proposition. Until open interest in the contract builds up to some reasonable total, price may be susceptible to undue influence by what amounts to extremely small buying or selling pressures.

The long position which was taken on January 3 was based mainly on the fact that December represented about a 5¢ "discount" under the September futures. However, since December represents *new crop*, and September represents *old crop*, such a differential does not—by itself—provide a sufficiently compelling reason to undertake the risks present at this early stage of contract life.

When the price dropped to 118⅜ on March 14, the stop-loss should have been moved down to the vicinity of 120½, even though no addition could be as yet made to the position. The "even dime" is a highly significant price-barrier in commodity trading. If buying pressure is sufficient to *penetrate* the 120 level, it might be expected that, once having overcome this hurdle, it will then be sufficient to carry the price somewhat higher.

Moving the stop-loss up to 144⅝ on July 26 was an excellent decision, but adding to the position in the middle of what was clearly a "short squeeze" was not good judgment. It is worth pointing out that this trader bought into another short-squeeze on June 21. Following a trading *program too closely* can sometimes lure one into such a "trap".

There are times when these flurries of short off-setting will be sustained subsequently, as prices move higher on the crest of additional buying demand. Far more often, however, once the shorts are chased in, a down-side reaction immediately follows. The reverse is equally true when the longs have largely departed in the face of falling prices: an up-side correction is to be expected in the next session or two. *Whether or not* the anticipated reaction occurs, the trader should make plans for it, by either moving to the sidelines temporarily or placing his stop-loss in *expectation* of such a counter-move.

In connection with stop-losses, it should also be pointed out that after the two exceedingly broad swings on June 20 and 21, a wider trading range than the 4¢ to 5¢, which was more-or-less constantly pursued, should have been contemplated and followed for the next several months. The more volatile prices are, the greater the risk on the basis of maximum swings. The only safe rule is to keep your stops *close enough* to adequately *protect a profit* or protect against a *major loss*. But, at the same time, keep your stop *far enough away* to accommodate *anticipated fluctuations* in the trading situation which exists. Daily limits on fluctuations offer a useful *maximum* guide.

Soybean Trading

We have made repeated mention of price behavior in the November, 1966 soybean contract. While not taking a major interest in that particular maturity, the same trader whose corn activities we have just reviewed was almost constantly involved in the May, 1967 soybean contract. A review of the price chart and a recapitulation of his trading activities contains some dramatic market lessons.

Here again, the quantities involved are different from the quantities the speculator actually traded. Also, the prices designated represent the levels at which his orders were *placed*. Executions varied slightly, but there was only one major aberration; a stop-loss which called for offset at 334⅝ placed on September 9 was "missed". Neither could he sell the position out on the 12th—there were no buyers in the permissible trading range. When execution was finally accomplished on Tuesday, the 13th, it was done at 322⅝.

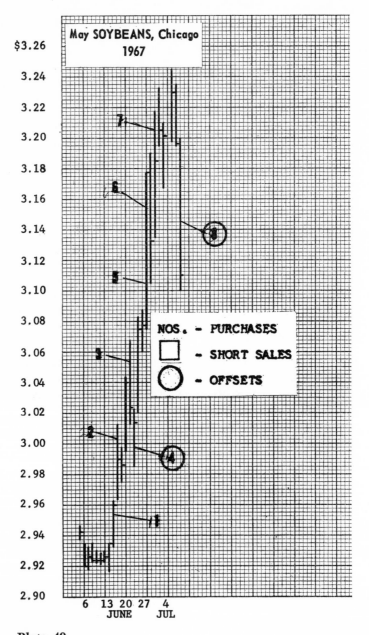

Plate 49

178

Trade No.	Date	Trades in May 1967 Soybeans	Bought	Sold	P/L ¢ per bu.	P/L Dollars
1	6/15/66	Buy: 15M @ 295⅜; stop-loss @ 291⅝	15M @ 295⅜		4¼	637.50
2	6/16	Move stop-loss to 295⅜ Buy: 10M @ 300⅜	10M @ 300⅜		(¾)	(75.00)
3	6/21	Move stop-loss to 299⅝ Buy: 5M @ 305⅜	5M @ 305⅜		(5¾)	(287.50)
4	6/22	Stop-loss hit @ 299⅝; total position offset		30M @ 299⅝		
				Position Result		275.00
				P/L to Date		275.00
5	6/27	Buy: 15M @ 310⅜; stop-loss @ 304⅝	15M @ 310⅜		4¼	637.50
6	6/28	Move stop-loss to 309⅝ Buy: 10M @ 315⅜	10M @ 315⅜		(¾)	(75.00)
7	6/29	Move stop-loss to 314½ Buy: 5M @ 320⅜	5M @ 320⅜		(5¾)	(287.50)
8	7/7	Stop-loss hit @ 314½; total position offset		30M @ 314½		
				Position Result		275.00
				P/L to Date		550.00

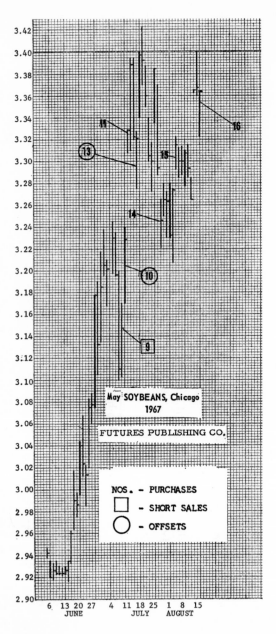

Plate 50

180

Trade No.	Date	Trades in May 1967 Soybeans	Bought	Sold	P/L ¢ per bu.	P/L Dollars
9	7/8	*Sell:* 15M @ $314\frac{5}{8}$; stop-loss @ $320\frac{3}{8}$		15M @ $314\frac{5}{8}$		
10	7/11	Stop-loss hit @ $320\frac{3}{8}$; total position offset	15M @ $320\frac{3}{8}$		$(5\frac{3}{4})$	(862.50)
					Position Result	(862.50)
					P/L to Date	(312.50)
11	7/13	*Buy:* 15M @ $332\frac{3}{8}$; stop-loss @ $327\frac{5}{8}$	15M @ $332\frac{3}{8}$		$(2\frac{3}{4})$	(412.50)
12		*Move stop-loss to* $329\frac{5}{8}$				
13	7/15	Stop-loss hit @ $329\frac{5}{8}$; total position offset		15M @ $329\frac{5}{8}$		
					Position Result	$\overline{(412.50)}$
					P/L to Date	(725.00)
14	7/27	*Buy:* 15M @ $324\frac{3}{8}$; stop-loss @ $319\frac{5}{8}$	15M @ $324\frac{3}{8}$		$12\frac{1}{4}$	1875.00
15	8/3	*Move stop-loss to* $324\frac{5}{8}$ *Buy:* 10 M @ $330\frac{3}{8}$	10M @ $330\frac{3}{8}$		$2\frac{1}{4}$	225.00
16	8/15	*Move stop-loss to* $329\frac{5}{8}$ *Buy:* 5M @ $335\frac{3}{8}$	5M @ $335\frac{3}{8}$		$(2\frac{3}{4})$	(137.50)

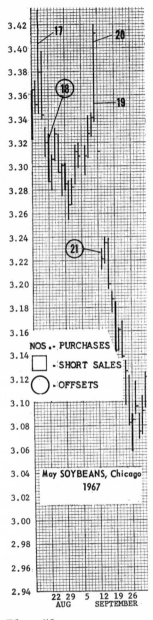

NOS. ◦ - PURCHASES

▢ - SHORT SALES

◯ - OFFSETS

May SOYBEANS, Chicago
1967

22 29   5   12 19 26
AUG   SEPTEMBER

Plate 51

182

Trade No.	Date	Trades in May 1967 Soybeans	Bought	Sold	P/L ¢ per bu.	P/L Dollars
17	8/17	*Move stop-loss to* 332⅝ *Buy:* 5M @ 340⅜	5M @ 340⅜			
18	8/20	Stop-loss hit @ 332⅝; total position offset		35M @ 332⅝	(7¾)	(387.50)
				Position Result		3600.00
				P/L to Date		2875.00
19	9/9	*Buy:* 15M @ 335⅜; stop-loss @ 331⅝	15M @ 335⅝		(13)	(1950.00)
20		*Move stop-loss to* 334⅝ *Buy:* 10M @ 340⅜	10M @ 340⅝		(18)	(1800.00)
21	9/12	Limit down day — (stop-loss can't be executed)				
	9/13	Stop-loss executed at 322⅝		25M @ 322⅝		
				Position Result		(3750.00)
				P/L to Date		(875.00)

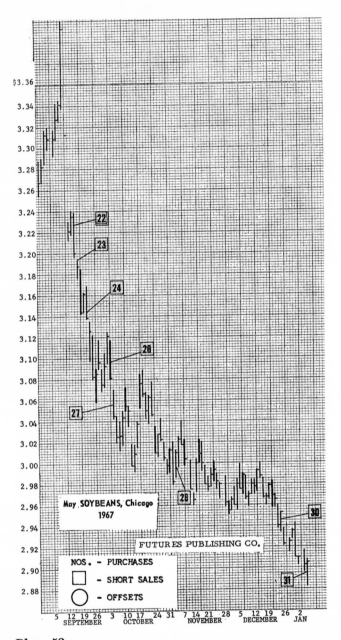

Plate 52

Trade No.	Date	Trades in May 1967 Soybeans	Bought	Sold	P/L ¢ per bu.	P/L Dollars
22	9/15	Sell: 15M @ 323⅝; stop-loss @ 330⅜		15M @ 323⅝	31¼	4687.50
23	9/16	Move stop-loss to 325⅜ Sell: 10M @ 319⅝		10M @ 319⅝	27¼	2725.00
24	9/21	Move stop-loss to 320⅜ Sell: 5M @ 314⅝		5M @ 314⅝	22¼	1112.50
25	9/28	Move stop-loss to 315⅜				
26	10/3	Sell: 5M @ 309⅝		5M @ 309⅝	17¼	862.50
27	10/4	Move Stop-loss to 310⅜ Sell: 5M @ 304⅜		5M @ 304⅝	12¼	612.50
28	11/2	Move stop-loss to 305⅜ Sell: 5M @ 299⅝		5M @ 299⅝	7¼	362.50
29	11/22	Move stop-loss to 300⅝				
30	12/22	Sell: 5M @ 294⅝		5M @ 294⅝	2¼	112.50
31	1/4/67	Move stop-loss to 295⅝ Sell: 5M @ 289⅝		5M @ 289⅝	(5¾)	(137.50)

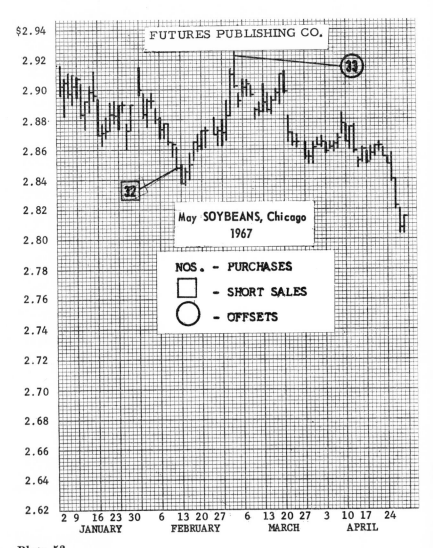

Plate 53

186

Trade No.	Date	Trades in May 1967 Soybeans	Bought	Sold	P/L ¢ per bu.	P/L Dollars
32	2/10	*Move stop-loss to* 292⅜				
33	3/2	*Sell:* 5M @ 284⅝		5M @ 284⅝	(7¾)	(387.50)
		Stop-loss hit at 292⅜; total position 60M @ 292⅜ offset.				
				Position Result		9950.00
				P/L to Date		9075.00
		Less Brokerage Commission on 42 contracts @ 24.00				1008.00
				Net Proceeds		8067.00

Using Charts in Trade

If You Can't Stand Heat . . .

This is the sort of commodity contract that can turn a speculator gray, and move him a long step closer to the poorhouse, unless he can keep his wits about him under great stress.

The May soybean contract took off explosively almost from the start. The trader was "in step" from the outset, but was unfortunately stopped-out by wide daily price swings on both of his first two long positions. On July 8, he decided that the "bull move" had run its course. This is where his real troubles began. Two successive July positions both proved to be in the wrong direction. Then, on July 27, he re-established a long position at 324⅜ which was "right". In approximately three weeks, he had made $3600 on it, which covered all earlier losses in the contract and produced a comfortable net profit.

There is an old saying in trading circles that "the market can give it to you in a hurry—and take it back even faster." On September 9—that fateful Friday in advance of the Government Crop Report—a run-up began in soybeans, aided in the last few minutes of trading by a short-squeeze of gigantic proportions. This trader bought at 335⅜; then moved his stop-loss up and bought again at 340⅜. When the closing bell ended the session, he was long 25,000 bushels with a stop-loss at 334⅝ and, all things being equal, should have been in good shape. But appearances can be deceiving.

When the crop report figures came out, the soybean market broke dramatically. The stop-loss order which was placed at 334⅝ was meaningless. Prices fell the full 10¢ permissible on Monday, September 12, and no trading was done because there were *no buyers* in the *permissible trading range*. On Tuesday, the 13th, he was at last able to get an offset made at 322⅝. The three sessions had left him with a 13¢ loss on 15,000 bushels, and an 18¢ loss on the 10,000 bushels additional.

Now that the house had literally "fallen in", it took no particular genius for this disenchanted "bull" to recognize that prices were more than likely headed lower. The trader went short on September 16 and stayed short until March 2. The results were gratifying to say the least.

Always Learn The Lessons You Pay For

Several points which should be apparent in this sequence of events deserve careful underscoring. First of all, *trading into a major crop report can be brutal.* Having said this, it must also be recognized that when the market gets a major surprise, its effects are not likely to be *all* reflected *at once.* In this case, the demoralization which was contained in a higher-than-expected soybean production forecast led to progressively lower prices throughout the balance of contract life. It is also notable that from September 14 until the maturity went off the board, a 40¢ price deterioration took place *without a single major upside reversal!* Unfortunate longs kept re-establishing their positions (or absorbing their steady losses) at ever-lower levels, but they could never win back the initiative in the market. On three different occasions during late November and early December, the market rallied precisely to the $3 per bushel level, but was unable to break above the line. From that point on, it was all downhill.

Look For The Wide Price Pattern

The key to successful "program-trading" stands revealed in this soybean chart. The opportunities a "program" speculator should seek are found in those contracts which reflect a tendency to make major *trend* moves of a *seasonal, fundamental,* or a *technical* nature. Program-trading in a situation like the one presented during the first four months of this particular contract is fraught with too much hazard to be very enticing. While major price "gaps" which occur in your favor are most gratifying, gaps which open in the "right direction" also foster other gaps that may open in the "wrong direction".

The safest course to follow when the price chart begins to "open up" is to close out your position and wait for a more *consistent* pattern to develop. Failure to do so invites the possibility of your getting "out of step" with price movements and being subjected to the well-known "whip-saw". In such a situation, the *more persistent* you are in establishing *new positions,* the *more punishment* you may be forced to take.

Don't Worry About a Bad Trade

There is another lesson to be learned from this example: You can be wrong *several times*—and for substantial amounts of money—but if you can catch a significant long-term trend, a profitable outcome is virtually assured. The crux of the matter rests in *proper management* of the position. This calls for *adding* to the winning position at regular, predetermined intervals, and keeping your stop-loss orders close enough to avoid taking a large loss. Finally, of course, *never* try to decide when the market has "gone far enough". It will be its own authority on this topic, and *you will know it* when your stop-loss is finally activated.

CHAPTER XIII

ADDING TO A PROFITABLE POSITION

A position which exceeds the predetermined limit on a permissible loss is *always* closed out. However, as we have seen, a position which justifies the speculator's profit expectation offers an *opportunity for enlargement* at designated price intervals, so long as it continues to perform in the proper fashion. The designation most often given to the practice of methodically adding to a profitable trade is "pyramiding". The term implies beginning with an initial trade base and adding to it successively, as returns on the initial commitment justify. In diagraming the procedure, the "pyramid" will always appear to be upside-down as concerns short-selling and right-side-up when it portrays trading from the long side.

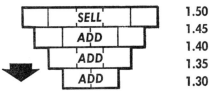

1.50	
1.45	
1.40	
1.35	
1.30	

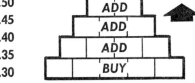

Plate 54

Adding to a Profitable Position

In addition to offering increased profit opportunities as the position builds, the trader's leverage situation is progressively enhanced also, since each succeeding commitment is made with a combination of his own risk funds and accrued "paper profits" previously realized from the trade "foundation".

Picking "Sell" and "Buy" Spots

For our example, let's consider an initial short sale of 10,000 bushels of May soybeans at 2.94⅝ executed on December 22, on Plate 55.

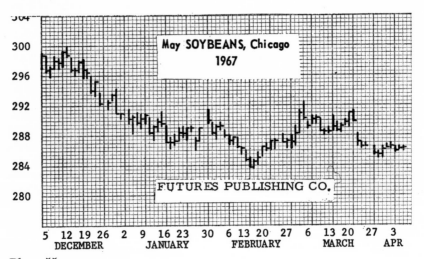

Plate 55

After fluctuating within a trading range, prices break through the $2.90 level on the down-side, on January 3, while never succeeding in going over $2.99¼ on the up-side. The price pattern convinces the trader that strong *resistance* exists in the $2.99 to $3.00 level. Once prices have fallen below the $2.90 level, the trader is likewise of the opinion that the price is even more on the *defensive* than it was before; and due for further down-side movement. He follows the rule, "sell weakness and buy strength", but rather than just placing a "resting order" to sell an additional quantity of May beans at $2.89⅝, the trader may attempt to obtain a *better selling price.* His method for doing this brings us to another fundamental rule of speculation: Sell "bulges" and buy "dips".

Seeking to generally "sell weakness" and specifically "sell a bulge" may sound like a contradiction, but it is not. The significant development with respect to the down-side price move was in breaking the $2.90 barrier. Having gone through this level, the speculator may be of the opinion that price is far more likely to penetrate the $2.90 level again—and *then* move lower, than to either keep dropping or work its way clear back up to the $3.00 level. Stated another way, his "selling signal" was in the penetration of the $2.90 price level. In terms of executing the sale, however, if he wants the best possible selling price, he must try to sell on a "bulge" in the price pattern. To do so, he will have to keep a rather close watch on the situation.

As previously noted, prices endlessly fluctuate between narrow or wide range limits. Soybeans being a fairly expensive commodity, their trading ranges are proportionately broader than a more modestly priced commodity like wheat or corn, for example. Historically, the intra-session trading range on soybeans averages out around 3¢ to 5¢. This is to say that in *average* markets, the lowest price recorded in a given session will be some 4¢ under the highest price in the same session. In active markets the *greater volume* of trading may reflect itself in a proportionately *wider trading range,* as we have seen. The speculator, in order to realize the best possible return from

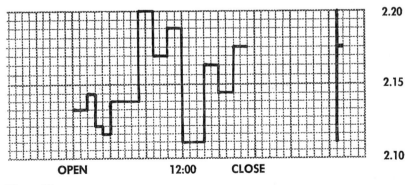

Plate 56

Adding to a Profitable Position

his position, must always consider this behaviorism in placing orders to buy and sell.

Down-side penetration of the $2.90 level on May soybeans has convinced the speculator that prices will go lower but in the meantime, prices will continue to fluctuate. The trader has decided to sell more May beans short, but he wants to sell them at the *highest possible price within the descending range.* His method for doing this might be to place an order which specifies, "Sell 5 May beans $2.91½ when the market touches $2.89⅝—day order." This kind of order could be placed with a broker several days in advance of the event; or could actually have been placed with the broker at the same time the initial position was taken. If so, this additional selling order would be a "resting order", the same as the stop-loss which was placed to contemplate possible upside movement in the contract.

By checking trading ranges each day, the speculator will be able to see if the price on May beans is approaching the specified level— $2.89⅝—which will automatically activate the "resting" sell order. The crucial day might produce a session in which prices begin working lower from the opening. The sell order is "touched off" and then, as is often the case, prices may turn around and move higher, reaching $2.91½ on the May soybean contract. At this point, the additional 5,000 bushels of May beans would be sold. After the sale is made, the price might continue to move upward to $2.92¼; then turn around once more and sell off towards the close of the session.

In the face of events set forth earlier, a lower price ($2.89⅝) would *activate* the sell order, but its *execution* could not take place until prices move 1⅞¢ higher on the specified contract.

The second means of accomplishing a short sale of this kind is by using a "time- and price-limit order". This order might instruct the broker to "Sell 5 May beans after 11:00 a.m. $2.91½—stop." The thinking behind this second handling could be that the trader looks for lower prices at the opening, followed by a turn-around, and higher prices during the mid-session. He only wants to make his short sale *after* the anticipated "bulge" has had a chance to have developed and passed. Moreover, while he has no real dope for "picking the top" of the upward fluctuation, he hopes to get his short sale made *near* the top of the *trading range* which has persisted for the preceding two to three sessions. Of course, if prices do not move to the specified "tick", he will not get execution. In fact his price may be hit and one or two sales executed at the level of his sell order; but his floor broker may still be unable to get a "fill".

"Tops" & "Bottoms" Can Be Thin

It is worth noting that the volume of trade which takes place at the higher and lower limits of the trading range are usually quite small. A single 5,000 bushel contract may change hands to post the "high" for the day; the same sort of minimum trade may post the "low" for the day. Inexperienced traders are often disappointed to see that the price specified in a limit-order was reached, but their order was still not executed. The explanation invariably is that offerings or bids at the maximum level were simply not sufficient to accommodate all orders "resting" at the top or the bottom of the market.

So, whether through placement of the first kind of combined order, or the time-and-price-limit order, we will assume that the trader has succeeded in selling an additional 5,000 bushels of May soybeans short at $2.91½. His total position at this point is "short — 15 May beans". Execution of the second order requires total margin of $2250, since margining of each subsequent trade demands that *initial margin to cover the total position* be on deposit with the broker. Initial margin on soybeans, as previously noted, is at this writing 15¢ per bushel; hence, $2250 initial margin is required to cover the 15,000 bushels. Of this total amount, only $1,850 represents the speculator's cash money on deposit with his commission house. The remaining $525 is represented by "paper profits", made on the initial 10,000 bushel short position as it dropped from a price of $2.96¾ (the first short sale) to $2.91½ (the second short sale). At this point, the speculator has increased his position in the market by one half, but his cash margin requirement is not proportionately larger. It has increased by less than one fourth, due to the fact that he is "trading on profits" in the amount of $525.

Whenever an opportunity for "pyramiding" presents itself, it materially increases the already substantial leverage situation in commodity trading. Coincidentally with selling the additional 5000

Adding to a Profitable Position

bushels of beans, a new look must now be taken at the speculator's stop-loss. On each 5000 bushels of grain — long or short — each price change of 1¢ results in a profit or loss of $50. By increasing the position to 15,000 bushels, each 1¢ movement in price will result in a profit or loss of $150. (Margins are ignored in this discussion.) At $2.91½ per bushel, the speculator has a $525 paper profit in the trade. This is to say that, commissions ignored, he can lose this amount "back" to the market before the position would represent a "zero-profit" situation. Having added a second 5,000 bushel sale, an upward price movement of about 3½¢ per bushel will dissipate the $525 paper profit. Hopefully, the addition will only be made if the trader feels he can safely move his top-side stop-loss down from $3.00½ per bushel to about $2.95½. At the point he adds the *third* contract of 5000 bushels, he has again risked the $525 paper profit — but his objective should be to get as close as possible to nothing worse than a "break even" on the trade.

Unless a stop-loss can be moved down, a position should *not* be increased, since doing so increases risk exposure without bringing any real offsetting advantage. Moving the stop-loss "insures" your pyramid.

Commodity speculators usually turn in far better performances in the placement and management of initial positions than they do in making the secondary judgments which call for additions to the primary trade. This fact is oftentimes directly related to their tendency to over-trade on limited funds.

Keep Part of Your Powder Dry

It was earlier pointed out that an initial position should never require commitment of more than fifty-percent of a trader's margin money. The reason for this rule now becomes apparent: the fifty-percent reserve is a guarantee that if prices move in the trader's favor, he will have the funds required to *enlarge his position* and take advantage of the greater leverage in pyramiding — "trading on profits". A modest beginning on a commodity position entails modest risks. As price movement validates traders' judgment and paper profits accrue, larger exposures are justified — but *only* if safeguards can be

196

invoked to reduce potential hazards. Maximizing profit opportunities calls for both financial *ability* and *willingness* to *enlarge a profitable position*. But — to repeat for emphasis — never pyramid unless you can *simultaneously* move your stop-loss and cut loss potentials substantially.

Each time a position is added to, a different situation exists. Most importantly, the contract is now trading at a somewhat different price level —and the range may be wider or narrower than previously. Consequently, profit and loss expectations may be altered. The position now deserves careful appraisal, along with increased attention on the part of its holder, since there is more at stake. This fact hardly requires emphasis, however, since there is nothing that will concentrate a speculator's attention like a large and profitable position which has been accumulated in several steps.

Don't Try to Stay Forever

The importance of "getting in" at the right time cannot be over-emphasized. "Getting out" at the right time is of even greater moment with respect to profits. Inexperienced speculators have a long and undistinguished record of *staying too long* in losing positions. During 1966, thousands of speculators established long positions in corn futures at prices ranging from $1.35 to $1.50 per bushel. Corn prices moved sharply higher through August and September, peaked out in the $1.55 to $1.58 range and fell precipitously into the $1.30 to $1.40 range in November. Public traders who — at the contract highs — had profits of 15¢ or 20¢ in their corn positions, sat patiently and watched their paper gains dissipated. They consoled themselves with the forlorn thought that they still "had a profit in it". A trading rationale of this kind is senseless. Regardless of paper profits remaining, every one-eighth down from the contract high was a loss for the longs.

A speculator buys something to sell at a higher price; or sells it in expectation of buying it back at a lower price. In either case, *profit is the sole motivation*. Any time prices move sharply against a commodity position, the time has come to close it out, whether or not there is some profit left at lower price levels. (Certain situations

197

Adding to a Profitable Position

which involve long positions in commodities and that are closely approaching the six-month period required for long-term capital gains treatment, constitute the only possible exception to the rule. But a different tactic is called for here. An intra-market hedge can be esablished to protect profits and still allow holding of the position which is being subjected to price deterioration.)

The best and surest way to guard against erosion of profits already accumulated is by careful placement of a stop-order which will automatically get offset on the position any time prices move out of an acceptable trading range. Speculative profits must be *protected* as zealously in existing positions as they are *sought* in new positions. Failure to do so will only succeed in turning profitable trades into "break-evens" — and the losing trades will continue to deplete risk funds. The predictable result will sooner or later be disaster, of course.

Daily Price Behavior

The matter of "selling on bulges" and "buying on dips" has been referred to previously. Now we shall consider this matter from a different standpoint. (See Plate 56.)

Examination of a bar chart on price movement in any commodity is convincing proof that prices rarely move up or down in a smooth and unbroken path. The *trend* may be clearly higher or lower, but the *path* followed by price in producing this trend is an unending succession of directional reversals. Depending on the commodity, and influenced to a large extent by its relative price, swings in value will be narrow or broad. Generally speaking, the more actively a contract is traded, the wider its price swings may be; since a high volume of speculator interest in a given commodity has a tendency to emphasize the short-term extremes within which its price fluctuates: The highs are rendered somewhat higher, and the lows are rendered somewhat lower, than is likely to be seen in a modestly traded situation. The long-range effect of speculation is to *reduce price fluctuation;* but the short-range effect of high-volume speculation may be just the opposite.

198

Plate 57

A public order reaches the pit broker for execution.

Adding to a Profitable Position

"Position" and "Day" Traders

At the very hub of the market — in the pits — will be found several categories of full-time, professional traders, including those who pursue a speculative program which involves taking positions in selected contracts and holding them over several weeks or several months, pending *major price movements*. These people are usually spoken of as "position traders". These individuals may establish a long or short position early in the season and hold it until maturity. "Day-traders", on the other hand, may be "long" for the first hour or so, then offset and go "short" for the balance of the session. In any case, the day-trader intends to offset *all* positions and be *even* with the market at the closing bell; the day-trader carries no positions overnight if he can help it. His speculative program is pointed exclusively to taking advantage of whatever profit opportunities exist between the opening and the close; by which time he will be evened up and out of the market.

"Scalpers"

The shortest of all short-term traders is the pit "scalper". This individual performs approximately the same function in the commodity pit that the "specialist" performs on the securities exchanges, with one important difference: the scalper has *no official designation* from the commodity exchange itself. The scalper buys and sells in search of profit, with no special privileges accorded him from any quarter. He may make dozens or hundreds of trades in the course of a single session. Generally speaking, the scalper is prepared to *sell* at ⅛¢ or ¼¢ per bushel *above the last trade;* he is usually a ready *buyer* ⅛¢ or ¼¢ *below the last trade.* His success depends on exceedingly small profits on a big trade volume. He views the minimum price fluctuation in grain — ⅛¢ a bushel — as an acceptable transaction, and considers ¼¢ per bushel an *excellent* return!

Commodity scalpers, like stock specialists, provide a source of supply when orders to buy exceed orders to sell. Likewise, scalpers (and specialists) constitute demand, when offerings exceed willingness to buy on the part of the public or longer-term traders. Neither the scalper nor the specialist can prevent prices from moving higher or lower in the face of altered supply/demand equilibrium, and they would not wish to do so even if they could. These somewhat similar market participants do, however, help maintain market liquidity and aid in sustaining orderly progression of prices from one level to another level. In so doing, they contribute immeasurably to the well-being of the market itself.

Like the day trader, the scalper carries no positions overnight. By the closing bell, he will have offset all of his previous trades and calculated his profits or losses on the individual session, as a trading interval which stands by itself.

From the foregoing, it should be seen that the position-trader, the day-trader, and the scalper, all seek profits from properly anticipating price movement. Each, however, approaches the market with a different period of time in mind. The position trader looks for a situation which he may carry for weeks or months; the day trader seeks positions which he may carry for, at most, a few hours; the scalper may buy 50,000 bushels of grain and sell it ten seconds later, or sell 50,000 bushels short and "cover" it in the same breath. All three classifications of traders have one thing in common. They will hold a position until profit expectations are realized, or the market moves adversely enough to require "covering the loss".

It is the interaction of these buying and selling forces, along with the actions of public speculators, commercial hedgers, producers, and processors, that determine the course of price movement, minute by minute. If selling pressure gains momentary ascendancy in a pit, prices will move lower until the lower (and more attractive) price prompts new buying sentiment. When this happens, the "bears" may suddenly lose the initiative to the "bulls"; a price reversal will occur and values will move higher. The result is a constant see-saw action.

Daily trading ranges in corn rarely exceed 2¢ or 3¢ per bushel. In soybeans, as noted above, the trading range is more like 3¢ to 5¢ a bushel. These swings are approximately parallel by reason of the fact that soybeans usually trade at about twice the price of corn. A 2¢ price change in $3.00 soybeans is the same order of magnitude as a 1¢ per bushel change in $1.50 corn. It may be well to note here also that margins anticipate these differences. The initial margin on corn at this writing is 10¢ per bushel, compared to 15¢ per bushel for the beans.

Adding to a Profitable Position

Day traders strive earnestly to pick points of price-reversal, since their greatest chance for a profit lies in properly forecasting price direction during the current trading session. Scalpers care little about "tops and bottoms", so long as they can anticipate price *direction*. Position traders tend to give major emphasis to relatively long-term price trends.

The public speculator is well advised to pursue the *position trader's* operational philosophy; however, selling on intra-session price "bulges", and buying on price "dips" can easily add another cent or two to profits — and reduce loss exposure accordingly. Granting this automatically gives rise to a question related to order placement.

Limited vs. "Market" Orders

A "market order" to buy or sell will be immediately executed at the best level offered in the pit at the time the broker receives it. This price may or may not be advantageous in view of the private speculator, but it is the "market price" when the order is called. In the face of rapidly moving prices, the trader may have no alternative but to accept whatever price the market gives him. This situation will usually apply when losses are mounting, due to a rapidly rising or falling price level. Establishing a new position, however, can ordinarily be approached somewhat more deliberately.

Experienced traders usually prefer specifying a fixed price (or better) at which they are willing to buy or sell. Obviously it will only rarely make sense to place an *entering order* far below — or above — the trading range, in the flimsy hope that something cataclysmic will happen to bring prices to the level of the order. Resting-orders well outside the trading range are commonplace, but their execution may be deferred for days or weeks. Or they may never be filled. The commodity speculator must try to find some middle ground between the price he *would like* and the price he can reasonably *expect to get* in the marketplace. There are many instances, in fact, where, for example, December corn at $1.42 per bushel represents a much more promising buy than the same contract at $1.38.

Depending on the tone of the trade, the chart pattern, and the general price trend on the futures involved, $1.42 per bushel, might be a clear indication to *buy* corn, while $1.38 per bushel could be an equally strong reason to *sell* the contract short. The speculator who is attempting to get all possible profit "mileage" out of his position, will put a price limitation on his orders to buy or sell, whenever he can *prudently* do so. In return, he will often be exposed to the unspeakable frustration of seeing prices come within a small fraction of a penny of his "limit" and then move away. Missing execution by ¼¢ or ⅛¢ can be an upsetting experience; and the speculator who constantly places limit orders will know the feeling often. However, the positions he is able to acquire on the basis of his limits will ordinarily be better — more profitable — than those taken "at market".

Don't Be Too Anxious To Execute

There is an old saying in speculative circles that you "can't lose a dollar on a position you don't have". Another axiom which bears on the same consideration is — "Whenever you reach, you will probably find trouble". Boiled down to their fundamentals, these two admonitions simply mean that a speculator is entitled to determine the price at which *he is willing* to undertake a given risk. If the market won't fill the order and do business at this level, then the speculator will either have to refuse to do business at all — or reconsider the situation and develop a second price appraisal.

The role of the speculator is that of forecasting price movement; nothing else. The only time a speculator can look forward to profits is when he catches the market quoting the "wrong price" on a given contract. The speculator must, in other words, catch the trade in error. Obviously if the market price is the right price, then it can only be expected to persist and there is no speculative profit to be made out of price consistency. It takes *change* to ring the speculative cash register. Doing this requires that the speculator's "price idea" be *better than composite market judgment* in the short-term, the medium-term, the long-term — or all of these.

It is no small assignment, which again underscores the thought that a wise speculator will be highly selective about the positions he undertakes. Additionally, and most important, unless he can find something palpably "wrong" with an individual price or a price relationship, he will stay on the sidelines and patiently wait for an opportunity to "catch the market with jam on its face". Anyone who insists on being constantly involved in commodity futures speculation should make a full-time business of it. Certainly there are situations every hour of every trading day which have exciting profit potentials, but finding these opportunities calls for careful study and critical analysis; in short — a *full-time engagement*.

The public speculator is, more often than not, an individual who has the financial wherewithal and the analytical turn of mind to make commodity speculation an interesting, exciting and rewarding *avocation*. This is to say that market activities will probably *not* receive *first priority*. Granting this, the prudent public speculator will limit his market forays to those situations which show the best opportunities for profit. He will leave the more limited, more hazardous, short-term commitments to those who have the time and the professional expertise with which to deal with them.

Plate 58

Filling the average order is usually a matter of seconds.

CHAPTER XIV

SPECIAL TRADING SITUATIONS

The trading lives of commodity contracts are about a year, or more. Within this relatively short time span, a commodity contract comes into existence, develops some discernible "personality" traits, and expires. While it can be said that all wheat contracts, for example, demonstrate somewhat similar characteristics, it is a serious mistake to look at all contracts in a given commodity in the same light.

Old Crop/New Crop

Some of the most glaring idiosyncracies in futures contract characteristics relate to the point in the *crop or production year in which they mature.* As a case in point, the May wheat contract represents "old crop wheat". The grain delivered against open long positions in May wheat will have been harvested in late summer or fall of the preceding year. The relative adequacy or scarcity of wheat stocks will exercise the most significant influence on the way May wheat "goes off the board". If the harvest was ample and crop disappearance through consumption and export was not excessive, it might be expected that wheat stocks in commercial channels would be sufficient to meet ordinary demands, pending the "new crop" which begins to arrive in volume in late June and July.

If, on the other hand, the preceding harvest was meager or disappearance of the crop has proceeded at an accelerated rate, wheat stocks may be seriously depleted. The result may be that food processors and others who need the grain face some degree of crisis in fulfilling their requirements until the new crop becomes available. In the face of ample or excessive residual stocks, stable or lower May wheat prices can be confidently anticipated. Scarcity of the grain will bring higher prices for the cash product, as well as for old crop May futures contracts which represent the commodity.

July wheat futures represent "new crop" grain. "Old crop" considerations are, at best, a *secondary* influence. The market's appraisal of the adequacy of the pending harvest in light of existing and projected *new* demands will be the major concern, reflected in relatively high or low prices on the July contract. If it appears that a significant imbalance is shaping up, as between expected supplies and estimated demands, wide price swings will usually document the building market consensus.

Trading in *old crop* grain commodities brings the speculator to grips with the fundamental adequacy of commodity *inventories remaining* at the *end* of the crop year. *New crop* contracts relate to *future needs.* Making these appraisals calls for careful analysis and meticulous arithmetic. Both past and projected exports must be studiously added up, along with past and projected domestic consumption figures. Appraisals require that *annual* data must be compared to the historical *averages* over not less than a five-year period. Government programs which affect acreage controls, export policy, "food for freedom", etc. must also be included in any meaningful price/value equation.

Harvest Time May Vary

Reference has already been made to the fact that September contract in soybeans can be *either old crop or new crop,* depending on how early planting was concluded and subsequent weather patterns during the growing season. A soybean is a "photo-periodic" plant. The mature beans will be ready for harvest a specified number of weeks after planting, so long as temperatures remain in an acceptable range and moisture is adequate to sustain plant development.

In view of the foregoing, the September soybean contract can be expected to reflect some volatility not present in other commodity categories. Should it appear that factors are favorable for an *early harvest*, proportionately *lower* prices on the September contract usually are seen. (The effect is one of enlarging old-crop carryover.) Should subsequent events alter this outlook, higher prices are quick to develop. This characteristic in September soybeans affords an excellent opportunity to examine the phenomenon known in commodity trading as a "weather market". The term is descriptively accurate.

Trading in September soybeans begins in September of the year preceding harvest. Usually the new contract comes "on the board" at some discount to the expiring November contract. This is prompted in large measure by the continuing trend to greater soybean acreage, and increasing per-acre yields. Once trading begins in the new crop beans, a pattern of price behavior quickly begins to develop. At the outset, disappearance of the old crop is the most important factor in pricing the new crop, since it governs the size of the carry-over which may be expected at the end of the current crop year. Government activities directed toward increased or reduced acreage are also a major factor, along with projcted yields per acre. Relative prices commanded by soybean meal and oil must be given full weight, too, since these may provide an index to increasing or decreasing *demand trends* for the products; and which may be sustained for several months or a year later.

Ordinarily, through the winter September soybean prices will follow the leadership of the July contract. September begins to develop a personality of its own in March, when the U. S. Department of Agriculture Crop Reporting Service releases figures on soybean planting intentions. A significant *increase* over the past year in projected soybean acreage will usually exert a predictably "bearish" influence on prices. The *same* or *reduced* planting intentions will ordinarily have the opposite effect.

Once the plantings intentions report is out, weather quickly becomes the most important single influence in the contract and will remain so for some four or five months. In a year when an early spring and dry fields permit putting seed in the ground in late March or early April, the impact on the September price is substantial. By virtue of the photo-periodic nature of soybeans, early planting almost insures an early harvest — and will usually bring somewhat lower prices on both the old-crop (July) contract and the new-crop (September).

Should bad weather and wet fields delay planting, the opposite effect can be expected to result. If the condition persists, harvest will be delayed; and September contract now becomes "old-crop", and its requirements will have to be filled out of carry-over stocks. Prices on the September maturity will — in this situation — reflect the market's appraisal of the adequacy of remaining supplies, projected to November — two months beyond the statistical end of the crop year. Understandably, the effect on price can be tremendous.

Growing Conditions Are Crucial

Early planting does not by itself lay all of the worries to rest. Ideal growing conditions for soybeans, as well as other grains, usually require temperatures between a minimum of 55° Fahrenheit and a maximum of 100° Fahrenheit. Additionally, of course, sufficient moisture must be present in the soil to sustain plant development.

Heavy early rains may threaten to wash seed out of the ground. In the face of such a possibility — provided the threat hangs over an important soybean region — prices will rise in recognition of the hazard. In the opposite weather situation, protracted periods of drought will also send prices upward in reflection of the possibility that dry weather may destroy the crop or seriously retard its growth. Each plant has its own development characteristics. The soybean is distinguished by an amazing recuperative power. While an extended period of dry weather will damage the growing plants — even to the extent of causing leaves to dry up and fall off — once the rains return, soybeans will usually put out new growth and "pick up where they left off."

As summer progresses, however, soybean farmers, processors and speculators keep a careful eye on weather forecasts. September bean prices in particular rise and fall in response to the thermometer and the soil-moisture scale. Traders repeat the market truism that "every soybean crop is lost three or four times before it is harvested." The statement merely underscores the susceptibility of market psychology to weather influences. When a period of dryness develops, market response tends to *over-emphasize* its significance in the form of a price bulge. When needed rain interrupts the period of drought, prices drop in something like *equal disproportion* to their previous increase. In short, the market tends to *over-buy* bad weather and *over-sell* good weather, offering an excellent opportunity for a speculator to "buy the dips" and "sell the bulges" through several months of the growing season.

The weather-market in soybeans is especially volatile due to the fact the September contract may be accelerated or retarded by weather patterns, to the extent of making the maturity fall into one crop year or the next. Similar considerations are also present in some other grain commodities, although to a lesser extent.

As this material is being prepared (December, 1966), July wheat futures (new crop) is trading at historically high prices under the influence of a protracted dry spell in the southwestern wheat belt. Spring wheat (for 1967 harvest) is already planted, but moisture is now needed to develop root growth and permit initial establishment of the plant before winter sets in. If rains do not come, the spring wheat yield will be harmed and high prices on the July contract will, in all likelihood, persist. Substantial risks are present. In the words of one market authority, "one good rain storm in western Kansas and eastern Colorado will drop July wheat futures to the support price level." (His prediction later proved absolutely accurate) and it serves to emphasize the importance of weather considerations in commodity prices, and alerts the trader to the fact that *excellent trading opportunities* — and proportionately *large risk exposures* — grow out of weather influences. There is a further anomaly which deserves mention in this connection.

Weather Psychology In The Market

The impact of weather on growing crops is self-evident, of course, but the weather psychology which permeates the market during the growing season should also be recognized. No grain is raised in Chicago, but a rain storm *in Chicago* during the crop growing season will almost invariably reflect itself in *lower commodity prices* on pertinent contracts! The explanation must be that traders consider moisture "bearish" and lack of rain "bullish" and react accordingly — almost automatically.

The foregoing should not lead the speculator to the unfounded conclusion that weather extremes are always of only transitory importance, to be later corrected by nature, and the affected crops saved. This is not the case. Extensive and persistent droughts have occurred in the past, and will most assuredly be seen in the future. The balance between supply and demand tends to be so sensitive that even a 2% or 3% difference in harvest yield can make a most significant difference in the adequacy of supplies; and alter the price the product commands in the marketplace out of all proportion to the percentage crop loss or gain. It is true that weather news tends to be *magnified in the short-term;* but it is equally true that weather must be accorded the highest priority as concerns longer-range prices of "new crop" commodities. Growing crops are absolutely dependent on benign combinations of temperature and moisture. Unless nature provides the proper climatic mix, human efforts are of no avail.

"Seasonal" Balance in Hedging

Of all of the special trading situations which challenge the courage and insight of the speculator, *maturing contracts* must be put at the head of the list. Within the contract trading life of about a year or so, open interest grows from zero to what may be impressive proportions. For each seller of a futures contract, there must also be a buyer, and the *foundation* of most futures trading is provided by hedging on the part of the producers, processors, dealers and shippers.

At the end of harvest, commercial interests are large buyers of commodities from producers, and they hedge their cash grain acquisitions in the market by sale of futures. Thus, the post-harvest situation usually finds commercial interests overwhelmingly *short* in the market — and speculative interests equally *long.* Toward the end of the crop year, this situation tends to be substantially moderated or, if a shortage of the commodity exists, it may be actually *reversed.*

In order to understand this development, we must review the reasons which prompt commercial hedging. By definition, a hedge is an *equal and opposite* position in futures, to the position held in cash commodities. If a grain dealer has a million bushels of corn in storage, a hedge against this cash corn position would require that he have a million bushels of corn futures sold short in the market. Obviously a commercial grain broker or processor must rely on speculators to buy his short-hedge offerings. It may also be assumed that speculators will only buy futures contracts at prices which appear to be sufficiently low as to offer a reasonable expectation for profit, in payment for assumption of the ownership risk.

It is a historic fact that prices during the harvest season tend to be lower than the yearly average. As the year progresses, the cash grain previously purchased by commercial interests is consumed and exported. As this takes place, the holders of cash grain reduce their inventories and "lift their hedges" by buying back — offsetting — their previously sold commodity futures contracts. Repurchase of these contracts by commercial interests takes place somewhat later in the crop year, after the harvest glut of the commodity has been materially reduced. One effect of this recurrent market pattern is a more or less perceptible "seasonal" increase in prices for most agricultural crops.

Plate 59

Inventory control is endless in a cash commodity operation.

Special Trading Situations

Maturing Contracts

Quite naturally, speculators who previously purchased the short-hedge offerings of the commercial interests will attempt to hold out for a price which will enable them to realize maximum profits. Note that this statement reflects a *hope* which may or may not always be realized. The price on futures contracts at maturity is closely related to the value of the cash product. *Cash and futures prices tend to converge in the market on the last day of trading.*

The holder of a short position in a maturing commodity contract has the choice of offsetting by an equal or opposite futures transaction, or he may satisfy his contract commitment by delivery of the physical commodity. The price which prevails on futures contracts at maturity will be a composite reflection of the willingness of the shorts to make delivery and the willingness of the longs to accept delivery. Excessive deliverable stocks "in position" will force prices down. Shortage of deliverable stocks "in position" will carry prices higher.

It should be noted at this point that only about *one percent* of the futures contracts bought and sold are actually satisfied by delivery of the cash commodity. Commercial hedgers are reticent to make delivery, since doing so entails costs and inconvenience which are acceptable in cash-market trading; but they *prefer offset* in the futures market to any other kind of settlement, *provided* this can be done without economic penalty.

Speculators are ordinarily in no position to make delivery of cash commodities because they hold none; they likewise wish to avoid accepting delivery of cash commodities, since they neither own storage facilities nor have use for physical product. Hence it will be seen that commercial interests merely *prefer* offset of their futures positions; speculators usually *insist* on offsetting in preference to taking or making delivery.

As a contract reaches its delivery period and the "last day of trading" approaches, holders of both long and short positions are coming down to the "moment of truth". Once trading is terminated in a given contract, all remaining shorts must *make delivery* and all remaining longs must *accept delivery*. Doing so may constitute a

212

major catastrophe for either or both. If a *shortage* of the product prevails, the *longs may stand firm* and threaten the shorts with having to deliver. This situation is known in the trade as a "short squeeze" and may send prices sky-rocketing as the shorts scramble to offset their open positions, which will remove the necessity of their delivering the cash commodity.

In the reverse situation, an *excess* of commodities in deliverable position may prompt the *shorts to stand firm* — threatening delivery — and forcing the longs to sell out their holdings at a disadvantage in order to avoid taking delivery. Sharply lower prices may result from such a "long squeeze".

One of the best indicators of a potentially explosive situation in a maturing contract is the amount of *open interest* remaining in the last few days of contract life. Ordinarily both hedgers and speculators will begin offsetting heavily during the month preceding maturity. Should open-interest remain usunually high beyond the "first notice day", it can be taken as a good indication that "somebody is in trouble". The problem for the speculator now is to decide whether it is the "longs" or the "shorts" who are likely to be caught in the squeeze which may be developing.

In appraising this kind of situation, it must be remembered that *only commercials* are usually ready to accept delivery in large quantities; likewise, *commercial* interests have both the facilities and the grain stocks to make delivery to the shorts.

In light of this, it will be seen that the public is more susceptible to "squeezing" than commercial interests. Therefore, in order to profit from the situation, the speculator must decide whether the public is *net long* or *net short;* and whichever decision he arrives at suggests that he take precisely the *opposite* position.

If the *public is short,* the speculator *may buy* the contract because the shorts *will buy* back their positions. Their doing so will likely send prices higher. If the *public is long,* the speculator *may sell* the contract short. He knows the public longs *will sell* out their positions, and doing so will probably send prices lower.

Needless to say, if the speculator takes a position in the closing days of a "tight" maturing contract — and improperly judges the

FUTURES TRADING AND OPEN CONTRACTS

On the CHICAGO BOARD OF TRADE, Monday, July 3, 1967.

Daily volume of trading (sales), including exchanges of futures for cash, and open contracts (one side only) as reported by clearing members, excluding long and short open contracts of significant size held by a reporting trader in the same future, as of the close of business. Figures subject to minor corrections.

Grain	Future	Volume of trading	Open contracts		
			At close	Change from previous close	Deliveries
(In thousands of bushels)					
WHEAT	July	7,320 (345)	25,165	− 2,925	3,000
	Sept.	11,205 (50)	44,020	+ 350	
	Dec.	19,185	56,305	+ 2,230	
	Mar.	5,230	33,370	+ 920	
	May	1,655	12,170	+ 825	
	Total	44,595 (395)	171,030	+ 1,400	
CORN	July	7,690 (205)	45,980	− 4,365	1,985
	Sept.	6,850 (80)	53,060	+ 985	
	Dec.	12,340	65,720	− 30	
	Mar.	2,220	21,130	− 350	
	May	680	11,650	− 10	
	Total	29,780 (285)	197,540	− 3,770	

The Commodity Exchange Authority releases this data daily on all regulated commodities.

Stocks of Grain in Deliverable Position at Chicago, Illinois, represented by outstanding warehouse receipts (except ungraded grain), as reported by Licensed Warehouses, as of June 30, 1967.

(In thousands of bushels)

Grain	Grade	June 30, 1967	Week ago	Year ago
	Total deliverable grades - - -	5,931	5,943	3,882
	Non-deliverable and/or ungraded	1,351	1,436	731
	Total	7,282	7,379	4,613
	1 Yellow	—	—	47
CORN	2 "	304	320	7,496
	3 " *	5,519	5,654	1,097
	Total deliverable grades - - -	5,823	5,974	8,640
	Non-deliverable and/or ungraded	3,681	4,769	2,488
	Total	9,504	10,743	11,128

The Commodity Exchange Authority releases this data weekly on all regulated commodities.

215

WHEAT FUTURES

Commitments of Traders, specified markets, May 31, 1967

(In thousands of bushels)

Classification	May 31, 1967		Net change from April 30, 1967	
	Long	Short	Long	Short
Chicago Board of Trade				
LARGE TRADERS				
Speculative				
Long or short only	8,060	10,455	− 335	+ 1,940
Long and short (spreading)	42,550	45,555	+ 5,175	+ 3,265
Total	50,610	56,010	+ 4,840	+ 5,205
Hedging	21,475	48,445	+ 7,875	− 1,840
Total reported by large traders	72,085	104,455	+ 12,715	+ 3,365
SMALL TRADERS				
Speculative and hedging	89,560	57,190	− 6,595	+ 2,755
TOTAL OPEN CONTRACTS	161,645	161,645	+ 6,120	+ 6,120
Percent held by: Large traders	44.6	64.6	+ 6.4	− 0.4
Small traders	55.4	35.4	− 6.4	+ 0.4

The Commodity Exchange Authority releases this data at the end of each month, in selected markets.

situation — he may only succeed in joining the other position holders who are caught in the squeeze. He may also find himself in the position of making or taking delivery, which almost always is a serious mistake. The reason should be clear:

Commercial interests control the lion's share of the cash commodity throughout most of the year, and they control practically all of the storage capacity at all times. They can, therefore, exercise almost complete discretion about their delivery decisions; and they do. The public speculator can rest assured that he will only *get delivery,* or be required to *make delivery,* when doing so is to his *economic disadvantage;* and when it is to the *advantage* of the commercial interest to obtain or dispose of cash goods.

There may be an occasional exception to the contrary, but it will be most rare, when becoming involved in physical delivery is less than a *great mistake* for the public speculator.

Government Crop Reports

Of major importance and occasionally devastating effect are the Government Crop Reports which are released at intervals throughout the agricultural crop year. This data is compiled by the Crop Reporting Board, a part of the United States Department of Agriculture. The figures are gathered from thousands of highly qualified observers under a cloak of the greatest secrecy. Once the individual reports are in hand, the Crop Reporting Board meets to analyze the composite situation and forecast total harvest probabilities.

These government figures always reach the trade at a time at which no trading in futures is underway. If the crop projections contain important surprises in the form of unexpected increases or decreases in a crop, the following day's futures market openings will clearly reflect the shock.

Carrying a position, either long or short, into the teeth of a Government Crop Report can be a soul-shattering experience. The market is regularly given credit for "discounting" future events and adjusting prices to anticipate forthcoming news. Based on past history, futures markets have less than a flawless record in "reading the minds" of the government crop reporters.

In the opening days of September, 1966, November soybeans were trading roughly in a range from $3.00 to $3.15 per bushel. The trade generally expected a 1966 harvest of 880 million to 900 million bushels of soybeans. The Government Crop Report was scheduled for release at 3:00 p.m. on Friday, September 9. The public was short a lot of soybeans when the trading session opened Friday morning. Prices on the new crop November contract began to climb perceptibly, and the farther they rose, the greater the pressure on the shorts to buy back their November soybeans. As more and more shorts were "chased in", the greater the upward pressure on November (and other) soybean futures prices. The last thirty minutes of Friday's session constituted a classical "short squeeze". In about forty minutes, the November bean price went from $3.19 per bushel to $3.28⅛ — and closed near its high for the day.

At 3:00 p.m. Eastern time, the Government Crop Report was released, indicating a projected soybean harvest of 926 million bushels — some 36 million bushels more than the trade had anticipated. The effect was cataclysmic.

After what must have seemed like an interminable week-end to holders of open positions, November soybeans opened Monday morning, September 12, down the full 10¢ limit allowable, and with virtually no trade in the contract. "Longs" who wanted to sell the November contract and extricate themselves from the losing position could find no one willing to buy within the permissable trading range. The following day, Tuesday, September 13, began as a repitition of Monday. November beans again opened down the full 10¢ permissable, then a trickle of trade began which gradually increased. At the close of the second session — following the Crop Report — the price on the November bean contract stood at $3.08¾ per bushel.

In two days' time, as a direct result of a 36 million bushel "surprise" in soybean crop expectations, price on the commodity plummeted about 20¢ per bushel. It is salient to note that in the succeeding three weeks, prices on the November contract worked their way on down to an interim low of $2.88½.

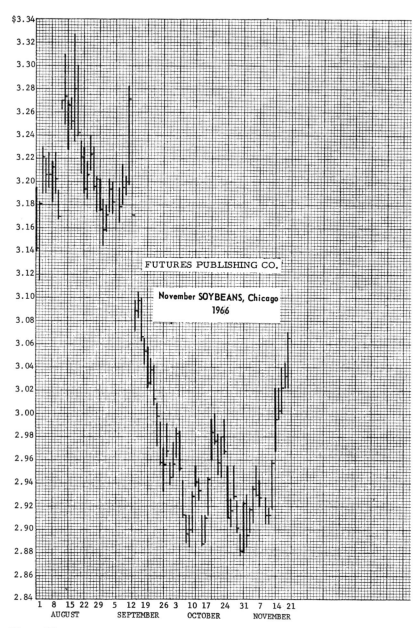

FUTURES PUBLISHING CO.

November SOYBEANS, Chicago
1966

Plate 60

Special Trading Situations

Beware The "Whip-Saw"

This chain of events is recounted in some detail for two purposes: First, to demonstrate the great hazards present in carrying a commodity position into a Government Report; and second, because it represents a classic example of the market "whip-saw".

Holders of short positions in nearby soybean contracts were "right" as later events unarguably proved; the soybean harvest *was* to be larger and lower prices *were* to be the result. In the interim, however, ascending prices caught the shorts who, in their desperate efforts to buy back their positions and offset, merely added more fuel to the flames of rising prices. Thousands of shorts *did* offset at the higher prices and they took impressive losses.

Then, some of them completely reversed their position: they bought back their short contracts and then bought more, switching to a long position; after which the crop report came out — and prices fell precipitously.

When events had run their course, there were some traders who had lost 7¢ or 8¢ per bushel in the upside "short raid" and lost another 20¢ in two succeeding days of limit-down price movement. Such may be the effect of unexpected "news" from a highly respected source.

Hind-sight always enjoys twenty-twenty-vision, and at 3:10 p.m. on September 9, every short who had weathered the "squeeze" and held his position knew that his judgment had been vindicated and that impressive profits were to be expected when the market opened next. Every short who offset knew now that he should have "stuck with his guns". Every long could look at the crop-estimate figure and know that he made one of the worst misjudgments of his trading career. But by the time the information upon which action could be predicated was available, the time had already passed when any corrective move could be taken. Once the figure was out, there was nothing to be done except sit back and watch profits or losses mount, depending on whether one was situated on the long or short side of the soybean market.

220

"Suckers" and "Plungers"

There may be some millionaire plungers who are sufficiently enamoured of high risks and super-charged economic adventure to welcome an exercise of this sort. However, it has no place in the speculative program of a prudent individual. Profitable speculation demands conservative behavior. Conservatism dictates that any open position — long or short — be closed out in advance of a potentially explosive event which cannot be — to some acceptable degree — appraised. A speculator will occasionally be caught flat-footed by a declaration of war, a general strike, sudden devaluation of money, or other developments which spring from political or natural events. Their results may be written in great profits or great losses. But at least the speculator has the satisfaction of being able to say that "no one could have foreseen this thing." There is *no such justification* for the losses which grow, for instance, out of a Crop Report surprise.

These figures are released at stated intervals. The secrecy which surrounds them makes fore-knowledge impossible and, yet, their impact may be ruinous to the interests of the individual who is on the wrong side of the market. In brief, carrying a substantial open position into a Crop Report is not really speculation, unless the situation is susceptible to close pre-evaluation, in the light of other known factors. Doing so is a sucker's exercise.

The wise speculator — unless he holds the firmest opinion — will offset his positions, be out of the market, and able to watch events from the safety of the sidelines. Once the new information is public knowledge, ample opportunities will exist to re-establish a position in light of altered knowledge which is reflected in the new numbers.

Week-End Trading

Students of commodity price behavior know that week-ends offer interesting opportunities for speculative endeavor, particularly during periods of relative commodity shortage or over-supply. Carrying a position over a week-end demands a healthy nervous system, but it can prove highly rewarding for those who are up to it.

Most public speculators and professional pit traders prefer sleeping Friday, Saturday and Sunday nights, to contemplating possible

221

price developments on a large open position. Proof of this is seen in the fact that commodity prices (and stock prices, also) demonstrate a quite consistent sell-off on Friday of each week, often followed by a discernible resurgence early the following week. Several reasons underpin the phenomenon. Major announcements from Washington are often released on the week-end in order to give the financial community an opportunity to "digest" the news before business is resumed in the next week. The week-end hiatus in trading is also a sufficient period of time to permit major changes in the weather pattern to take place.

Friday Sell-Off

While important events may not be actually concentrated in the Saturday-Sunday period, their public impact is often magnified because people spend more time listening to radios, reading newspapers and watching television on week-ends than during any other two-day period. In light of all of these reasons, coupled with the fact that the public tends to be long far more often than it is short, a sell-off oftentimes occurs on Friday as public speculators and pit traders close out their positions before going home Friday night "even with the market". To the extent that this evening-up action introduces abnormal selling pressure into the marketplace, Friday prices may be forced lower than composite information logically would justify in a relatively under-supplied market situation.

By taking a *long* position on the Friday close and carrying it until the following Monday or Tuesday, a very respectable profit can often be realized in *selected situations*. Close examination of a vertical bar-chart, which reflects daily prices, can provide a useful clue to this type of price behavior.

Week-End Arrivals

Another week-end situation which deserves speculator attention often materializes early in the harvest season. Each harvest usually begins in the face of depleted stocks in the market complex. Old-crop futures prices may be at relatively high price levels, in reflection of the current supply shortage. As harvest activities increase, crop movement into the market increases also and the largest "arrivals" tend to take place on week-ends and be reported on Monday. Nothing disenchants the faint-hearted longs more noticeably than impressive build-ups in local stocks.

Trading on this situation might attract a speculator who can carry a position over a week-end and still sleep. He may give consideration to selling a selected commodity short on Thursday or early in Friday's session (to take advantage of the higher market prices which often prevail prior to the week-end sell-off) and buy back the short position at or near the opening on Monday, when lower prices are often a reflection of the heavy week-end arrivals. Again, a vertical bar-chart showing daily price movements is an invaluable tool in appraising such a speculative possibility.

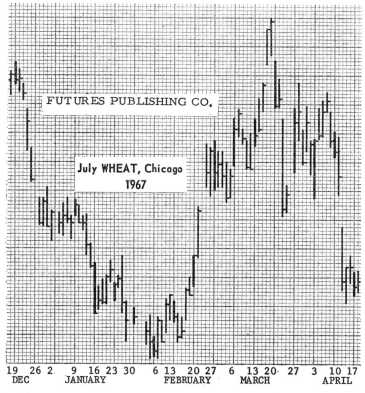

FUTURES PUBLISHING CO.

July WHEAT, Chicago
1967

19 26 2.   9   16 23 30   6 13   20 27   6   13 20· 27   3   10 17
DEC   JANUARY   FEBRUARY   MARCH   APRIL

Plate 61

Special Trading Situations

Better to Lose Money Than Lose Sleep

One final — and general — word needs to be said with respect to all special trading situations. As the label implies, "special situations" are somewhat unique, may be unpredictable, and — as such — involve unusual opportunities for profits and perhaps commensurate opportunities for losses. Speculation necessarily involves risk, but the prudent speculator constantly evaluates the order of risk he is willing to accept in return for a given profit potential. More than money is involved in the kind of trading discussed in this section. There are those who have sufficient equanimity to carry a large open commodity commitment and never give it a thought, except at such times as the matter comes under routine scrutiny. Another type of person may find that even a small commodity position preempts his attention and eclipses matters of vastly greater importance.

Strangely enough, the number of dollars involved does not seem to be controlling. Human psychology varies widely. The differing capacities of people to withstand — or ignore — the stresses of speculation, while getting on with their business — and obtaining a good night's sleep — is all too evident. A single 5,000 bushel contract of corn futures may suffice to keep one individual awake half of the night, while 50,000 bushels will not spoil the dreams of someone else in essentially the same economic circumstances.

The only safe rule in speculation is to "lighten up" to the point where sleep comes easily. Time, experience, and increasing success will raise the speculator's *level of tolerance* for carrying open positions, just as surely as repitition of any experience robs it of novelty and reduces its distractive nuisance value.

All this is but another persuasive argument in favor of protecting every new position with a stop-loss order — and perhaps a stop-buy or stop-sell to put the "second story" on the pyramid. Once this has been done, most traders find it easier to play the patient game and await developments. So long as a position is unprotected, every change in price suggests re-examination of the problem. Endless re-hashing of the same problem is neither conducive to good trading decisions — nor good mental health.

CHAPTER XV

SPECULATION IN PRICE RELATIONSHIPS

Most commodity speculation on the part of public traders involves taking either a long or short position, in the expectation that prices on the selected contract will subsequently rise or fall, and in so doing will produce a profit. There is another form of commodity speculation which deserves most careful consideration by the public speculator, but which to this point in time has largely been an activity left to the professional in the market: it is known as "spreading" in the grain market, "straddling" in certain other markets, and is synonymous with *arbitrage*, which is the term used to identify the activity in securities trading.

Time Differential

In a "normal" commodity market, we can expect to see the nearby futures selling at a price fairly close to that which prevails in the cash market for spot merchandise. Later maturities in a normal market will be priced progressively higher than the nearby contract, in reflection of the carrying charges entailed in holding the commodity until the scheduled delivery date. In corn, for example, we might find the nearby December futures quoted at $1.40 per bushel with the March contract at $1.42½; May $1.45; July $1.47½. In such a case, we would have a clear reflection of 2½¢ carrying charges included in the price of each more distant contract month.

Geographic Differential

Likewise, in a normal market we might expect to find December corn in Chicago quoted at $1.40 and Kansas City corn at $1.35 for December delivery, in which event the 5¢ per bushel differential or "spread" would be reflective of the cost of transporting the commodity from the "interior" Kansas City location to the terminal market. A theoretically "normal" market would be one which constantly reflected the economic costs of holding and/or transporting a commodity over time and/or geographical distance. Since these costs are easily calculated, it is no particular problem for the speculator to arrive at a firm notion of what constitutes a reasonable price differential or spread relationship on commodities deliverable at different points in time, or physically located at various geographical points.

Market reality is seldom so uniform, however. As a practical matter, *full carrying charges are rarely reflected in commodity prices,* although actual transportation costs are usually all included in the pricing structure. The reason is that competition exists between commodity warehouses, with the result that the price of storage, insurance and interest on money — which comprise carrying charges — move up and down in response to the proportion of storage space occupied, money availability, etc. One warehousing firm may elect to take in grain at less than its full carrying cost, and in so doing the carrying charges are partially "absorbed". Transportation costs, on the other hand, are firmly established by interstate commerce regulations and freight schedules issued pursuant thereto. Hence competition in the transport of commodities usually only exists between different modes of transportation; rail versus barge, or truck versus rail.

Supply/Demand Imbalance

There is a further consideration which exerts great influence on price differentials over time, as well as between geographical locations. Immediately following harvest, for example, wheat prices in

Topeka, Kansas, can be expected to reflect a substantial excess of supplies over requirements in that city. Until the harvest glut is clearly out, depressed prices on the crop in such surplus areas are a natural result. Chicago, on the other hand, is a *wheat deficit* location for virtually twelve months out of the year, removed as it is from the great wheat producing areas of the country. As harvest supplies begin moving, the relative shortage of wheat in Chicago is relieved. On rare occasions, an over-supply of the commodity will develop in Chicago which will have the effect of making the product no more valuable in the market city than it is in the interior location.

Stated another way, the market *must* pay the owner of cash grain in Kansas for his ransportation costs, else he will not move it. The market *may* also pay a large or a slight premium on the product for moving it out of the wheat surplus location and into the wheat deficit location, depending on *relative needs.* Consequently we usually expect to see Kansas City grain prices *under* Chicago grain prices by at least the amount of transportation and handling costs involved in shipping. We may also expect to see a slight or a substantial premium on the commodity — above and beyond transportation costs, depending on supply/demand balance in the two localities being compared.

With respect to price differentials between *different contract months* in the *same commodity* and in the *same location,* supply/demand considerations are the only influences which need be considered. It has been said that the market always "puts first things first". Presently existing shortage or over-supply reflects itself in higher or lower prices; and while an over-supply of wheat, for example, may bring lower prices to *all contract maturities* in the current crop year, the *nearby contract will usually be affected more* than the more deferred maturities. In the case of scarcity, prices on the nearby contracts will always rise more sharply than prices on deferred deliveries. Over-supply will depress nearby contracts more than prices on more distant maturities.

Price Rations Use

It is this action in the marketplace which accomplishes the rationing function so vital to matching supplies with needs. When a shortage of wheat exists, higher prices result, with the effect of reducing wheat consumption in total amount. Ordinarily, a cerain amount of wheat is fed to livestock and poultry, but if the price on wheat climbs far enough, chicken and livestock producers may find it to their economic best interests to switch to some alternative food supply for their flocks and herds. In the face of high prices, only the higher priority usages are filled. "Low end" usage tends to be satisfied by substitute products or, in the case of meat and poultry, livestock populations may be deliberately reduced in numbers until feed costs return to acceptable levels.

With the higher prices prevailing in a market, sparsely supplied by a given commodity, additional producers are attracted to the field of endeavor. Their entry brings greater production, which tends to solve the temporary shortage and forces relative values, as measured by prices, downward.

In an over-supplied market, again using the wheat simile, cheap wheat may be fed to livestock and otherwise used in low-end feeding activity. The increased consumption reduces the excessive supplies. Low prices discourage a certain proportion of the producers, resulting in a smaller harvest. As the surplus disappears through greater consumption and somewhat restricted production, prices rise once more. Thus it is seen that *the cure for high prices is high prices; the cure for low prices is low prices.* All of this depends, of course, on sufficient market freedom for supply and demand to assert itself in trade between buyers and sellers — allowing higher prices to ration and conserve inadequate supplies, or permitting lower prices to encourage consumption and discourage excessive production.

When shortage brings higher prices, the highest prices of all will be seen with respect to current or nearby considerations. When this happens, the "premium" which usually prevails on distant contracts may "move up" to the nearby contracts. The distant maturities may show an appreciable "discount".

For example, in a situation of extreme shortage, the nearby May wheat contract may be priced at $1.75 per bushel with the July contract at $1.70. The 5¢ *inversion* is a clear indication that concern over present shortage is taking priority over whatever problems may surround the July period. In other words, the 5¢ premium for immediate supplies is a measurement of the market's appraisal of the "tight" May situation as compared with the still largely unknown July situation. Both futures prices may, in the face of shortage, rise dramatically — along with equal, or perhaps even greater, price increases in the cash market. When this happens, usage of the product will be curtailed, out of the purest economic considerations. In thus rationing available supplies, the supply crisis may have been solved by the time July rolls around. If it is not, further price increase in the July contract is a logical expectation in a free market.

Trading in Price Difference — "Basis"

Speculation in spreads involves evaluation of relative prices as between different points in time, or different geographical locations. A fundamental measurement — and all prices are merely measurements of relative values — is the price differential between cash products for immediate delivery and the nearby futures contract. This differential or price spread is identified as "the basis". Basis, in turn, is the most reliable continuing indicator of near-term supply/demand balance. If dealers in cash commodities need more supplies, they will, of course, raise their bids sufficiently to attract a greater volume of offerings. So long as their stocks are sufficient, they will stand on lower bids, and perhaps refuse to buy at all, except at what appears to be a bargain price "discount".

Bids in the cash market (in Chicago or in the "country") are quoted using the nearby futures contract as a reference point. For example, if the nearby futures (May) price on corn is $1.40 per bushel, the cash market price will be communicated at a designated premium "on" May, or discount "off" May. A cash grain merchant might be bidding for corn at "2¢ under" with the nearby contract selling at $1.40. He is therefore bidding for corn of contract quality, for immediate delivery, at $1.38 in Chicago. The bid would be proportionately less in country locations where transportation would have to be figured into the Chicago price.

As trading in the futures proceeds, the price on the May corn contract might go to $1.42; if so, the cash bid, being pegged at 2¢ under, would now automatically stand at $1.40 per bushel. Thus, cash bids and futures prices move up and down together. Should the higher price attract large offerings on the part of farmers and country elevators, a cash grain merchant might decide to lower his "basis" to "3¢ under" the nearby futures.

The same things which have been said concerning cash and the nearby futures also pertain to a lesser extent to price relationships between nearby and more deferred futures contracts.

Spreading A "Normal" Market

The speculator who wishes to trade on price relationships in a "normal" market should begin with a normal carrying-charge as his point of departure. If he believes that the price spread between the nearby and the more deferred contract will narrow in days to come, he will *buy the nearby contract* and *sell the deferred contract*. (This is called a "bull spread".) If he believes the spread will widen in the future, he will *sell the nearby contract* and *buy the deferred contract*. (This is called a "bear spread".)

Spreading An "Inverted" Market

In an inverted market, with the nearby carrying a premium over the deferred, the procedure is exactly reversed: If the trader thinks the *inverse will increase,* he will *buy the nearby* and *sell the deferred*. If he expects the *inverse to narrow or disappear,* he will *sell the nearby* and *buy the deferred*.

Once such a spreading position is taken, correlative price changes can be ignored. By being long one contract and short another, a price increase of 2¢ per bushel in both leaves and speculator in the same position he was at the outset. The 2¢ price increase results in a 2¢ loss in the short position, which is exactly made up by a 2¢ profit on the long side of the spread. However, if a "bear spread" position was established anticipating a widening of the basis (short the nearby and long the deferred), a drop in price of ½¢ on the nearby contract and an increase of ½¢ on the deferred maturity produces a 1¢ profit for the spreader. By the same token, a 1¢ fall in the nearby — while the price on the deferred remains unchanged — also produces a 1¢ profit. The spreader will lose on his position when price differential *widens or narrows in the direction not anticipated.*

230

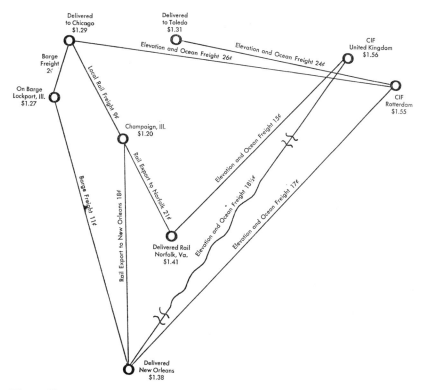

THEORETICAL PRICE SURFACE FOR CORN

Plate 62

Transportation is a major and inescapable element in the price of all agricultural — and most other — commodities. Relative prices attract supplies from surplus to deficit areas, and a good deal of the price differentials is a reflection of transportation costs. Locational shortage or oversupply also affects price differences between geographic points.

231

Speculation in Price Relationships

No Limit to Inverses

It is worthwhile repeating that the theory of carrying charges in the commodity market limits the premium that a *deferred* contract may carry to the amount of carrying charges involved in holding the merchandise over the period of time involved. There is no such theoretical limit, however, to the extent of an inverse, depending on the seriousness of the shortage which produces it. Cash or nearby contracts may reflect *any amount* of price premium over more deferred maturities.

Inter-Market Spreads

Most spreading takes place between contracts in the same commodity and on the same exchange. For example, Chicago May corn spread against Chicago July corn, or Kansas City September wheat against Kansas City May wheat. These positions are referred to as *intra-market* spreads. *Inter-market* spreads may also be placed. Such a position involves the purchase of Chicago May wheat against the sale of Kansas City or Minneapolis May wheat. In this situation, *relative scarcity* or *over-supply* in the two selected locations would be the major consideration in evaluating the price spread opportunity, along with transportation costs on the commodity. Inter-market spreading can present some exceedingly complex problems, but on occasion offer outstanding profit opportunities with minimal risk exposure.

Inter-Commodity Spreads

There is still a further spreading opportunity which involves a basic commodity and its manufactured or semi-manufactured products. Soybeans offer a good example for demonstration purposes. A soybean has little value in its natural state. Only through crushing and conversion to soybean meal and soybean oil does the legume become practically useful. The economic value of the soybean can be said to be the composite value of its products. Spreaders in the soybean market have developed a formula which permits them to deter-

232

mine the "normal value" relationship between soybeans, and soybean meal and oil. The equation involves the following arithmetic:

Oil price per pound $\times$ 11 = oil value per bushel

Meal price per ton $\times$ .0235 = meal value per bushel

Oil value + meal value = product value per bushel

Product value per bushel — soybean price per bushel =
Gross Processing Margin

Applying the foregoing formula, it will be seen that when soybeans are selling for $3.20, soybean meal is selling for $71.00 per ton and soybean oil at 12¢ per pound, the crusher stands to lose 21¢ per bushel for each bushel he processes; a most unrewarding endeavor! In a situation of this kind, the spreader would be likely to buy the *under-priced products* and sell the apparently *over-priced soybeans* (known as a "reverse-crush spread").

Oil price — 12¢ per pound
12¢ $\times$ 11 = $1.32 per bu. oil value

Meal price — $71.00 per ton
$71.00 $\times$ .0235 = $1.67 per bu. meal value
                          $2.99 per bu. product value

                          —$3.20 per bu. soybean cost
          Loss = $ .21 per bu., Gross
                          Processing Margin

However, in a different price situation, with soybeans selling at $2.40 per bushel, soybean meal at $71.00 per ton, and soybean oil at 9¢ per pound, the crusher stands to make a handsome profit—identified as Gross Processing Margin (GPM)— and so would undoubtedly be an eager buyer of soybeans. In this situation, the spreader would also be inclined to buy the relatively *under-priced soybean futures,* and sell the relatively *over-priced products* (called a "crush spread").

Speculation in Price Relationships

$$\text{Oil price} = 9\cancel{c} \text{ per pound}$$
$$9\cancel{c} \times 11 = \qquad \$ .99 \text{ per bu. oil value}$$

$$\text{Meal price} = \$71.00 \text{ per ton}$$
$$\$71.00 \times .0235 = \underline{\$1.67} \text{ per bu meal value}$$
$$\underline{\$2.66} \text{ per bu. product value}$$
$$\underline{-\$2.40} \text{ per bu. soybean cost}$$
$$\text{Profit} = \$ .26 \text{ per bu., Gross}$$
$$\text{Processing Margin}$$

In either situation the spreader's hope for profits would depend on a return to more normal relationships between the price on the basic commodity and the component values of soybean meal and oil. About 25¢ per bushel GPM is usually considered a useful profit point— but actual margin has varied widely.

Historic price behavior in these inter-related futures offers valuable guidance in detecting imbalances, nonetheless. Spreads between soybeans and the products have in the past provided one of the most attractive opportunities for multiple-position speculation in commodities.

Possibilities Are Numerous

The opportunities for spreading are limited by little except the ingenuity and imagination of the trader. For instance, there is a much discussed and broadly recognized "hog-corn ratio", which relates to the efficiency of pigs in converting corn into pork meat weight. Spreaders sometimes find situations in which high priced corn and cheap pork prices suggest selling the grain futures and buying the animal futures. Still other spreaders take multiple positions between wheat and corn, oats and wheat, pork and beef, gold and silver, soybean oil and cottonseed oil—the possibilities are almost unlimited.

The best spreading opportunities tend to be those in which a high degree of *substitutability* or *convertibility* exists between the commodities involved. A shortage of one and a surplus of the other will produce high prices on one hand and lower prices on the other. A spreader's profits in any case grow out of *changes in price relationship* over time in a single location, or at different geographical points.

It must be said that, inasmuch as price relationships tend to be more stable than flat prices, both *risk exposure* and *profit potentials* in spreads are likely to be *less* than those present in speculation on flat prices. This is *not always* the case, however, and the spreader will do well to choose his opportunities with great caution. This is especially true when considering spreads between *different commodities* and in *different markets*—where significantly *different forces* may operate on price/value relationships on the two sides of the open position.

Spreading Margins Are Smaller

The generally smaller order of risk present in positions which represent spreads between multiple contracts in the same commodity, or different markets in the same (or related) commodities, gives rise to a different level of margin required to bind performance on the part of the trader. For example, with straight position margin on wheat at 15¢ per bushel, the spreading margin would likely be about 10¢ per bushel—and this would apply to only *one side* of the position. To demonstrate, consider a trader who spreads 100 wheat between "old" and "new" crops. He might *buy* 100,000 bushels of May futures and *sell* 100,000 bushels of September futures. At 10¢ per bushel spreading margin, he would need to put up $10,000 to establish the position and, in all likelihood, would need to maintain the 10¢ per bushel "in the clear" for so long as he holds it.

Rules vary, but it is usually true that in spreads between *different* commodities, (e.g., wheat and corn, or corn and oats) the margin required is the margin applicable to the *one side* of the spread which calls for the *larger margin*. Thus, a spread between wheat and oats would be marginable at the wheat rate. It should also be remembered that, in order to take advantage of the lower margin requirements, amounts on each side of the position must be *equivalent*. One contract of May wheat would be necessarily spread against one contract of some other month—or some other grain.

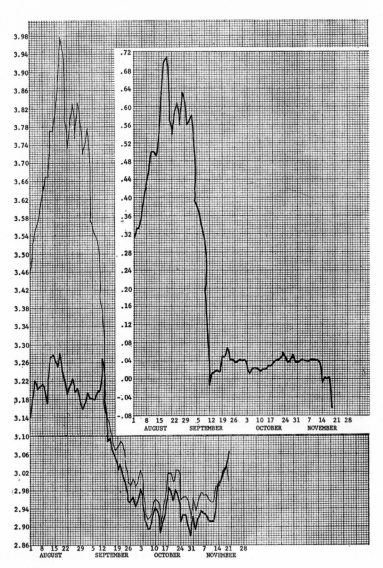

Plate 63

Both of these charts reflect the price differential between cash soybeans and the November '66 futures. From a 71¢ inversion in mid-August, prices returned to "normal" in September, and the November contract expired at a 6½¢ discount.

236

CHAPTER XVI

ORDER PLACEMENT AND EXECUTION

Transaction of customer orders in the pits is the exclusive function of a highly skilled group of professional floor brokers. The greatest testimonial to their efficiency is found in the exceedingly small number of errors which they commit, even while trading in the highly charged atmosphere of fast moving, volatile markets. There are a few things, however, that even the best pit broker *cannot* do. Heading the list is the occasionally forgotten truth that a broker cannot read a customer's mind.

Commodity orders, like orders in the securities market, follow *precise forms* and are accorded *specific handling* depending on certain *key terminology*. It therefore behooves a speculator to be completely familiar with the subtle and obvious differences which exist, for example, between a "stop" order, a "limit-only" order and a "market-if-touched" order. Failure to recognize the difference in handling each of these orders will receive can produce serious disappointment on the part of the trader—and waste an infinite amount of time in futile discussions between the brokerage house solicitor, the customer and the pit broker.

Errors in execution will occasionally occur. When they do, exchange rules ordinarily require that the broker *absorb* his mistakes when they operate to the disadvantage of the customer; however, when a mistake is to the *advantage of the customer,* market rules direct that the *customer* be given the "windfall" profit. As concerns the customer, it amounts to a sort of "heads I win, tails you lose" situation. In view of this fact, it is only reasonable that the pit broker be provided orders which are completely clear and in conformity with good order writing practice. If this is done, the public customer can almost invariably count on meticulous execution.

The first consideration in any order, of course, is the quantity involved. In the grain market, for example, orders are communicated in terms of *thousands of bushels*—"Buy 5 March wheat" means to buy 5,000 bushels of March wheat futures—one contract. Oil orders are stated in *contracts.* "Buy 5 March soybean oil" directs the broker to buy five 60,000-pound soybean oil contracts. This single example should be sufficient to emphasize the importance of specifying the quantity *in accordance with established practice in the market.* Failure to do so can result in a fill which you don't want, but which could by no means be interpreted as a trading error on the part of the broker who handled the transaction. To repeat, *don't expect a broker to read your mind!*

Don't Mix Lots

On Exchanges which deal in both "round lots" and "job lots", it is important that the customer *specify the combination* of each included in any given order. For example, if an order is placed for 8,000 bushels of soybeans on an Exchange that trades job-lots, it should be placed as "1 round lot and 3 job-lots". The round lot is 5,000 bushels. Each job-lot is 1,000 bushels, making 8,000 bushels total. Unless this is done, the fill may be made in the form of eight 1,000-bushel "jobs". The reason for this is that job-lot trading is usually handled by a separate broker who specializes in it. Often times, also, job-lot execution may only be feasible at some slight *premium* to the round-lot market price.

Commodity orders are subject to a broad range of limitations as to time of execution, price, etc. The following list is by no means all-inclusive, but it will comprise a recapitulation of the more common order forms and clarify the handling accorded to each.

Price Limits

1. *Market Order:* A market order is an *unrestricted* order as to price, which only requires that it be promptly executed upon receipt and at the *best price available* at the time it reaches the pit.

2. *Price-Limit Order:* A price-limit order is one which specifies the *maximum* buying price or the *minimum* selling price which the customer will accept. A limit-order may only be executed at the *limit price or better.* For example, a *limit-order to sell* at $1.40 can only be filled at $1.40 or *above* $1.40. A *limit-order to buy* at $1.40 may be executed at $1.40 or any price *lower* than $1.40.

Time Limits

1. *Day-Order:* A day-order is one which expires automatically at the end of the session in which it is placed. *Unless otherwise noted,* most houses treat all commodity orders as day-orders. In order to avoid automatic expiration at the end of the session in which it is activated, an order must usually be designated as "good-til-cancelled", "good for one week", "open", etc. It's good practice to *always specify* the life of an order at time of placement.

2. *Open-Order or Good-Til-Cancelled Order:* An open order or a good-til-cancelled order (usually referred to by the initials GTC) are orders which will remain in effect until the customer explicitly *directs* cancellation; or until the futures contract to which the order applies expires.

3. *Specific Time Expiration:* This order may be identified as an "off at a specific time" order, and is merely a day order with a designated time contingency. For example, "Buy 5 December corn $1.35 — limit, off at 12:15 p.m." This order tells the broker that he is to buy 5,000 bushels of December corn futures at $1.35 per bushel or better, at any time up to 12:15 p.m. However, if the order is not executed by 12:15 p.m., it is then to be cancelled.

Order Placement & Execution

4. *Time Of Day Order:* This is an order which is to be executed at a given minute in the session. For example, "Buy 10 May wheat 11:30 a.m. market". With this, the broker is instructed to buy 10,000 bushels of May wheat at 11:30 a.m. at the best price then available in the market.

In addition to specific limitations of the sort treated above, there is another category of special orders which will be accorded standardized handling as follows:

1. *Stop Order:* This is an order that is activated at a particular price level, usually *above* or *below* the current market. These orders are often referred to as "stop-loss" orders because they are most often used by customers who are interested in limiting a loss on an open long or short position. For example, a customer may have a long position involving 10,000 bushels of July corn which he purchased at $1.40. When the position is established, the customer may enter an order to "sell 10 July corn $1.35⅜ — stop — open". This order has the effect of calling for offset of the long position at any time the price on July corn futures falls to the *specified level or lower*. It is designated "open", hence it will be held in force as a "resting order" until price movement decrees its execution— or it is *specifically cancelled* by the customer.

   A word of warning in connection with such an order should not be amiss: Should the long position to which the stop-sell order applies be closed out at the verbal direction of the customer, the "resting" stop-order must also be specifically cancelled. Unless cancelled, it will continue to "rest" until executed. *Should the price move down to its limit level, it will be filled.* By not cancelling the "stop", the customer would suddenly find himself "short" 10,000 bushels of July corn, which he would have to accept.

2. *Stop-Limit Order:* This one gets almost the same execution as the stop-order explained above. A stop-limit order goes into force as soon as there is a sale at the "stop" price or "worse"—but the stop-limit order can only be filled at the *limit*

price—*or better.* To demonstrate, an order to "sell 10 July corn at $1.35⅜ stop-limit — open" will be a resting order until the specified contract sells *at or below* $1.35⅜. Once this price is reached, the stop-limit order is activated, but it cannot be executed at a price lower than $1.35⅜. It can, however, be filled at *any price above* the one designated. The danger in a stop-limit order is that in a rapidly rising or falling market, execution may prove to be an impossibility; hence the limit requirement may defeat its central purpose of extricating a customer from a losing position at the quickest and most advantageous point.

3. *"Quick" or "Fill or Kill":* This is an order which must be executed at once, and at a specified price, or it is to be cancelled. Obviously a market order is subject to prompt execution as soon as it reaches the floor broker, since it is not subject to either time or price limitation. A "fill or kill" specifies a limit price and usually takes this form: "Sell 10 July wheat $1.69½ Fill or Kill". At the time the order is placed it must be presumed that the wheat contract is quoted in a range of perhaps ½¢ above or below the "fill or kill" limit price. In practice, when the order is received by the pit broker he will usually call the "quick" bid three times. Unless he finds a taker on his three calls, he marks the order cancelled and (most brokers) immediately notifies the customer "unable" or "can't quick", and follows this advice with the current price quotation in the maturity involved. Some houses refuse to accept quick-orders for execution in the first few minutes of trade or the last few minutes during each session. This is a decision which each house must make, and usually reflects their appraisal of the possibilities for execution, depending on the volume of the trade and price behavior in the selected contract.

4. *M.I.T. or Board Orders:* M.I.T. means "market-if-touched" and "Board" means the same thing. Therefore, if the specified price on such an order is "touched", it becomes a market order—and is filled at the best price then available. The execution price may be either *higher or lower* than the "touched" price. The M.I.T. designation is somewhat of a misnomer in

view of the fact that the specific "tick" may not be actually touched—and need not be—in order to activate the order. For example, such an order might read "M.I.T. $1.40¼ sell 10 July corn". The price on the July corn contract may move from $1.40⅛ to $1.40⅜, missing the ¼¢ tick entirely; but for purposes of an M.I.T. order the activating price level would be considered accomplished. Execution of the M.I.T. order would be touched off and the "fill" would be at the best price available in the contract.

5. *Cancellation Orders:* Next to the placement of an original order, *proper cancellation* of orders which are "resting" must be given only slightly lesser priority. In establishing a trade relationship with the broker, it is well to make certain that unless a longer time is specifically designated, *all* of your orders are to be considered *day-orders*. As such, they will automatically expire unless executed during the session in which they are placed. This handling is regularly accorded commodity orders in the vast majority of commission houses, but underscoring the procedure can do no harm, and it may serve to avoid subsequent misunderstanding.

Cancellation orders may take several forms, among which are the following:

a. *Straight Cancel Order:* A straight cancel order simply conveys the customer's directive that a previous order is to be stricken, and will ordinarily take this form: "Cancel (day) order to buy 5 July wheat at $1.69¾ stop". It is good practice to also give the solicitor your account number whenever placing orders or entering cancellations. Doing so is just one additional safeguard against error. As shown in the above example, the cancellation should recite *all* the pertinent elements in the previous order which is being cancelled. Do not rely on a mere request to your broker to "cancel the order I placed with you this morning". You may remember the details of the order clearly, but a solicitor is dealing with hundreds of such transactions every day. It is expecting too much that his memory will be up to the task of keeping the particulars of all of his customers' business freshly in mind.

b. *Cancel Former Order (C.F.O.) With Specific Instructions:* A "C.F.O." order is one which *cancels* an earlier order and *replaces* it with a new order or new instructions, usually involving a change in price specification. For example: "*C.F.O.* Buy 5 July wheat $1.69¾ stop. *ENTER* Buy 5 July wheat $1.70⅜ — stop". The above advice directs that the earlier order to buy one contract of July wheat at $1.69¾ — stop, is to be cancelled and replaced by a new order to purchase 5,000 bushels of July wheat at $1.70⅜ —stop. The only thing which has been changed is the price level at which the customer will accept execution.

6. *Spread Orders:* Execution of spreads always involves two separate considerations which may be two contracts in the same commodity, two different markets in the same commodity and futures month, two separate markets involving the same commodity and different contract months, a single market and two separate commodities, two separate commodities and two different contract months, etc., etc., etc. The possibilities are almost endless. The prime consideration in spreading is always one of *price differential* between the two "legs" of the spread; *flat price* levels are only of *secondary importance.*

As noted elsewhere, when the spreader believes the price differential will narrow (in a normal market) he will buy the nearby and sell the more distant future. When he believes the price difference will increase (in a normal market) he will sell the nearby contract and buy the more distant future. In an inverted market (with nearby fuutres selling at a premium to more deferred futures) the opposite procedure applies: If the trader believes the price inversion will increase, with the nearby futures going to an even greater premium over the more deferred contract, he will buy the nearby and sell the deferred. If he believes the inversion will disappear and prices return to a more nearly "normal" relationship, he will sell the nearby contract and buy the later maturity.

Order Placement & Execution

Framing a spread order calls for careful concentration on the part of the trader, just as it requires meticulous execution by the floor broker. A typical intra-market spread order might be as follows: "Buy Chicago 100 July wheat—sell Chicago 100 December wheat — 5½¢ — limit — G.T.C." This order instructs the broker to buy the deferred contract and sell the nearby contract in equal amounts, at any time he can do so, and without regard to the specific price on either. The order is a clear indication that the trader believes that a 5½¢ price spread between the two contracts is excessive—he thinks the spread will narrow. The trader is, of course, willing to accept the spread position at anything better than the 5½¢ differential, which the order "limit" identifies as his minimum allowable execution. "G.T.C." informs the solicitor and the floor broker that the order is *good until cancelled,* whether this be a few hours or a few weeks. *Unless* the order is cancelled, it will remain a resting order until expiration of the March contract.

7. *Inter-Market Spreads:* The placement of an order to buy in one market and sell in another is a more complex activity by far than establishing a spread position in a single market; the reasons should be obvious. In most situations, a customer will order his broker to "Buy Chicago March wheat and sell Kansas City March wheat" at a specific spread difference. Depending on how closely the customer restricts his broker, the spread order may prove to be unfulfilled—or unfulfillable—by reason of its *close limitations.* Inter-market spreading is occasionally handled on the basis of market-orders for execution at the same time of day. For instance: "Buy 20 Chicago March wheat and sell 20 Kansas City March wheat—11:05 a.m. — market". By reason of constant interchange of price information over their respective ticker systems, prices in the two markets tend to maintain quite consistent relationships, influenced, of course, by the relative supply/demand considerations in the two locations. By *timing execution* of the two orders in the two separate markets, the customer can be sure of having close time concurrency in his trades. If he is right in his "price idea" about the spread, getting the

fill will likely be of more importance than trying to get the last $\frac{1}{8}$¢ or $\frac{1}{4}$¢—and which could prevent execution of the order, in rapidly moving markets particularly.

8. *Inter-Commodity Spreads:* There is a form of commodity spreading which involves separate products and which, by strict definition, are not spreads at all; for example, wheat and corn. It is true that a certain degree of substitutability exists between these two commodities. Poultry, as a case in point may be fed wheat, or their diet can be comprised largely of cracked corn. The same is true in feeding pigs and beef. The fact has given rise to an equation which in the trade in known as the "wheat/corn ratio". Simply stated, this premise suggests that whenever the price differential between wheat and corn narrows beyond a certain point, reflecting a price/value abberation in their *respective nutritional values* as live stock feed, wheat should be bought and corn sold in anticipation of a return to a normal price spread. In the opposite situation, where the price of wheat outstrips the price of corn in light of their *respective feeding values,* wheat should be sold and corn bought, in anticipation of their return to a more classical price/value relationship. Although buying or selling corn against sales or purchases of wheat have on occasion proved to be extremely profitable, doing so involves two separate positions—rather than a spread, as defined in the rules and regulations of some grain markets. Orders involving this kind of transaction may take any number of forms, including:

   a. "Buy 50 July corn and sell 50 July wheat at 25¢ — limit — G.T.W." This order form instructs the floor broker to buy corn and sell wheat at a specified price differential per bushel—or better. The specific price of the corn or wheat at the time the trade is executed is only of secondary importance: flat prices on the two commodities are not even mentioned. G.T.W. means "good this week"—until Friday.

   b. "Buy 10 July corn 1.40\frac{1}{2}$ — limit, and sell 10 July wheat 1.65\frac{1}{2}$ — limit." This order accomplishes the same thing set forth in the earlier example, provided it is possible to fill it at the precise prices specified. Stated in this fashion, however, (as a two-part order) *one side* of the trade can only be executed if the *other side* of the trade can also be filled at the designated price.

A broker obviously cannot be expected to execute the corn trade in the hope that the July wheat price will come into range and permit him to get the second fill. Should he execute the corn trade, and July wheat fail to show the required limit-price on his spread order, he would be left with the long position involving 10,000 bushels of July corn in his own account. As a practical matter, specifying prices on two sides of a spread usually only adds to execution difficulty and often results in less advantageous fills for the customer than would be obtainable on a purely price-differential basis.

9. *One-Cancels-Other (O.C.O.):* This is a two-part order which covers both ends of a pair of alternatives. An O.C.O. order might be used by a trader who has an open 20,000 bushel short position in corn, for instance, with the price hovering around $1.35. If the price goes down, he wants to add to the position; if the price goes up, he wants protection against loss. An O.C.O. to accomplish both objectives might read: "Sell— 10 May corn $1.33½—Stop—or—Buy 20 May corn $1.38¼—Stop . . . O.C.O."

If the price hits $1.33½ or less, the *sell* side will be filled and the *buy* side will be cancelled. If the price rises to $1.38¼, the stop-loss will be activated; the 20,000 bushels short position will be bought in, and the *sell* side of the order will be cancelled.

The orders listed above are only a small representation of all the possibilities which exist. Each form, of course, has a great many variations which can be employed to meet specific requirements. The possibilities are only limited by the imagination of the customer and the *practicalities of understanding and execution* on the part of the broker. In the best interests of both, orders should be kept as simple and unfettered as possible. The greater latitude you can give the pit broker, while still protecting your own interests, the *better* executions you will likely receive.

After all, if a pit broker *can't fill* an order—or *can't understand* it— placing it is a waste of everyone's time.

Plate 64

World commerce in comodities involves a broad spectrum of risks, not the least of which is the matter of price fluctuation while a cargo is in transit. It is for this reason that international traders in food, fibers and minerals are among the largest users of futures markets. They hedge their cash cargoes before the merchandise is even loaded, and the hedge is "lifted" only after the shipment is at its destination.

CHAPTER XVII

WHAT A BROKER CAN AND CAN'T
DO FOR YOU

Public speculators *must* trade through brokers, and selection of a broker involves considerations which call for a careful and critical analysis of your personal needs, in light of the facilities a given commission house offers. Relationships between customers and brokers follow no consistent pattern. Some traders view their brokers as little more than functionaries, through whom they must pass orders; neither seeking nor wanting anything from them except meticulous *order-writing* and efficient *execution* on the trading floor. Other public traders take every opportunity to "pick the brains" of the brokerage house representatives. They may not follow their broker's suggestions, but they want to hear his comments concerning the market in general, and about particular contracts which may be under scrutiny as presently existing or potential positions.

Discretionary Accounts

In still other situations, public traders occasionally abdicate the entire decision-making function to the brokerage house and *rely totally on the broker's judgment* in buying and selling. An arrangement of this kind, under the rules of most commodity exchanges, requires that the customer sign a "Discretionary Trading Agreement" which, in

Broker Services

effect, gives the broker power-of-attorney to buy and sell on behalf of a customer—*with or without* the customer's knowledge or approval. Rules and regulations of the Chicago Board of Trade additionally require that any discretionary trading account involving commodity contracts on the Board of Trade be personally supervised by a brokerage house *partner*. It is also mandatory under the rules of most commodity exchanges that confirmation slips, P & S statements, and all other trading documents be supplied the discretionary customer in the same manner as if he were promulgating his own trades.

Broker Services Differ

The essential services provided by the brokerage houses are much the same, insofar as they all receive, transmit and execute customer orders. From this point on, however, similarities begin to diminish.

Each organized exchange establishes minimum margin rules in each commodity traded. Brokerage houses may *not* set customer margins *below* the minimums established by the exchanges—but they may, in their own discretion, require *larger* margins—and many of them do.

Some brokerage houses are highly selective in the kinds of orders they will accept for execution in particular circumstances. For example, some houses refuse to accept limit-orders "on the open" or "on the close". Or they may refuse to accept anything but market-orders in the last hour of trading in a maturing contract. Still other houses may refuse to accept spread-limit-orders between two different commodities (for example, to simultaneously buy wheat futures and sell corn futures at a designated price difference).

Within the rules and regulations of the exchanges upon which a brokerage is transacting business, the regulations imposed by the Commodity Exchange Authority, and within the limitations of statutes which apply to agency relationships and contracts generally, a brokerage house enjoys a broad area of self-determination. There are rules a licensed broker *must* follow and which set forth things he *must do* to avoid running afoul of the several levels of authority under which he operates. Likewise, there are things he *must not do*. However, except for the specific "thou shalt——" and "thou shalt not——" a commission house is free to determine its own policies and order its relationships with customers to suit itself. The customer, in turn, has the continuing prerogative of choosing the broker who suits him best. He may elect to maintain the relationship or interrupt it at any point he sees fit to do so.

Commission houses, like other human institutions, reflect varying strengths and weaknesses. It is up to you, the customer, to determine where your interests will be best served and select your broker accordingly. Primarily, of course, efficient transmittal and execution of orders are the most important considerations. Brokerage houses are occasionally faced with the same manner of staffing problems which plague other kinds of businesses. Excessive staff turnover may fill a "wire room" with inexperienced people. Inexperience breeds mistakes and while a mistake can usually be reconciled through discussion, doing so can be time-consuming and frustrating in the extreme. Inexperience or lack of care on the part of a solicitor can result in order-writing errors; lackadaisical performance on the part of a pit broker can have disastrous results in order-filling.

These seems to be no substitute for trial and error in selecting a broker who best meets your personal needs. The quality of their advertising is certainly no guide! Finding the right broker may involve two or three changes in your account; and if necessary, have no hesitancy in doing so. Commodity speculation is not a hobby; *it's a business.* Substantial amounts of money are at stake and the brokerage commission you will pay on every transaction should entitle you to professional treatment all the way from the customer man's desk through the wire room, to the pit and back again. If you settle for less than this, you are needlessly jeopardizing *your* funds and *your* speculative future.

Broker Advice

Inexperienced speculators oftentimes look hopefully to their broker for "inside information" that can produce "guaranteed results". Obviously they rarely find it. If such authorities on market behavior exist, they aren't likely to spend their time behind a brokerage desk. People who can "read the market" are trading for their own accounts—and making millions doing it! Brokerage house employees are *rarely* traders. Most commission houses, as a matter of fact, specifically *pro-*

hibit their employees from *trading on margin* in either stocks or commodities. The philosophy seems to be that a "position" in the market is likely to color the judgment of one who should—at all times and under all conditions—maintain an unbiased view in serving his public customers. The point is valid.

Despite the prohibition against employee trading, a great many brokerage houses produce and disseminate daily, weekly or monthly *advisory letters* which briefly recap pertinent developments in selected commodities and offer some interpretation of these events, as concerns their possible impact on price behavior. Depending on the capabilities of the staff people who research and prepare these materials, a broker's "letter" may be exceedingly valuable; or it may be worth less than nothing.

In addition to recounting the news and highlights which relate to fundamental market matters, some houses offer opinions concerning chart conditions which will bear on future price patterns. Here again, depending on your own particular appraisal of charting as a speculative tool—and the technical competence of the chartist commentator—this information may be worthy of consideration or downright misleading.

A "Grain of Salt" is Advisable

It all adds up to the fact that there is no *consistent authority on prices except the market*. While a highly skilled and well-experienced brokerage house representative may have an excellent "price idea" concerning a particular contract at a particular time, if he has the occult ability to consistently forecast prices, you might well ask yourself, "Why is he *giving* such valuable information away?" The market will certainly pay him more for such knowledge than any possible combination of customers. All he needs to do is back his judgment with some money and take the same positions for *himself* that he is advising *others* to assume.

Relying exclusively on a broker's advice—or giving him authority to exercise his own discretion in trading for your account—has one point to commend it: Since the decisions he will be making do not involve his own funds, it stands to reason that it might be easier for him to follow the trading axiom, "cut losses short and let profits run" than it would be for you. The broker is not likely to become "emotionally involved" with someone else's money. But, if this is the strength in the procedure, there are several weaknesses.

To begin with, a brokerage house exists to *transact business*. Each order placed involves a firmly established brokerage fee which usually covers the "round trip". This is to say that the brokerage fee on 5,000 bushels of soybeans (one contract) is $24 and covers execution of the *sale or purchase* which establishes the position, and the subsequent *purchase or sale* which will offset and close it out. The brokerage fee is the same whether a position is kept open five minutes or for the life of the contract. The brokerage fee is not affected by whether a given trade produces monumental profit or a jarring loss. It costs a pre-determined amount to obtain execution of each order—and the success of any brokerage operation depends directly and exclusively on the *number of trades* they handle during each business day.

Brokers Are on "Both Sides" of the Market

It's disquieting to many newcomers to commodity speculation to discover that his broker is both *buying* and *selling* the *same contract* for different customers at virtually the *same time,* day in and day out. Of course each purchase must, at some point, be offset by a sale. Furthermore, when hedging is involved on the part of commercial interests, a sale or a purchase may be dictated by *changes in cash inventory* rather than by independent appraisal of market condition or even probable price behavior. Thus, a commission house is usually on "both sides of the market" buying and selling simultaneously.

This should not be surprising, since the only business of a brokerage house is the execution of orders in the marketplace. It would be Machiavellian to suppose that a broker would be so unfeeling as to have no interest in whether or not his customer showed a profit, but such an interest, even when it exists, is actually humanitarian rather than economic. A *customer* does not have to succeed in his search for profit in order for a *brokerage house* to realize the profits it wants.

Broker Services

Giving a broker informal carte blanche to make your trade decision, or formal *discretion to trade in your behalf* puts you at the mercy of both his judgment and his avarice. Once a discretionary trading agreement has been signed, the broker who holds it can trade you in and out of successive positions with such rapidity that your margin funds may literally disappear in commissions. Such "churning" can break you, without regard for the vicissitudes of price fluctuation. In fairness, it must be said that deliberate "churning" is a rare occurrence; however, instances of it are sufficiently numerous as to put any prudent speculator on his guard against the possibility, however remote.

Listen Carefully — Decide For Yourself

There are exceptions to every rule; still the *best* rule in commodity speculation is to only follow the advice of a broker—or anyone else—to the extent that its validity is *proved to be reliable in practice.* Then, place your own orders for execution on the basis of the best composite information obtainable, tempered in light of your own judgment of events to come. The mere fact the someone occupies a position of responsibility and accepts orders for execution on commodity exchanges is no proof of either technical competence in evaluating market conditions or skill in the management of risk capital. Automobile salesmen only rarely understand the internal workings of the machines they sell. By the same token, the average commission house employee is not likely to be an expert on *price forecasting* in the markets in which he deals. He *need not be* to perform his function efficiently and well.

It's a Lonely Business

Newcomers to commodity speculation have a deep and continuing need for reassurance, regardless of whether prices are going up, down, or nowhere. If prices on a position are moving against its holder, the broker can expect regular quizzing which asks the question (in perhaps a dozen different ways), "How far do you think prices may go?" Of course the customer is attempting to evaluate his ability to hold on and absorb the "paper loss" pending a price reversal.

There is nothing more distasteful to an inexperienced trader than converting any "paper loss" to a *real loss,* by closing out the position. There are situations in which the signs are so unmistakable that anyone may be able to flatly advise selling out or offsetting through purchase. More often, however, the advisor may be only slightly less confused than the customer; in which case the "advice" may be altogether too equivocal to have any real value. The distraught trader will often seem to listen carefully to his broker's words, but he really only hears the things which support a decision which he has *already arrived at* independently.

In short, the trader in such an instance is looking for *companionship* rather than *advice;* and he can usually depend on finding the companionship he seeks. Warm and reassuring as such a conversation may be, it doesn't alter the fact that *if* the position is a bad one, its hazards may persist and its resulting losses may grow apace. *A bad trade is not to be cured by conversation.* The only way to cut a loss short is by offset.

The people who most often are caught in a dilemma of this kind are those who have taken an open position in a commodity contract without a *beginning plan.* They have not appraised the situation from the standpoint of profit potentials and loss maximums. Therefore, they honestly have no opinion as to where they should "give up", take a loss, and look for more rewarding opportunities in a different position. They hope their broker—or someone—will be able to provide some sort of miracle which will retrieve them from their own initial folly—and save the day. Needless to say, they are usually disappointed, since commodity salesmen are not soothsayers, and the market prices tend to pick their own directions without respect to what any of the "experts" might appear to believe at any given moment.

Broker Advice Can Be Valuable

The purpose of his discourse is not to downgrade the value of broker information. Some of it is extremely valuable. But even the best of the price forecasters and market analysts are guilty of great misappraisals which, if followed *blindly,* will result in certain disaster. The only safe course in commodity speculation is, as has been stated earlier, to assume a position with a firm notion about its profit potentials and loss limits. Having done this, when prices move against the position, it *must be closed*; when prices move in favor of the position, it *may be enlarged.* "Cut losses short and let profits run" is the *only* formula for speculative success.

If advice from any quarter proves to be consistently profitable to you, it will more likely be a result of rigid application of this trading axiom, than a reflection of vastly superior knowledge of market fundamentals or technical considerations. By rigid application of the analysis procedure and trading program set forth earlier, a trader can develop his own position-management techniques with some experience. By careful adherence to the trading rules, his results will be much better than if he relies on his own judgment *part* of the time and leans on the advice of others the *rest* of the time.

The telephone is an indispensable element in commodity trading. Once you have established yourself with a broker and taken a position, you are an "active account". If you are maintaining a "free balance" of margin funds in reserve with your broker, you can expect to receive telephone calls from him regularly. The purpose of these calls will be to inform you of any significant market information which will have come to the broker's attention and to generally impart a "feel" of the fundamental trading situation to you.

These calls may often contain an implication or an outright statement that a "good opportunity" exists in connection with one or more commodity contracts. Your brokerage representative may be personally convinced of the validity of the advice he is giving you—or it may represent an "official" opinion developed in the firm's research department and passed to the solicitors for relay to their customers. Regardless of where the "price idea" comes from, and without respect to whether subsequent events prove the information to be right or wrong, brokers make telephone calls to customers for the purpose of generating new business. The mere existence of free funds in your margin account is an open invitation to greater activity in the market on your part.

The regularity and the length of the broker calls you receive will probably have a direct relation to the size of the "free" margin balance you maintain on deposit. The information contained in such telephone calls should be viewed as only that: *information.* Your decision as to whether action is or is not justified should still depend on your private appraisal as to whether the "opportunity" is one which intrigues you as a professional risk-bearer.

It should be remembered that *interesting opportunities* come in two forms: those producing *profits* and those producing *losses.* It's hard to imagine a more *interesting* situation for a speculator than being on the wrong end of a bad position. However, excitement and profits are *not* the same thing!

Margin Account Segregation

Even experienced securities and commodities speculators are oftentimes unaware of an important protective device which exists in connection with *regulated commodity margin deposits.* Under the Commodity Exchange Act, commodity margin funds must be "segregated". This is to say that, from the time you open an account with a broker and deposit funds with him in a regulated commodity margin account, those funds must be kept *distinctly separate* from all other funds in the brokerage firm. They may not be "pooled" by the broker. Neither may they be used by the broker for any purpose other than margining your regulated commodity positions, payment of your trade commissions for executions, and covering whatever trade losses you sustain.

The distinction between the segregation requirement in *commodity* deposits and the handling given *securities* deposits is most significant. Under the latitudes of governing statutes, security margin funds may be used by a brokerage house to pay its rent, light, water, salaries, etc. No problem exists so long as the firm meets the applicable requirements of solvency; customers' securities' "free balances" may be used by the broker in virtually any fashion he sees fit. The securities customer's margin deposit appears in the records of the firm and, of course, constitutes a legal obligation. But the *money itself* may or may not be on hand at any particular moment.

Financial failure of brokerage houses is a comparatively rare phenomenon, due to the restrictions under which they operate and the kind of business in which they are engaged. However, bankruptcies have occurred in the past and presumably some of them will take place in the future. Whenever this happens, security margin funds *may* be lost in the financial collapse; commodity margin funds *cannot* be. This, by reason of the CEA requirement which spells out an iron-clad protective procedure for holding all regulated commodity accounts separate and distinctly apart from all other funds; for as long as they are in the broker's custody.

Many traders who deal in both commodities and securities follow the practice of opening a regulated commodity account and then, as stock purchases are made, or when positions are taken in *un*-regulated commodities, they authorize transfer of the required amount of money *from the regulated commodity account to the other category.* Doing so merely requires the signing of a standard transfer form. Likewise, profits realized on un-regulated commodities or profits from securities transactions are directed to be *re-deposited into the regulated commodity account.* In so doing, a customer can rest assured that his margin funds, although they are not earning interest, are every bit as safe as they would be if on deposit in a bank.

Errors Do Happen

It has already been noted that brokers, like other mortals, can make mistakes; moreover, that a broker's error may result in either an "accidental" profit or loss. The major commodity exchanges unanimously take the position that when an error in execution occurs, the profit, if any, *belongs to the customer*; and the loss, if any, *must be absorbed by the broker.* The existence of the rule exerts a profound influence on brokers in their striving for efficiency.

There is no reason, nor would it be possible, to outline all the various kinds of errors which might occur in the course of trading; nor to identify the individuals who could, in some train of events, be found culpable. An order may be improperly framed, resulting in an execution in the wrong contract month, in the wrong amount or at the wrong price. A pit broker may misread an order, which results in an "over-fill" or an "under-fill"; he may inadvertently buy, when the order directs him to sell.

Operating in the highly charged atmosphere of a busy market offers countless opportunities for mistakes. The fact that so few errors do occur is the best possible testimony to the expertise of the whole chain of funcion from the solicitor's desk to pit execution, and back. When errors occur they are usually resolved immediately in the brokerage house—and in accordance with the exchange requirement cited previously; that the customer receives the profit from the error, if any, but is saved from any possible loss in the opposite situation.

Arbitration Procedure

When resolution of the difficulty cannot be worked out with the brokerage firm, each organized commodity exchange has an *aribtration committee* which sits as a referee between the interests involved. After listening to the evidence, the arbitration commitee is empowered to render a decision and enforce its ruling upon a *member firm*. It is important to note that matters involving both members and nonmembers are eligible to be brought before this kind of exchange fact-finding body. The infintesimal number of issues that remain unresolved following arbitration can still be taken into the civil courts for disposition.

To sum up, a broker is neither a god nor a devil. He is, in the vast majority of cases, a well-trained agent in a highly specialized and most demanding activity. His primary function is to meticulously carry out the instructions of his customer-client. Common practice regularly casts him also in the role of counselor, fortune teller and price prognosticator. The success he may have in these latter-named fields will depend upon a great many things, none of which may be directly assessable except on the basis of demonstrated reliability—or lack of it. A speculator who believes that careful selection of a broker removes the need for his *own* attention to, and study of, the market and the positions of risk he is considering, is placing an inordinate measure of faith in a second party. There are some public traders who have richly profited by pursuing this kind of program. There are a great many more who have experienced the opposite result.

Unless a person has the time, the means and the incentive to manage his own speculative program, he should probably not speculate in commodities at all. Or he should retain an individual in whom he has unlimited confidence, turn over a designated amount of money for speculative activity, and pay no attention whatsoever to the market situation on a day-by-day basis.

The most successful public trader is one who is willing to listen to advice, evaluate *all* of it, discard *most* of it, use *some* of it, and make his own judgments in light of his own willingness to assume risk exposure. Most important of all, to reiterate for emphasis, he is one who cuts his losses short and lets his profits run, knowing that if he can be "right" even half the time, the speculative strategy will produce a most rewarding composite result.

Appraising Advice in General

This section cannot be closed without a modest warning against placing too much confidence in the opinions of *anyone* who has a stake in the issue under discussion. Courts recognize that there are those who are automatically disbarred from sitting on a jury, since they have an *interest* in the outcome. The same rule should be applied in discussing the market.

From a practical point of view, how *can* you expect a trader to answer a question which bears on a position he holds? Ask a "bear" what he thinks the prospects are for sugar, and he will tell you he thinks prices will work lower. A "bear" almost always looks for lower prices. But ask the "bear" what he sees in sugar prices when he *happens to hold a long position* in the commodity and he will tell you that he thinks *higher prices* are in prospect. Any other response would be unthinkable. Moreover, the larger his position and the *larger his loss*—if any—in the position, the more eloquent he is likely to be in presenting the higher-prices argument.

The *only* time you can really expect to get an unbiased opinion about a trading question is when you ask it of someone who has *no position* in it. The statement should not be taken as a charge of dishonesty. Anyone who is long desperately *wants* prices to go up; anyone who is short equally *wants* them to go down. Economic interests are bound to cloud the objective judgment of even a veritable saint, if he holds a market position.

Before asking someone what he thinks about the price of anything, ask him if he owns any of it. If the answer is "yes", go elsewhere for an unbiased opinion. He can't give you one.

Plate 65

All pit trading is by "open outcry." It's too noisy to hear much, but hand signals help solve the problem.

CHAPTER XVIII

SPECULATIVE PITFALLS

Several of the topics which will be treated in this chapter have already been referred to directly or by implication in material which has come before. But the importance of being able to identify pitfalls which exist in commodity speculation justify the risk of any degree of repetition.

Most of the *serious* losses sustained by public speculators in commodities are *avoidable*. They ordinarily grow out of lack of caution in establishing a new position and/or failure to unflinchingly apply the strategic rules of position management when the danger signals appear. The greatest losses which speculators sustain in commodity positions are those which are directly related to stubbornness; refusal to recognize facts, take a small loss, and close out the proposition that has gone sour.

As previously noted, it isn't necessary that one be "right" even half of the time, in order to make handsome profits in speculation; assuming stringent application of the trading technique which maximizes profit opportunity and minimizes the chances for loss. If one third of the positions taken prove to be right—and provided they are managed properly during the period of time you hold them—your speculative success over time is virtually assured. But the market is

263

a hard teacher and your performance in it will be graded closely—and constantly reflected in profits or losses. When you make a mistake, it will cost you money—*every time*. By the same token, good decisions always save money—or bring cash rewards.

Over-Trading

Money is the basic tool of speculation, since speculation involves dealing in valuable property held over some period of time. The property may involve a physical asset or it may be represented in a futures contract, which stands as a measurement of *ownership risk*. In either case, a prudent speculator will carefully determine the extent of his capital which can be earmarked for speculative activity and everything he does in his speculative program will be *first* checked against these risk resources. If he errs, it should always be on the side of conservatism. *Under-trading can't break you*; over-trading surely will.

Impressive personal fortunes have been amassed very quickly in commodity speculation. Philip D. Armour, for example, is authoritatively said to have cleared two million dollars in less than ninety days by selling pork short during the last few weeks of the Civil War. The market price of pork stood around $40. Armour was convinced that the war was about to be ended and, with its end, he was confident that pork prices would fall. In pursuit of this "price idea", he thought $40 pork to be unrealistically high; so he sold trainloads of the commodity for future delivery at prices ranging from $40 down to $30 per cwt. Suddenly the Civil War did end and the price of pork promptly fell to $25; then to $20, and finally settled around $18 per cwt. Armour was able to buy back his pork contracts—or buy the physical product—for about half his previous selling price. In so doing, he laid the foundation for one of the world's great companies—and one of America's greatest personal fortunes.

But for every dollar Armour *made* on his speculation, the same dollar was *lost* by a buyer of pork—who must have been equally convinced that demands for food to supply an army and sustain the civil population would drive prices up; and that the war would continue. Had Armour's speculative notion proved wrong, his loss might have been as monumental as his gain.

From the standpoint of professional speculation, over-trading is *always* a bad policy, because it can be fatal. Reversals can occur, opinions can be wrong, and what might merely be an incidental reversal under more conservative practices, in the face of over-trading, can constitute a catastrophe from which financial recovery is impossible.

You Can Never Be Sure

A professional speculator always recognizes the fact that *any* position may prove to be untenable at some point. The rosiest outlook may, for the most unpredictable reasons, turn to one of unrelieved despair. When this happens, a loss must be taken, and the *sooner* it can be taken, the better. By holding position commitments within conservative bounds, several successive losses can be sustained, but there will still be additional risk funds in reserve to enable the speculator to seek out another attractive opportunity—and back his judgment with the required capital.

Over-trading is done too often on the basis of "hunches". The over-trader is depending on luck to deliver him a windfall profit. It's a "sucker's" game. There are occasions when luck meets the hopes placed in her, but the speculator who intends to *stay* in the business and *succeed* in the business will pin his future to more solid criteria. He will never permit his open position commitments to exceed sensible bounds, regardless of how sure he feels. As a rule of thumb, the following measurements represent a useful set of maximums:

1. An *initial* position should never tie up more than 50% of your available risk capital.

2. An *enlarged* position should never tie up more than 90% of your available risk capital.

Over-trading is like Russian-roulette: One loss can take you out of the game—forever. A smart speculator always leaves himself some *latitude for loss.*

265

Speculative Pitfalls

Margin Calls

There are two levels of margin which must be on deposit in connection with an open commodity futures position. *Initial margin* is usually about 5% of the value of the contract, and must be deposited at the time the purchase or sale is made. Once a position has been established, a minimum margin must be kept "in the clear" throughout the period of time you hold it. This is referred to as *maintenance margin* and is usually about one-third less than the *initial margin* requirement.

As prices fluctuate on the contract held, the speculator's margin deposit is increased when prices move favorably—and is decreased when prices move adversely. Thus, when prices fall on a contract in which a long position is held, the speculator's margin funds are said to be *impaired*; the same would be true in connection with a short position in which prices rise. A trader's equity in a position fluctuates almost constantly: increasing when the price of a contract held long increases, and falling when prices rise on a contract which has been sold short and vice-versa.

With respect to grain futures, all brokerage houses follow the practice of calling for additional "variation margin" as soon as price change has impaired the speculator's margin equity to less than the designated maintenance margin requirement. For example, initial margin on wheat is currently set at a minimum of 15¢ per bushel. (This is subject to change.) In order to buy or sell a wheat futures contract, the trader must deposit 15¢ per bushel with his broker to indemnify his performance on the terms of his market obligation. One contract (5,000 bushels), therefore, requires an *initial margin* deposit of $750.

Maintenance margin on wheat is currently set at 10¢ per bushel. This is to say that once a position in wheat futures is taken, the price on the selected futures may move 5¢ per bushel to the disadvantage of the holder of the contract before the latitude which exists between *initial* and *maintenance* margin is wiped out. Under the practices of all brokerage houses, whenever prices have moved against the holder's wheat position to the extent of 5⅛¢ per bushel, a call would go out for additional margin funds. In order to hold the position, more money must be deposited with the broker, to bring the margin amount *back up* to the *initial margin level of 15¢ per bushel.*

Failure to answer a call for additional margin within the period of time specified by the broker may result in the position being closed out by the broker. In the case of the larger accumulations involving several contracts, the entire position will not necessarily be closed out; but a portion of it will be, in order to reduce the total risk liability present, and reduce the amount of margin funds required to cover the reduced position.

Never Answer A Margin Call

It is difficult to envision a situation in which answering a call for additional margin on a deteriorating position could be viewed as anything except bad speculative practice. Such a call for additional margin will not be made unless prices have already moved substantially in the *wrong* direction. The trader's price idea has already been proven to be *invalid by the facts.* Holding a losing position is bad enough; *staying* with a loser, when doing so requires putting up additional funds to hold on, cannot be defended on any basis. Faced with a call for additional margin as a result of price variation, two courses of action, and only two, deserve consideration:

1. *Close out part of the position* in order to free up existing margin funds and bring margin on the reduced portion of the position back up to standards.

2. Recognize the "loser" for what it is, and *close out the entire position.*

Traders occasionally justify answering variation margin calls with the fiction that they "intended to add to their margin account deposits, anyway." If you truly intend to deposit additional risk funds with your broker, do so at any time *except* when price changes face you with the demand for additional margin to meet broker or exchange requirements.

To repeat for emphasis, *never answer a variation margin call!* Doing so is almost always open flirtation with speculative disaster.

Moving a Stop-Loss Order

We have previously discussed the procedure involved in evaluating the establishment of a new speculative position, and pointed out that in doing so an *initial profit objective* should be identified along with a *maximum loss limitation*.

When a contract is bought or sold, a stop-loss order should be placed above the trading range (in the case of a short sale) or below the trading range (in the case of a long purchase). The exact point at which the stop-loss is placed may be reflective of your personal appraisal of price movement within a daily or weekly trading range; or may be determined with the help of chart patterns, or otherwise. However the stop-loss level is arrived at, once fixed it should be left in force — barring the most dramatic change of circumstances.

Inexperienced speculators have an inglorious record of enlarging their losses by "moving" stop-losses higher or lower, thus offering the opportunity for prices to move even *further* to their disadvantage.

As prices move in your favor, serious consideration must be constantly given to the possibility of moving a stop-loss *up* in connection with a long position, and moving it *down* to protect profits in a short position. Failure to do so will leave your "paper profits" exposed to the vicissitudes of subsequent price fluctuation. And a profit which is yours on one day may, in the face of later price change, be taken away from you as prices rise or fall.

Move a stop to *protect a profit* — but a stop-loss order should never be moved upward or downward to *enlarge the opportunity for loss*. If a position is wrong, the *closer* the stop-loss, the less it will cost you to learn the bad news.

Adding To A Loss — "Price Averaging"

Neophytes in speculation find ingenius ways to rationalize failure. One of the recurrent means they seize on is the notion that their "effective price" in an overall commodity position is subject to *averaging*, up or down, through successive purchases or sales.

For example, a speculator buys 10,000 bushels of corn at $1.30.

This price then falls to $1.25, which amounts to a 5¢ loss. At this point, the unskilled speculator may decide to buy another 10,000 bushels at the lower price. In so doing, he may consider that his "effective" price on 20,000 bushels of corn is $1.27½. Arithmetically the figure is correct, but in terms of speculative tactics, the procedure is absolutely and irretrievably wrong. *Each* acquisition must be realistically viewed as *separate* and apart from each subsequent acquisition. The first decision to buy corn futures at $1.30 per bushel clearly stands as a mistake, since prices fell 5¢ per bushel under the purchase price. The purchase of 10,000 additional bushels at $1.25 *may* prove to be profitable, but this will not be known until subsequent price behavior is revealed. In any case, the *first* purchase is still "wrong" *until price moves above $1.30;* buying more, at *any* price, won't change this.

Price patterns, like weather patterns, have a well-recognized tendency to "persistence". Prices that are moving downward tend to continue downward; prices that are moving upward tend to maintain an upward direction; prices that are moving sideways are inclined to maintain a horizontal channel. Establishing a long position in a descending market is simply the wrong thing to do. When it is done, the trader is probably attempting to "pick the bottom". Tops and bottoms are elusive things, and trading *against the trend* can be a fine road to bankruptcy.

Adding to a losing position, whether long or short, can only *multiply* negative risk exposure; it can escalate a modest loss into a debacle.

When prices are going against you, close the position out — or let your stop-loss limitation stand as protection. If the stop-loss is reached, the position will be closed out — and it *should be!*

Moving a stop-loss higher or lower to accommodate adverse price movement is mere folly; *adding to a losing position* in the face of a trend which is already working against you can only be considered speculative *madness.*

The only time an initial position should be added to is *after* it has produced a *paper profit,* which can then be re-committed, to increase your leverage situation on an additional purchase or sale.

Speculative Pitfalls

When adverse price developments identify a position as a loss, it must be considered as a candidate for close-out or, at most, something to be left alone pending improvement of its performance.

(Commercial grain dealers can buy or sell up or down "on scale" and profit from it. Speculators should leave the practice strictly to them.)

Adding To A Profit

While adding to a loss position should never be done, adding to a profitable position may greatly enhance your chances for large profits.

As detailed earlier, once a position has generated a paper profit, these profits can be used to margin additional contracts in the same futures. In so doing, you will have reduced the total amount of "cash" margin required — thus increasing leverage on the cash you must put up to bind your contract performance. In times of major price movement, excellent opportunities may offer themselves to "accumulate" substantial holdings with profits from previous acquisitions or sales.

In adding to a winning position, the possibility of price reversal converting a paper profit into a loss must always be borne in mind. Therefore, *whenever* an initial position is enlarged, there should also be an opportunity to limit loss potentials by *moving the stop-loss* order somewhat "closer" on the *total* position.

For example, a trader in May wheat in 1966 had an opportunity to sell the contract short at more than $2.00 per bushel. The price on the contract subsequently fell below $1.70 per bushel. The price move covered more than 35¢ per bushel and was accomplished without a significant reversal. A trader who followed the procedure of adding to a profitable position in May wheat may have sold 10,000 bushels (two contracts) short at $1.95. He may have sold another contract at $1.90; still another at $1.85, etc. Each time the position was enlarged, the stop-loss should have been moved downward *somewhat proportionately.*

270

For example, in selling the first two contracts, the position might have been "stopped" at $2.00⅜ per bushel, indicating the trader's belief that the "even dollar" would represent a major resistence level — but with the stop placed ⅜ higher to contemplate the possibility that the even-dollar level might also prove to be a major "magnet" in an active trade.

His loss on the first two contracts would, therefore, be limited to about 5¢ per bushel (the difference between initial margin of 15¢ per bushel and the required maintenance margin of 10¢ per bushel). When the third contract is sold at $1.90, the stop-loss should be moved down into the vicinity of $1.95 — the price level on the first short sale. Having done so, the trader has now virtually removed the opportunity for *any* loss, since he intends to get out of the position if prices should get back to the level at which he initially sold it.

As the fourth contract is sold short, the stop-loss is once more moved lower. A loss is now out of consideration — the objective is to *protect and build profit:* the stop-loss is placed well "inside the profit area". By adding to the position in this fashion, the trader is repeatedly using *paper-profits* to margin subsequent sales. His *paper profits, profit opportunities, and margin leverage* are *all increasing.* When he adds to the initial commitment, he trades on a profit of 5¢ per bushel on the first two contracts. The second 5¢ move involves three contracts; the third 5¢ move, four contracts, etc.

Once he gets his stop-loss order moved into "the black", he has assured himself a profit on the composite position and all he needs to do is pursue the incremental pyramiding program and let prices take their course. The skilled trader will realize that the *persistence factor* in price movement is operating for him: the longer prices fall, the more likely they are to *continue* falling. In the face of any definitive price reversal, his stop-loss order is "resting" to effect a quick close-out on the entire accumulated position and protect the majority of his profits.

Closing Out Too Fast

A major pitfall for inexperienced speculators is in the area of *premature* closing of a winning position. It takes steady nerves to resist the temptation to "dump" a winner after having picked up a small, quick profit on it. Such an inclination must be stoutly resisted.

The first objective is to get a profitable position going; secondly, move your stop-loss order into the profit area, and thirdly, *sit back and wait*. Each time you can move a stop-loss order to your advantage, you have "locked in" an additional profit. Do not attempt to determine when prices have "gone far enough". The market is the only authority on the *right* price. If the position is being managed properly, you will know when prices have reached the end of the move. When this has happened, and the price trend has reversed itself, your stop-loss order will be activated and you will be offset out of the position. Now your *paper profit* is ready to be counted; it's a *cash profit*.

Let A "Stop" Take You Out

A profitable position should nearly always be closed out by the activation of a stop-loss order. Rigid adherence to this rule will save you from the frustrating knowledge that you have needlessly cut profits short when a little more patience would have paid off.

Reversing Position in the Market

A major object of pity in commodity markets is the unfortunate soul who rides a price trend up, or down, for a period of time; then closes out the position with a profit — and *immediately* establishes a new position in the *opposite direction*.

For example, to use the wheat situation noted earlier, a trader of the author's acquaintance sold May wheat short at $2.00 per bushel — extremely close to the contract high for the year. The trader stayed with his short position and added to it until the contract price fell to around $1.85. At this point he closed out his short position, having realized some 15¢ per bushel profit on the down-side movement. Then he immediately re-established a *new* position by going "long" May wheat. He was convinced that the market had "found bottom".

Instead of the price on the contract reversing itself — as the trader expected — prices paused for a few sessions, then the situation continued to deteriorate. After having profited from a 15¢ down move in his *short* position, he then proceeded to lose 18¢ by being *long* May wheat. He stayed with the losing long position virtually all the way to the bottom. Every day he felt "the price has go up." But it didn't.

The hard fact is that prices *don't have to do anything* except fluctuate! There is no right price for anything except the price the *market puts on it,* and while the 35¢ slide in May wheat prices which occurred in 1966 was an historic move, new market history is constantly being made.

The trader referred to above undertook to *argue* with the market. He was "in step" with the price move when he sold May wheat short. As price moved lower, he added to his position, which increased his opportunities for profit, and prices continued to move in his favor. Then, based on his decision that it was now *time* for a price turn-up, he closed out his May wheat holdings and established a long position in the face of a dramatically deteriorating price structure. The long position cost him all of the profits he had realized on the earlier short position — and then some.

Take Time-Out Between Positions

There is a great deal to be said for calling a "rest period" between speculative exposures in a given contract. If prices have been moving higher, at the point at which a reversal occurs a price *plateau* is likely to develop before a full-fledged down-side correction occurs. The sideways price pattern may persist for a few hours, a few sessions, or several weeks. There is no speculative purpose served in maintaining a position in a market which is going nowhere. By remaining on the sidelines and observing price development, you will have risk capital available to step in at the point at which a new pattern does appear.

In the interim, the *best position* is *no position.* Above all else, steer clear of establishing any new position contrary to *demonstrated market direction.* Persistence in price movement can be a terrible enemy, and there is nothing which can prove as ruinous as being "out of step" with the market.

Speculative Pitfalls

"Quick change artists" in speculation usually defeat themselves through their search for price *tops* and *bottoms*. Successful speculators look for a discernible trend and *then* get aboard. They don't worry about "missing" part of the move, so long as they can be "with the parade" over most of its route. The highest risk exposure in price behavior is at the reversal points (at each successive top and bottom). The prudent speculator *selects* the *lesser risks*. He leaves top and bottom picking to those who believe they possess "second sight" or have a crystal ball which is well-nigh infallible.

Trading on "News"

Inexperienced commodity speculators are oftentimes distressed to discover that prices sometimes fall sharply in the face of "bullish" news or climb suddenly on "bearish" news. When this kind of thing happens, the phenomenon may be viewed as a contradiction of the facts.

In order to understand the behavior of market prices in the face of "news", it must be remembered that a primary function of the market is to "discount the future". Stated another way, the market presumably "knows" everything which is known by *all of the people buying and selling in it*. Their orders to buy and sell are a direct reflection of each trader's personal *knowledge and appraisal* of events to come. The market, like a computer, accepts all of these positive and negative inputs, adds up the total and delivers an answer in the form of price *stability,* price *increase,* or price *deterioration.*

An inexperienced trader might consider a story in The Journal of Commerce, which announces the fact that a foreign government has placed an order for several million tons of U. S. grain, as being an excellent reason to buy the grain futures concerned. In checking with his broker, however, he may discover that prices on the commodity involved are actually *lower as a result* of the publicity. The cause and effect relationship is obvious on closer examination:

It might be assumed that the trade has been generally aware of the pending business for several weeks. As negotiations proceed, traders hear bits and trickles of information and, from these, piece together an idea concerning the size of the export order involved.

274

Now the publicity appears; at last the story is out. It may be that the size of the order actually placed by the foreign interest is *smaller* than the trade had *expected.* Disappointment is best written in lower prices.

GRAIN PRICES DECLINE ON CROP REPORTS

Most grain futures prices declined again last week on the Chicago Board of Trade, influenced by favorable harvest and growing weather and crop reports that 1967 production will hit new highs.

When trade closed Friday at the exchange, wheat was ⅛ lower to ¼ cent a bushel higher, corn ⅛ lower to ¼ higher, oats ⅛ lower to ⅜ higher, rye ¼ lower to ½ higher, and soybeans 1⅛ cents lower to ¼ higher.

Weather was the most important factor in commodity prices earlier in the week. On Friday, the Quaker Oats crop summary tended to influence higher prices, reporting that wheat, corn and soybean production this year might show some losses because of rain damage to fields. Prices advanced about 1½ cents a bushel.

However, about 30 minutes after Friday's opening, another trade-respected statistician, Conrad Leslie of Lamson Bros. & Co., estimated 1967 corn production and all wheat production would hit new highs.

With Leslie's report, prices declined and at the close Friday were near lows for the day.

Government Program For Wheat Next Year Is Almost Unchanged

By a WALL STREET JOURNAL *Staff Reporter*

WASHINGTON — Agriculture Secretary Freeman authorized a 1968 wheat program almost unchanged from the one in effect for the current crop.

The price-support loan level continues at $1.25 a bushel. Wheat also may again be planted on feed-grain acreage on farms participating in both programs, and feed grains may be planted on wheat allotments. As in 1967, too, a farmer may plant up to 50% in excess of his allotment and still be eligible for the program, provided the excess production is stored and other conditions are met.

Domestic marketing certificates, which are designed to provide farmers with full parity prices on wheat consumed in the U.S., will be issued on an estimated 530 million bushels that the nation is expected to consume in the coming year. As before, the certificate will be valued at the difference between full parity and the $1.25 loan value. For the 1967 crop, certificates worth $1.36 a bushel are to be issued on 520 million bushels of wheat.

Mr. Freeman termed the 1968 program adequate to "assure an ample supply of wheat to meet all needs, both domestic and foreign, and protect farm income." Farm revenue from wheat next year will match that from the current year's crop, he predicted.

275

Speculative Pitfalls

The market has a tendency to "over-buy" good news and "over-sell" bad news. As knowledge of the pending export business gained currency among trading interests, a flurry of excitement resulted and its immediate effect is seen in rising prices. As prices do ascend, holders of short positions in the affected contracts will be impelled to reduce their holdings or close out their positions entirely. In either event, the previous sellers of the grain now must become buyers as they attempt to offset. As their orders reach the market, prices are driven up even further as a result of the imbalance in sell/buy pressures which result.

The market is "discounting" the "good news" about export activity. In addition to the *new* buying orders which the good news triggers, a slight — or significant — "short squeeze" may also develop. In combination, prices may move somewhat higher than the size of the export business which started it could, by any reasonable appraisal, justify.

With public announcement of the export order which has been placed, there is no longer any room for speculation about the trade details; although the quantity involved may be sizeable, it may, nevertheless, be *well under trade hopes*. At the same time, many of the disadvantaged shorts may have been "chased in" in the face of rising prices. Thus, both the *new* "long" buying and *offsetting* by "shorts" that support higher price levels have disappeared; and without these elements, *prices must fall.*

There is an old saying among commodity speculators that "by the time you have heard the news, it's too late to use it." With few exceptions, the axiom will prove itself in practice. The market does not often reward a trader for being able to read a newspaper. Most people can do so. The market does reward a trader for being able to weigh unknown but forthcoming events and draw conclusions about composite effects; provided, of course, that the trader has the courage to back his judgment by taking a market position.

It Pays to Keep Informed

The foregoing should not be taken to mean that following the news is a waste of time. Most emphatically, it is not a waste of time.

276

The value of following news developments closely, however, lies in sharpening a trader's overall perspective and "feel" for the supply/demand situation, and enhancing his ability to forecast probable actions on the part of governments and other official and public interests who can exert great weight in the marketplace. The events about which a trader must conjecture and from which will emanate his greatest profits — or losses — concerns things of which the market is *not yet aware;* or about which the traders have a *wrong idea.* It is also worth emphasizing that, while market prices are always authoritative, the *traders* can be, on balance, *badly wrong* in their overall appraisal of a particular situation which is developing.

We will now deal with one of these examples in detail.

Trading Into Major Crop Reports

There are few considerations which take precedence over supply/demand balance in the major commodities. Populations must be fed, clothed and housed, and commodities constitute the raw materials with which these activities are made possible. The United States Government, through the U. S. Department of Agriculture, has very properly concerned itself with making regular statistical projections of crop size and consumption at designated intervals. Through the periods which cover crop planting, growth and harvest, estimates are made by the Crop Reporting Board which are designed to keep producers, consumers and commercial interests apprised of the overall situation surrounding our major commodities.

Crop reports are always released at 3:00 p.m. Eastern Standard time, after the commodity markets have closed throughout the country on the selected report day. Since the information is gathered from thousands of sources and maintained in the strictest confidence, the figures are absolutely available to no one before their public release to all who want them. The impact of these government reports on price can be *tremendous;* especially if the data contains a major "surprise" for the trade.

The reports always follow an established form, and the release schedule is equally firm. The first estimate is a forecast of *winter wheat* and *rye* plantings — and is made available about December

277

20, of the year preceding the projected harvest. The initial wheat and rye forecast is followed up by revised projections which are released at monthly intervals from April through August. Monthly forecasts of production on all *spring grains* are commenced in March, and comparable statistics are released at monthly intervals thereafter until the harvest is completed and the final, actual production is known.

Each crop report includes estimated production in the current crop which is either being planted, raised, or harvested; and each report compares the latest crop prospects with the estimate which was released a month ago — and the previous year's actual production figure. The projection reflected in each crop forecast is the government agency's best judgment at the *end of the month just passed.* If weather, for example, has been disadvantageous in the meantime, the forecast figures may need to be adjusted downward, somewhat below the projection, as a result of two or three weeks of poor growing conditions, *after the data was assembled.*

It goes without saying that a sizeable increase or decrease in anticipated crop size, as compared with previous crop averages, can be a mighty influence on price. In 1966, as a case in point, the trade expected a soybean crop of about 890,000,000 bushels as everyone awaited the September crop forecast. In the trading session immediately preceding release of the official figures, the price on nearby (September and November) soybean contracts climbed precipitously, posting more than 8¢ per bushel gain in the last half-hour or so of trading. A surge of new buying was stimulated by people taking *new* long positions in the market — and shorts added to the upward pressure as they were forced to buy back their contracts. A "squeeze" developed aginst the disadvantaged earlier sellers. Higher prices ruled to the closing bell.

When the government figures were released 45 minutes after the close, the 1966 soybean crop was estimated at 926,000,000 bushels. Soybean prices dropped the limit of 10¢ per bushel during each of the next two trading sessions and continued to steadily deteriorate for three weeks thereafter. Traders who had properly anticipated a big increase in the soybean crop sold the commodity short and stuck to their guns in the face of the "squeeze" were richly rewarded for having done so. The market was "wrong" in having posted high prices on the commodity in expectation of a small crop. The "longs" who stayed with their long positions made large "paper profits" during the immediate pre-report period, but *sustained major losses* when the crop facts were known.

Never Underestimate An Important Report

This discussion is largely repitious of material which appears elsewhere in this volume, but its repetition is deserved for the purpose of underscoring a most valuable warning: Unless you are unquestioningly convinced that you have caught the market in error, NEVER CARRY AN OPEN POSITION, EITHER LONG OR SHORT, INTO A MAJOR CROP REPORT. The hazards involved are far too great! The events which may follow may be *ruinous!*

Success in speculation does not require that a speculator "plunge" himself into possible financial ruin for the opportunity of realizing profits. The wise speculator will only undertake those risks which he feels offer a better opportunity for profit than for loss. A risk which is *incalculable* is a "sucker" risk; and a crop report *may* involve this order of risk. If so, it ceases to be speculation in the true sense; it comprises a gamble. And, as such, it should be studiously avoided.

Beware Trading on the "Opening"

Commodity markets are not continuous. Trading is conducted for only a few hours each business day. Overnight, pressures build up in the form of accumulated orders waiting for execution when the next session begins. The balance between orders to buy and orders to sell will be seen in price levels — and can produce price aberrations which are *dramatic* but *short-lived,* lasting only a few seconds or a few minutes. If buying pressure substantially exceeds offerings in a given commodity contract, it may open at a considerably higher price level than it closed on the preceding day. *Overnight news* which is known but has not yet had an opportunity to be introduced into the pricing equation will assert itself in the first seconds of the opening. Its influence will tend to diminish as the market has an opportunity to "discount" it. But, for the span of time during which it is being "digested", its effect may be out of all proportion to its longer-term implications.

Placing market-orders — fillable at whatever price prevails — on an opening may be an exceedingly hazardous practice, since no one really knows *where* prices will open. A prudent speculator should have a fairly solid notion about the price level at which he wants to buy or sell something. Opening prices are full of surprises; and surprises can be disastrous.

In view of these considerations, the better course to follow is that of waiting until the first flurry of trading has passed before drawing any solid opinions about prevailing price level. If this procedure is not desirable or feasible, then the use of price-limits on an order is the next best thing; although limits will sometimes deprive the pit broker of an opportunity to obtain split-second execution.

Beware Trading On The "Close"

A philosophy of caution should also apply generally to trading "on the close". As previously noted, pit traders fall into several categories including day-traders, position-traders, and scalpers. A good deal of "evening-up" takes place in the last minute or two of each session, particularly in actively traded contracts. If "the pit is long" toward the end of the session, it can confidently be expected that before the closing-bell rings there will be an appreciable amount of selling on the part of the day-traders and scalpers; this, since the pit participants concerned do not want to carry *any open positions overnight*. When this final wave of selling hits, prices are likely to be driven down. The reverse would be equally true if the close approaches with "the pit" being, on balance, substantially short. As the "locals" buy back their short contracts, the flurry of demand which results may drive prices upward.

Many of the same hazards exist with respect to a market order "on the close" as was pointed out in connection with the opening of a session. However, the closing moments of trade are *usually less volatile* than the opening, except in the face of special circumstances which may produce extraordinary results. As a general rule, market-orders at either the opening or closing of a session represent a *higher order of risk,* as concerns the levels at which they may be executed, than the same kind of order introduced into the market at *any other time of day.*

To recapitulate, then, price aberrations which represent the greatest departures from the normal trading range usually occur in the first (or the last) few minutes of the session. They grow out of pent-up overnight demand or offerings, which call for immediate execution (or may reflect position imbalance among the "locals" in the pit). There may be times when a public speculator will deliberately choose these situations for the accomplishment of a specific transaction, but as a general rule it should be recognized that the market's *reliability* in reflecting values tends to be at its *lowest ebb* at the *beginning* and the *end* of a session.

Beware the Last Days of Contract Life

The majority of all commodity contracts have a trading-life of about one year. During this period of time, the volume of trade in the contract tends to pick up, and the "open-interest" usually grows proportionately. The larger the open-interest in a given contract, the more unfilled positions outstanding in it. Open-interest, as reported by the Commodity Exchange Authority, represents only *one side* of open positions. For example, in a futures in which there are 1,000 contracts held long, there *must* also be 1,000 contracts held short; total *positions,* therefore, is 2,000 contracts. Open-interest would be reported as 1,000 contracts, equal to *either* the *long* or the *short* side of total contracts held open in the maturity.

Since less than 2% of all futures contracts are satisfied by actual delivery of the physical commodity, it stands to reason that *most* of the existing positions will be closed out by offset prior to the termination of trading in each particular futures. In the terminal phase of a maturing contract, a sort of tug-of-war develops between the longs and the shorts. Obviously, the longs want *higher* prices so they can sell out at a profit. The shorts want *lower* prices so they can buy back at a profit. The eventual outcome may rest importantly on which side is willing or able to "sit tight" the longest.

Speculative Pitfalls

In order to offset, the shorts in an expiring contract must buy back the thing which they previously sold. The best place to obtain the needed futures is from the longs who likewise, in order to offset *their* open positions, must sell out the contracts they previously purchased.

So the economic antagonists face each other in the pit and hope prices will move in the direction of their respective advantage. The exercise is certainly thrilling and can be highly profitable *if* you are fortunate enough to be with the "winners". Should you be a member of the vanquished camp, the results can be precisely the reverse — and great losses can be quickly sustained.

Leave the "Last Days" to Others

Public speculators should *leave the last days of trading to the full-time professionals* or to public traders who have yet to learn better. In so doing, the unpredictability of contract termination price behavior can be avoided, but this is not all. There is an additional hazard inherent in trading the tail-end of a commodity contract which can hardly be overlooked: all longs who have not offset by the "last bell" *must accept delivery* of the physical commodity; all shorts who have not offset *must make delivery* of the physical commodity.

A public speculator is rarely ever equipped to economically fulfill delivery requirements. *Taking or making delivery almost invariably represents a bad move for anyone except a producer or a dealer in cash merchandise.* Holding out to the bitter end in an expiring contract is speculative brinksmanship which cannot be recommended to the public trader on any basis. This, even though the final gyrations in price which may eventuate as a volatile contract "goes off the board" may look most enticing.

Trading Limits Don't Apply To Cash

It has already been noted that commodity futures markets impose limitations on the maximum amount that prices may change — up *or* down — on each contract in a single session. In corn, for example, each futures price presently has an 8¢ maximum allowable increase

282

or decrease in the *current* session, *above* or *below* the closing price of the previous session. While this provides a built-in protection for the trader in futures contracts, comparable *limitations do not exist in the cash market.*

A speculator who holds a short position until the expiration of futures trading must, once trading has come to an end, make arrangements to deliver the physical product. In order to do so, he must, if necessary, buy the commodity in the cash market and deliver it to a qualified long futures holder. Situations have existed where the market price on the maturing futures was at considerable variance with the effective price in the cash market. In September of 1966, for example, the shorts who were forced to deliver soybeans after the termination of trading in the expired futures had no choice except to buy them in the seriously under-supplied cash market. In order to obtain deliverable grades, many of the shorts who had failed to offset before the end of the trading had to pay as much as 25¢ per bushel *over the final futures price* to get the supplies they needed. Needless to say, by failing to offset, they sustained even greater losses in meeting their obligations to deliver.

The risks in last-day trading are great — and may be *incalculable;* and taking or making delivery involves both inconvenience and handling costs. A public speculator usually wants no part of either.

Weather Markets

Of all the imponderables which confront producers of growing crops and speculators in the commodities concerned, none is more fraught with uncertainty than weather itself.

It might be said that every crop has its own temperature/moisture combination which represents optimum growing conditions. Anything less than this ideal constitutes a greater or lesser threat to harvest prospects. From the time the new crop goes into the ground as seed until it's finally harvested, growers and traders watch weather developments eagerly—and they *hardly ever like what they see!* Anything which seems to threaten the well-being of the crop will send prices higher—in expectation of some relative shortage. As each successive problem is relieved by moderating temperatures or the arrival

Speculative Pitfalls

of much-needed precipitation, prices which were sent higher by a "weather scare" return to lower levels, in recognition of the fact that the particular danger has passed.

Weather markets usually take their cues from weather averages. This is to say that the trade will view as "normal" the *average* temperature ranges and precipitation, as reported by the U.S. Weather Bureau in a given area over a period of five years or ten years.

The Crop Reporting Service and agricultural extention agencies report intentions, planting progress, and crop development at regular intervals during the planning, planting and growing season. If excessively wet weather interferes with the "normal" planting pattern, a price response can be expected. With the seed in the ground, should dry weather delay germination or wind storms blow the top-soil away and expose the seed, prices will rise in direct response.

If the fields dry out and planting picks up; or should rain or snow fall in adequate amounts to germinate the seed and commence the growing cycle, the market will immediately note this in the form of reduced prices. Downturns always come in the face of conditions which seem to promise an improved or adequate harvest, and vice-versa.

Weather markets offer one of the best demonstrations of the trader's tendency to "over-buy" bad news and "over-sell" good news. The fluctuations in weather market prices can be sharply precipitous, and directional reversals can take place suddenly—either in response to *actual* weather changes, or a change in weather *prospects,* as reflected in overnight, five-day and thirty-day forecasts.

Nature is not really as perverse as weather-market evidence, reflected in commodity prices, would seem to indicate. Each year presents a somewhat different weather pattern in terms of the schedule of arrival followed by precipitation and temperatures; but when each crop year is over, the composite result *usually* varies only slightly from recent historic norms. Wide price aberrations, which are a distinguishing characteristic of weather-markets, grow out of the fact that supply/demand relationships must stay in fairly close equilibrium in order to maintain stable price levels. Any appreciable deviation in crop size brings highly *disproportionate effects* in price levels. It pays to remember, "every crop is usually lost two or three times before it is

284

finally harvested." Don't make *long-term decisions* on what may be only *short-term conditions.*

Weather-markets offer excellent opportunities for short-term trading activity. The recommended procedure is always to "buy dips" and "sell bulges". In view of the highly erratic price behavior which can be encountered during the pre-harvest period when weather is the major price influence, stop-loss orders must be carefully placed on *every position* taken, and adjusted as often as needed. Failure to do so is needlessly courting disaster. Once established, stay with a position until your stop loss is hit. You *may* ride a "weather move" right into a long-term trend, but usually it's shorter-term.

There is no blanket rule as to whether the long or short side of the market should be preferred, except to keep in mind that the major price changes will emanate from *changing* weather conditions. If temperature and moisture has been marginal and prices have risen in response thereto, a continuation of the situation can be expected to *gradually* escalate prices further and—should bad conditions persist, threatening disaster proportions—there is no telling how far they might go. At the *first hint* of a rain storm in the face of unusually dry weather, however, down-side price movement will come suddenly. The drop can cover the equivalent of several percentage points in product price, as the market "discounts" the effects contained in a changing weather pattern.

When weather conditions are good and the situation begins to deteriorate, the market will immediately read "bullish" implications into the change, and firmer prices will promptly result, in accordance with the market's re-evaluation of the overall picture. Remember that prices usually *fall faster than they rise,* though.

Weather markets offer exciting and profitable speculative opportunities, but weather-market prices are *always fickle.* The prudent trader must constantly view the weather-market trading situation as short-term. He must be prepared to take small losses as often as necessary for the privilege of being "on board" for larger profits on major moves. *One* such larger success will more than make up for *several* small disappointments.

Speculative Pitfalls

Trading Dull Markets

A quiet market, like a quiet youngster, is probably up to mischief. Several things may be involved in a market which appears in the doldrums. Whenever prices have been moving in a given direction for a period of time, and at fairly high trading volume levels, the trend usually can be expected to "wear itself out" eventually. A listless trade may signal the coming event.

For example, if corn begins an upward price trend at $1.20 per bushel and over a period of several weeks moves to $1.40 per bushel, it stands to reason that, in the process, the longs who bought at the lower levels will have made substantial profits; the shorts who sold in the face of the events outlined will have sustained equivalent losses.

A time will come when repeatedly disappointed shorts will move to the sidelines, unwilling to assume additional exposures. Some of the longs will provide offerings, as they elect to take their profits from the price move and drop out. But *liquidation on the part of existing longs will not be sufficient, in the absence of a real price reversal, to maintain high volume activity.* As the price move reaches the end of its interim cycle, trading will slow as if reflecting the market's opinion that "the price is about right". There is a trading axiom which usually can be accepted, that "A market which can't go up must go down." This gives rise to another trading rule which can save a speculator impressive amounts of money: *Never "buy" a quiet spell following a price rise.*

Conversely, when prices have been consistently deteriorating over a period of time, disenchanted longs will finally despair of "picking a bottom" and move to the sidelines to await a clear indication of reversal. When this buying is taken out of the market, trading volume will diminish and the only real buying demand will involve shorts who have profited from the down move, and are now ready to cash all or part of their paper profits. When trading volume dries up following a major down move, extreme caution with respect to the establishment of any new short positions is clearly indicated: "A market that can't go down must go up." As a general rule, *never "sell" a dull market which follows a significant downside move.*

286

The foregoing is merely a re-statement of the trading principle noted elsewhere, that it makes good sense to "*sell* bulges" and "*buy* dips". In doing so, however, the trader must always bear in mind that the *dip* or the *bulge* may be a small interval of *fluctuation* in a larger—and continuing—*price trend*. The only protection against this hazard is a well-placed stop-loss order which will close out the position, should prices resume their upward or downward channel after a "breathing spell".

Trade the Big Ones

The best trading markets are the big, active markets. In the first place, they offer the greatest liquidity. They more easily accommodate execution of buying and selling orders, with but minimal impact on price levels. Put another way, an active market has better "muscle tone". It is able to withstand greater counter-forces without being deterred from its price course. A dull market is likely to be a thin market; narrowly balanced on an equilibrium point between extremely limited buying and selling pressures. It may take only a slight nudge in one direction or the other to send prices sharply higher or lower.

If a trader is enamoured of the wispy hope for finding interim "tops and bottoms", *market dullness* is the principal symptom which should be looked for. These are the points in trading from which price reversals usually take place.

Plate 66

When an order reaches the pit it is only identified by a number. Neither the broker who fills it, nor the trader or broker who takes the "other side" knows — or cares — where it originated. All either is concerned about is that someone wants to buy, or wants to sell. For every buyer there must be a seller, and at some price level there always is.

Addendum

Hopefully, both the methods and the usefulness of professional commodity speculation have been clarified in these pages. It should be seen that in selling "short" the speculator is contributing to *demonstrated supply;* in buying "long" he is adding to *demonstrated demand.* Price stands as a measurement of these opposing forces, and the role of the market is to *discover* prices.

The role of the speculator is to *forecast* prices. Thus it must be said that in a given situation, the speculator can only fulfill his economic obligation by selling short. In the opposite frame of reference, he can only meet his economic responsibility by going long.

The question of morality will likely continue to be raised in connection with commodity speculation. Morality, it should now be clear, has little to do with either the form or the practice. Economics is not a moral discipline: High prices are only preferable to low prices when viewed through the eyes of the seller. Milk is worth more than water, because the market is usually willing to pay more for the white liquid. Whiskey is worth more than milk, proven by the fact that it commands a higher price in trade.

All manner of judgments can be made with respect to what is "good for the people", or "good for society", or "constructive" or "destructive". We may do so, but the market has no way to appraise side issues. The market accepts things offered by the sellers, presents them to buyers and discovers the price at which merchandise will change hands. The only valid price in any transaction is the price below which the seller would not sell and above which the buyer would not buy.

Addendum

The buyer of wheat may represent a starving nation and the seller of wheat may hold millions of bushels in storage. The price at which the transaction takes place only measures supply and demand. Conditions under which each trader enters the market are only important insofar as respective urgency may influence the level of their bids and offers. To put it most bluntly, the market can't "feel" hunger, which is merely propensity to consume; unless it is also coupled with *willingness* to buy and *ability* to pay.

Drawing qualitative distinctions between investment and speculation is about as reasonable as attempting to present outright purchase of an asset as being somehow preferable to renting the same facility. Each handling contains elements of both utilitarian strength and weakness, and the approach which is selected should be the one which best suits the needs and the inclinations of the individual concerned.

One last thing can be said, however; and without fear of successful contradiction from any source whatever; free markets have written a record of accomplishment which is unequaled by any form of administered prices, managed production or controlled exchange. Modern commodity markets have made a contribution to national and world well-being which will probably never be fully appreciated unless, on some unfortunate day in the future, commerce becomes the captive of official planners and the search for profit is outlawed in favor of some politically expedient brand of enforced sharing.

It should never be forgotten that the greatest crimes of the 20th Century have been perpetrated under the sweet-sounding economic dogma of Marxist socialism that swears fealty to "the greatest good for the greatest number". Free markets, on the other hand, enable each buyer and seller to pursue his *own* interests, with a decent regard for ethics and legalities.

There can be little room for argument as to which has performed best in the past. Or which offers more for the future of individuals, nations and the world at large.

The End

GLOSSARY

ACCUMULATE — Buying by traders who expect to hold the contracts for a period of time. Building up a position over time.

ACREAGE ALLOTMENT — The limitation on planted acreage established by the government for each farmer, for basic crops.

ACREAGE RESERVE — A part of the farm program which applies to Basic Commodities under which the farmer receives payment from the government for not planting part or all of his acreage allotment.

ACTUALS — The physical commodities, as distinguished especially from futures contracts.

AFLOAT — Grain which is loaded in vessels, in harbor or in transit, but which has not reached its destination and been unloaded.

ARBITRAGE — Simultaneous purchase of cash commodities or futures in one market against the sale of cash commodities or futures in the same or a different market; to profit from a discrepancy in price. Also includes some aspects of hedging. See "SPREAD".

BASIS — The spread or difference between the spot or "cash" price and the price of the near future. Basis may also be used to designate price differentials between "cash" and more distant futures, as well as different locations as specified.

BEAR — One who believes prices are too high and will decline.

Glossary

BEAR MARKET — One where large supplies and/or poor demand cause a decline in price.

BEARISH AND BULLISH — When conditions suggest lower prices, a bearish situation is said to exist. If higher prices appear warranted, the situation is said to be bullish.

BID — A price offered subject, unless otherwise stated, to immediate acceptance for a specific amount of commodity.

BOARD ORDER or **MARKET-IF-TOUCHED (MIT) ORDER** — An order to buy or sell when the market reaches a specific price. A Board-Order to buy becomes a market-order when the commodity sells (or is offered) at or below the order price. A Board-Order to sell becomes a market-order when the commodity sells (or is bid) at or above the order price.

BOARD OF TRADE (CHICAGO) — Licensed contract commodity exchange, located in Chicago, Illinois; affords facilities for both cash and futures trading — primarily in grains.

BOT — Abbreviation for "bought".

BREAK — A sharp price decline.

BROAD TAPE — A teletype reporting system which automatically prints out news, weather, markets, etc., as furnished from professional and government reporting services.

BROKER — An agent entrusted with the execution of an order. He may be employed in the office of the commission house that carries the account or a floor broker or pit broker who actually executes the order on the trading floor. See "CUSTOMER'S MAN".

BROKERAGE — The fee charged by a floor broker for execution of a transaction. The fee may be a flat amount or a percentage.

BROKERAGE HOUSE — See "COMMISSION HOUSE".

BUCKET, BUCKETING — The illegal practice of some brokers in accepting orders to buy or sell without executing such orders. Such a broker hopes to profit by pocketing the loss which a customer may experience when closing out the transaction. If the customer closes out at a profit, the broker pays the profit. The illegality lies in an agent's direct dealing with his principal without disclosing the fact.

BULGE — A sharp price advance.

BULL — One who believes prices are too low and will advance.

BULL MARKET — One where small supplies and/or strong demand cause prices to rise.

BUYING HEDGE — Buying futures to hedge cash sales in present or future. (Also see "HEDGING")

BUYER'S MARKET — A condition of the market in which there is an abundance of goods available and hence buyers can afford to be selective and may be able to buy at less than the price that had previously prevailed. (Cf. seller's market.)

BUY IN — To cover or liquidate a sale.

BUY ON CLOSE OR OPENING — To buy at the end or beginning of a session at a price within the closing or opening range.

CALL — (1) A period in which trading is conducted to establish the price for each futures month at a particular time, i.e. an opening or closing CALL.

(2) **BUYER'S CALL** — Purchase of a specified quantity of a specific grade of a commodity at a fixed number of points above or below a specified delivery month in futures, with the buyer being allowed a certain period of time within which to fix the price by either purchasing a futures for the account of the seller, or indicating to the seller when he wishes to price-fix.

(3) **SELLER'S CALL** — The same as BUYER'S CALL with the difference that the seller has the right of determining the time to fix price.

CALLS AND PUTS — See "PRIVILEGES". (Illegal in regulated commodity markets). "CALL," an option permitting its holder (who has paid a fee for the option) to call for a certain commodity or security at a fixed price in a stated quantity within a stated period. The broker is paid to bring the buyer and seller together. The buyer of this right to call expects the price of the commodity or security to rise so that he can call for it at a profit. If the price falls the option will not be exercised. The reverse transaction is a "put".

CALL LEVEL — The price level at which additional margin money must be put up by the holder of an impaired open position.

CARLOAD — For grains, may range from 1,400 to 2,500 bushels.

CARRYING COSTS — Those charges incurred in warehousing the actual commodity, generally including interest, insurance and storage.

CASH COMMODITY — Physical merchandise; goods available for delivery immediately or within a designated period following sale; includes a commodity bought or sold "to arrive".

CASH FORWARD — Sale of a cash commodity for delivery at a later date.

CASH PRICE — The current bid or offering price for a cash commodity of designated grade, and for immediate delivery.

CASH TRANSACTION — Purchase or sale of physical merchandise; can be in futures.

C.C.C. — The Commodity Credit Corporation.

C.E.A. — The Commodity Exchange Authority.

C.E.C. — Commodity Exchange Commission.

C. & F. (cost and freight) — Cost and freight paid to port of destination.

CERTIFIED STOCK — Stocks of a commodity that have been graded, have passed various tests and found to be of deliverable quality against futures contracts; which are stored at the delivery points and in warehouses designated regular for delivery by the exchange.

CHART — Any of a variety of systems by which prices, output consumption or related considerations may be plotted on paper for ease of visual reference.

CHARTER — An engagement of a vessel to a given destination at a fixed rate.

C.I.F. — Cost, insurance and freight paid (or included) to a port of destination.

CHICAGO BOARD OF TRADE — An organized commodity exchange which houses most of the world's futures trading.

CHURNING — Excessive trading in and out of commodity positions, when doing so has the main objective of generating commissions to the broker.

CLEARANCES — Total marine shipments from domestic and foreign ports.

CLEARING CONTRACTS — The process of substituting principals to transactions through the operation of clearing associations; in order to simplify the settlement of accounts.

CLEARING HOUSE — The (separate) agency associated with a futures exchange through which futures contracts are offset or fulfilled and through which financial settlement is made (also CLEARING ASSOCIATION).

CLEARING MEMBER — A member of the Clearing House or Association. Each clearing member must also be a member of the Exchange. Each member of the Exchange, however, need not be a member of the Clearing Association; if not, his trades must be registered and settled through a clearing member.

CLEARING PRICE — See "SETTLEMENT PRICE".

CLOSE — The period at the end of the trading session during which all trades are officially declared as having been executed "at or on the close". The closing-range is the range of prices on trades made during this designated period.

Glossary

C.O.F.O. — Commercially objectionable foreign odor.

COMMISSION — Fee charged by a broker for performance of specified market functions.

COMMISSION HOUSE — A concern that buys or sells for the accounts of customers. Also called Brokerage House, sometimes Wire House.

COMMODITY — An economic good of broad use and value; as distinguished from a service.

COMMODITY CREDIT CORPORATION (C.C.C.) — A wing of the U. S. Department of Agriculture which functions as the holding and marketing agency in connection with administered farm commodities.

CONSIGNMENT — An unsold shipment of grain placed with a commission man who will offer it for sale.

CONTRACT — (1) A formal multi-lateral agreement between two (or more) parties in interest, and which binds each to certain stipulated performances. In commodity trading, is usually synonymous with "futures contract".

(2) A unit of the commodity being traded. Orders must specify the number of bushels to be bought and sold; also "Round Lots"; Cf.: "Job Lots".

CONTRACT GRADES — The grades of a commodity listed in the Rules of an Exchange as those that can be used to deliver against a futures contract.

CONTRACT MARKET — An organized commodity futures market which qualifies under the Commodity Exchange Act.

CONTRACT MATURITY — Relates to a given month: July, September, March, etc.

CONSERVATION RESERVE — The section of the Soil Bank Program calling for long-term contracts for the conversion of crop land into grasses, trees and water conservation uses.

296

CONTROLLED COMMODITY — Commodities subject to Commodity Exchange Authority regulation; listed in the Commodity Exchange Act. The list is comprised of domestically produced agricultural products.

CORE SAMPLE — See "SAMPLE".

CORNER — (1) To corner is to secure such relative control of a commodity or security that its price can be manipulated.

(2) In the extreme situation, obtaining more contracts requiring the delivery of commodities or securities than the quantity of such commodities or securities actually in existence.

COST OF STORAGE — Rate charged for physical warehousing of a commodity; (may include in or out elevation charges). See "CARRYING CHARGE".

COUNTRY ELEVATOR — A grain elevator located in the immediate farming community to which farmers bring their grain for sale or storage, as distinct from a terminal elevator which is located at a major marketing center.

COUNTRY PRICE — The price which prevails in an area removed from the central market (usually quoted as being "on" or "off" a designated futures price).

COVER — The purchase of futures to offset a previously established short position.

CROP REPORT — Any of several forecasts made by both private and official sources. The major ones emanate from the Crop Reporting Board of the U.S.D.A and equivalent bodies in Canada, and elsewhere.

CROP YEAR — Period used for statistical purposes, from the harvest of a crop to the corresponding period in following year. U. S. wheat crop year begins July 1 and ends June 30; cotton, August 1-July 31; varying dates for other commodities.

CRUDE OIL — Oil which has undergone the first stage(s) of refinement.

Glossary

CRUSH (Soybeans) — The process which converts soybeans into meal and oil. Also, a term used to describe a particular spreading posture between soybeans and products.

CRUSH SPREAD — In soybeans, the purchase of bean futures and simultaneous sale of an equivalent amount of meal and oil futures.

CURRENT DELIVERY — Means delivery during the present month.

CURRENT QUOTATION — The last price, bid or offer on a designated futures, cash, etc.

CUSTOMERS' MAN — An employee of a commission house, also called a broker, account executive, solicitor or registered representative, who engages in soliciting or accepting and handling orders for the purchase or sale or any commodity for futures delivery on or subject to the rules of any contract market and who, in or in connection with such solicitations or acceptance of orders, accepts any money, securities or property (or extends credit in lieu thereof) to margin any trades or contracts that result or may result therefrom. Must be licensed under the Commodity Exchange Act when handling business in commodities covered thereby.

DAILY FLUCTUATION LIMITS — See TRADING LIMITS.

DAY ORDERS — Those limited orders that are to be executed the day for which they are effective, or are automatically cancelled at the close of that day.

DAY TRADER — One who carries no open positions overnight.

DEFERRED — Any contract which matures later than the "nearby".

DELIVERABLE GRADES — See "CONTRACT GRADES".

DELIVERY MONTH — The calendar month during which a futures contract matures.

DELIVERY NOTICE — The notification of delivery of the actual commodity on the contract, issued by the seller of the futures to the Clearing House.

298

DELIVERY POINTS — Those locations designated by commodity exchanges at which a commodity covered by a futures contract may be delivered in fulfillment of the contract.

DELIVERY PRICE — The price fixed by the Clearing House at which deliveries on futures are invoiced and also the price at which the futures contract is settled when deliveries are made.

DESIGNATED MARKETS — (By C.E.A.) See "CONTRACT MARKETS".

DIFFERENTIALS — The price difference between classes, grades and locations of a given commodity or commodities.

DISCOUNT — Applied to cash prices that are below the future, or to deliveries at a lesser price than others (May at a discount under July) or to lesser prices caused by quality differences.

DISCRETIONARY ACCOUNT — An account for which buying and selling orders can be placed by a broker or other person, without the prior consent of the account owner for each such individual order; specific authorization having been previously granted by the account owner.

DISTANT or DEFERRED DELIVERY — Usually means one of the more distant months in which futures trading is taking place. See also, "CASH FORWARD".

DOCKAGE — See "FOREIGN MATERIAL".

ENSILAGE — Chopped animal feed which is stored in bulk — usually in a moist condition.

EVENING UP — Buying or selling to adjust or close out an open market position, also called "offset".

EXCHANGE OF SPOT OR CASH COMMODITY FOR FUTURES — The simultaneous exchange of a specified quantity of a cash commodity for the equivalent quantities in futures; usually instituted between parties carrying opposite hedges in the same delivery month. Also known as "exchange for physical" or "against actuals",

Glossary

or as "giving up futures for cash". In grain, the exchange is made outside the "pit".

EXPELLER PRESS — A machine used in soybean oil extraction.

EX-PIT TRANSACTION — A trade made outside the exchange trading ring or pit which is legal in certain instances. It is primarily used in price-fixing transactions involving the purchase of cash commodities at a specified basis.

EX-STORE — Selling term for commodities in warehouse.

FAMILY FARM — In common usage, a non-specializing farm of modest size which is presumed adequate to support a rural family.

FARM PRICES — The prices received by farmers for their products, as published by the U. S. Department of Agriculture; determined as of the 15th of each month.

F.A.Q. — Fair average quality.

FIBERS — Raw materials, either natural or synthetic, from which a wide range of cloth and other products are fabricated.

FILL-OR-KILL ORDER — A commodity order which demands immediate execution or cancellation.

FIRST NOTICE DAY — The first day on which notices of intentions to deliver actual commodities against futures market positions can be made or received. First notice day will vary with each commodity and exchange. It usually precedes the beginning of the delivery period.

FIXING THE PRICE — The determination of the exact price at which a cash commodity will be invoiced after a "call sale" has previously been made based on a specified number of points "on or off" a specified futures month.

FLAKE — A soybean morsel from which the oil has been extracted.

FLASH — Hand signals used by pit brokers.

FLAT PRICE — Price on a single position; differing from "spread" price, which relates to a dual position.

FLOOR BROKER — Any person who, in or surrounding any pit, ring, post, or other place provided by a contract market for the meeting of persons similarly engaged, executes for others any order for the purchase or sale of any commodity for future delivery on or subject to the rules of any contract market, and who for such services receives or accepts a prescribed fee or brokerage.

FLOOR PHONE MAN — An employee of a brokerage house who serves as the communication link between his firm's office and the brokers in the pits.

FLOOR TRADER — An exchange member who executes his own trades by being personally present in the place provided for futures trading.

F.O.B. — Free on board. Usually covers all delivery, inspection and elevation costs involved in putting commodities on board whatever shipment conveyance is being used.

FORAGE — Natural pasture for livestock.

FOREIGN MATERIAL — Anything other than the designated commodity which is present in a lot.

FORWARD SHIPMENT — A contract covering cash commodities to be shipped at some future specified date.

FREE BALANCE — Margin funds on deposit with a broker, and which are not committed against existing open positions.

FREE MARKET — A theoretical trade situation in which buying and selling decisions, production and use judgments, etc. are un-fettered by any uneconomic considerations such as price controls, export quotas, etc.

FREE SUPPLY — The quantity of a commodity available for commercial sale; does not include government held stocks.

Glossary

FROST-DROP — Planned destruction of a designated portion of a growing crop for the purpose of restricting unwanted production.

FULL CARRYING CHARGE — (1) In market parlance, the cost involved in owning cash commodities over a period of time; including storage, insurance and interest charges on borrowed working capital. (2) In futures, the cost, including all charges, of taking actual delivery in a given month, storing the commodity, and re-delivering against the next delivery month.

FUNDAMENTALIST — A market participant who relies principally on supply/demand considerations in his price forecasting activities; especially one who tends to give "technical" considerations small weight in his decisions.

FUTURES COMMISSION BROKER — See "CUSTOMERS' MAN".

FUTURES CONTRACT — Agreement to buy and receive or sell and deliver a commodity at a future date, with these distinguishing characteristics:
1. All trades in the same contract, such as a 5,000 bushel round lot of grain, have the same unit of trading.
2. The terms of all trades are standardized.
3. A position may be offset later by an opposite trade in the same contract.
4. Prices are determined by trades made by open outcry in the pit within the hours prescribed, or visually posted.
5. The contract has a basic grade, but more than one grade may be deliverable.
6. Delivery is required during designated periods.
7. The trades are cleared through a Clearing House daily. (Traders in cash or spot goods usually refer to sales for shipment or delivery in the futures as "deferred" or "forward" sales. Such sales, however, are not standardized as are futures contracts just described above).

FUTURES PRICE — The price bid or offered for contract grade commodities, for delivery at a specified period in the future.

FUTURES TRANSACTION — Purchase or sale of a futures contract; exchange of a futures position for the cash commodity.

GIVE-UP — This is a contract executed by one broker for the client of another broker, which the client orders turned over to the latter broker. Generally speaking, the order is sent over the leased wires of the first broker who collects a wire toll from the other broker for the use of his facilities.

GOOD-TIL-CANCELLED (G.T.C.) — An order which will remain open for execution at any time in the future until the customer cancels it. For example: Sell one May soybean meal at $66.00 G.T.C.

GRAIN FUTURES ACT — A federal statute which regulates trading in grain futures. Administered by the U.S.D.A. and the C.E.A.

GRAINS — For purposes of the Chicago Board of Trade: Wheat, Oats, Rye, Corn, and Soybeans.

GROSS PROCESSING MARGIN — In the case of soybeans, GPM refers to the difference between the price paid for soybeans and the sum of prices received from the sale of oil and meal products after processing.

GROWTHS — Description of commodity according to area of origin; either refer to country, district or place of semi-manufacture.

G.T.C. — Good til cancelled. Usually refers to open-orders to buy or sell at a fixed price.

HARD SPOT — An interval of strength in the market, usually resulting from considerable buying.

HARDEN — A term indicating a slowly advancing market.

HEAVY — This is applied to a market where there is an apparent number of selling orders overhanging the market without a corresponding amount of buying orders.

Glossary

HEDGER — Usually a dealer in physical commodities who holds positions in futures which are opposite his cash positions: viz:

Long cash corn

Short corn futures

HEDGING — Briefly stated, hedging is the sale of futures against the physical commodity or its equivalent, as protection against a price decline; or the purchase of futures against forward sales or anticipated requirements of the physical commodity, as protection against a price advance.

Hedging on futures markets consists of buying (or selling) futures contracts in the amount to which one is long (or short) the actual commodity. Usually the futures transaction is nearly simultaneous with the spot transaction. Hedgers thereby fix or protect a "carrying charge", a processing margin, etc. The futures hedge is thus a temporary substitute for an ordinary transaction which will occur later. Hedging also provides opportunities for added profit.

HIGH — the highest price posted within the designated period: day, contract, etc.

I.C.C. — Interstate Commerce Commission.

INCENTIVE PAYMENT PLAN — The type of support program used for domestic clip wool in which a cash subsidy is paid to the wool grower based upon his selling price.

IN BOND — An inspected, sealed and cleared shipment, actually in transit or scheduled for export.

INITIAL MARGIN — The amount of money required to bind performance on a newly established futures position. (See VARIATION MARGIN).

INSPECTION — In commodity marketing, an official evaluation procedure which results in a grade or class designation being assigned.

INTER-COMMODITY SPREAD — A multiple position between two substitutive or related commodities; e.g. corn and oats.

INTER-MARKET SPREAD — A multiple position between two exchanges: e.g. Minneapolis wheat/Kansas City wheat.

INTERNATIONAL WHEAT AGREEMENT — A multi-government treaty arrangement which fixes the price of this commodity in international trade between the participating nations.

INTRA-MARKET SPREAD — A multiple position between commodities traded on a single exchange: e.g. Chicago soybeans/Chicago soybean oil.

INVERTED MARKET — A futures market in which the nearer months are selling at premiums to the more distant months; hence, a market displaying "inverse carrying charges". These price relationships are characteristic of situations in which supplies are currently in shortage.

INVESTOR — One who commits capital to a given business proposition, with his hopes for return tied exclusively to interest, dividends, rent, etc.

INVISIBLE SUPPLY — Uncounted stocks in the hands of wholesalers, manufacturers and producers which cannot be identified accurately; stocks outside commercial channels, but available for commerce.

JOB LOT — A unit of trading smaller than the regular round lot, usually, in grains, 1,000 or 2,000 bushels.

JUMPED STOP — See STOP-LOSS ORDER.

LAND-BANK PROGRAM — A government program which seeks to manage agricultural production by taking land out of use or returning it to use, depending on projected needs.

LAST TRADING DAY — The day on which trading ceases for a particular delivery month. All contracts that have not been offset by the end of trading on that day must thereafter be settled by delivery of the actual physical commodity, or by agreement; i.e., "WASH SALES".

LEVERAGE — In speculation, the increased power of money committed in a situation involving margin (which is less than the total value of the property covered in the commitment).

LIFE OF DELIVERY or CONTRACT — The period between the beginning of trading in a particular future to the expiration of that future.

LIMIT-ONLY — In trading, the definite price stated by a customer to a broker restricting the execution of an order to buy for not more than, or to sell for not less than, the stated price.

LIMIT (UP OR DOWN) — The maximum price advance or decline from the previous day's settlement price permitted in one trading session by the rules of the exchange.

LIMITED ORDER — One in which the client sets a limit on the price, as contrasted with a market order.

LIQUIDATION — The closing out of a long position. It is also sometimes used to denote closing out a short position, but this is more often referred to as "covering".

LIQUIDATING MARKET — One in which the predominant feature is longs selling their holdings.

LOAN PRICE — The statutory price at which growers may obtain crop loans from the government.

LOAN PROGRAM — The primary means of Government price support in which the Government lends money to the farmer at a pre-announced price schedule with the farmer's crop as collateral. The primary method by which the government acquires stocks of agricultural commodities. (See NON-RECOURSE LOANS).

LONG HEDGE — The purchase of futures, against sales of cash (usually for deferred delivery).

LONG THE BASIS — This is said of one who has bought cash or spot goods and has hedged them with sales of the futures. He has therefore bought at a certain basis on or off futures and hopes to sell at a better basis with the futures for a profit. (See HEDGING)

LONG SQUEEZE — A market situation in which longs are forced to liquidate in the face of falling prices.

LONG-TERM — A period of time adequate to permit unfolding of major trends in production, consumption, utility patterns, etc.

LOW — The lowest price posted within the designated period: day, contract, etc.

MAINTENANCE MARGIN — Same as VARIATION MARGIN

MARGIN — The amount deposited by buyers and sellers of futures, to insure performance on contract commitments; serves as a performance bond rather than a "down-payment".

MARGIN CALL — A request to deposit either the original margin at the time of the transaction, or to restore the guarantee to "maintenance margin" levels required for the duration of the time the contract is held.

MARGIN FUNDS — Moneys on deposit with a broker (or the Clearing House) to bind performance on commodity futures positions.

MARGIN OF CULTIVATION, EXTENSIVE — The situation in which unit doses of labor and capital applied to less and less productive land finally reach land of such poor quality that the product just pays for the labor and capital.

MARKET ORDER or BOARD ORDER — An order to buy or sell when the market reaches a specified point. A board order to buy becomes a market order when the commodity sells (or is offered) at or below the order price. A board order to sell becomes a market order when the commodity sells (or is bid) at or above the order price.

MARKET PRICE — The price which prevails in the central market, as compared to "country" price.

Glossary

MARKET PSYCHOLOGY — The composite attitude of "bulls" and "bears"; especially as it relates to prospects for price behavior.

MARKET TECHNICIAN — An individual who attempts to forecast prices through evaluation of supply/demand balances, and/or quality and volume of trade, etc.

MARKET TREND — General direction of prices, without regard to short-term fluctuations.

MARKETING QUOTA — A federally enforced restriction on the amount of a commodity that a producer is permitted to sell. Usually conforms to the quantity of wheat, corn, etc., the farmer can grow on his acreage allotment.

MARKETPLACE — Broadly, the area in which buyers and sellers deal in selected goods and in which transportation, exchange of information, common currency and methods of trade are sufficiently uniform to create a more or less distinct economic arena.

MATURITY — The period within which a futures contract can be settled by delivery of the actual commodity; the period between first notice day and last trading day. Often used as a synonym for contract (e.g. July corn maturity, December wheat maturity, etc.)

MEDIUM-RANGE — A period of time sufficient to accommodate fundamental changes in supply/demand balance. Usually one crop-year or less.

MEMBERS' RATE — The commision charge for the execution of an order for a person who is a member of and thereby has a seat on the exchange. It is less than the commission charged to a customer who does not have a seat on the exchange.

MOVING AVERAGE PRICE — A composite of individual prices over a given period of time. Often employed by chartists to define a **price trend,** as compared to short-term price fluctuations.

NEARBY — The futures contract which is nearest to maturity.

NEARBY DELIVERY — Means the nearest traded contract month.

NEGATIVE CARRYING CHARGE — See INVERTED MARKET

NEGOTIABLE WAREHOUSE RECEIPT — Document issued by a "regular" warehouse, which guarantees existence and grade of commodity held in store. Transfer of ownership can be accomplished by endorsement of the warehouse receipt.

NET POSITION — The difference between the open contracts long and the open contracts short, held in any one commodity.

NEW CROP — The projected harvest.

NOMINAL PRICE — A declared price for a futures month. Used at times to designate a closing price when no trading has taken place in that particular contract during the final few minutes of the trading session. It is usually the average between the bid and the asked prices.

NON-RECOURSE LOANS — A loan under the U. S. agricultural program to farmers on the security of surplus crops which are delivered to the government and held off the market. The loan must be liquidated as provided by the government's program but the government has no recourse against the farmer for a deficiency if the security fails to bring the amount of the loan.

NOTICE DAY — Any day on which notices of intent to deliver on futures contracts may be issued.

NOTICE OF INTENTION TO DELIVER — A document furnished by a short-seller indicating his intention to fulfill his contract obligation by delivering cash merchandise.

O.C.O. — One cancels other, in which filling of one order cancels customer's alternative order.

OFF — In quoting the basis, the number of points the cash price will be under a specified futures price. Example: 20 points off December.

OFF THE BOARD — Close of trading in a maturing contract.

Glossary

OFFER — An indication of willingness to sell at a given price. (Opposite of "BID".)

OFFICIAL INSPECTION — See INSPECTION

OFFSET — Usually the liquidation of a long or short futures position by an equal and opposite futures transaction.

OILS — In commodity trading, usually includes soybean oil, cottonseed oil, olive oil and other edible fats that are broadly substitutive.

OLD CROP — The past harvest.

OMNIBUS ACCOUNT — An account carried by one futures commission merchant with another, in which the transactions of two or more persons are combined rather than designated separately and the identity of individual accounts is not disclosed.

ON — In quoting the basis, the number of points the cash commodity is above a specified futures month. Example: 20 points on December.

ON-CONSIGNMENT GRAIN — Usually refers to grain conveyed to a broker for sale in the cash market.

ON THE CLOSE — The last few (two or three) minutes of each trading session (varies).

ON THE OPEN — The initial two or three minutes of trading in each session (varies).

OPEN CONTRACT — Contracts which have been bought or sold, without the transactions having been completed by subsequent sale or re-purchase, or actual delivery or receipt of the commodity.

OPEN-INTEREST — The total of unfilled or unsatisfied contracts, on one side of the market. (In any one delivery month, the short-interest always equals the long-interest, since the total number of contracts sold must equal the total number bought.)

OPEN-ORDER — See GOOD-TIL-CANCELLED

OPEN OUTCRY — Required method of registering all bids and offers in the pits.

OPENING BELL, CLOSING BELL — The signal which begins and ends each trading session on each exchange.

OPENING RANGE-CLOSING RANGE — In open auction with many buyers and sellers, commodities are often traded at several prices at the opening or close of the market. Buying or selling orders at the opening might be filled at any point within such a price range.

OPTION — A term sometimes erroneously applied to a futures contract. It may refer to a specific delivery month, as "the July option". Puts and calls or privileges which are now illegal in regulated commodity exchanges were true options, entailing no delivery obligation. Futures contracts are not options.

ORIGINAL MARGIN — The margin needed to cover a specific new position.

OVER-FILL — A trading error in which an excessive purchase or sale is made.

OVERSOLD or **OVERBOUGHT MARKETS** — When the speculative long-interest has been drastically reduced and the speculative short-interest increases, actually or relatively, a market is said to be oversold. At such times, sharp rallies often materialize. On the other hand, when the speculative long-interest has increased rapidly and the speculative short-interest decreases sharply, a market is said to be overbought. At such times, the market is often in a position to decline sharply.

OVERSUPPLY — A market situation in which available commodities exceed demonstrated demand. Result is usually seen in lowering prices. See UNDERSUPPLY.

PAPER LOSSES — The total extent of impairment in the margin deposited against an open position.

Glossary

PAPER PROFIT — The profit that might be realized if the open contracts were liquidated as of a certain time or at a certain price. Margin requirements are adjusted according to paper profits, hence they are to some extent "real".

PAPER-TRADING — A method by which market trading can be simulated, for purposes of gaining experience and background information in the activities concerned.

PARITY — (A theoretically equal relationship between commodity prices and all other prices.) Equality of relationship. Specifically, in farm program legislation, parity is defined in such a manner that the purchasing power of a unit of the commodity is maintained at the level prevailing during some earlier historical "base period".

PITS — Designated locations on the trading floor where futures trading takes place in particular commodities.

POINT — The minimum price fluctuation in futures. It is equal to 1/100 of one cent in most futures traded in decimal units. In grains it is ⅛ of one cent.

POSITION — To be either long or short in the market.

POSITION LIMIT — The maximum number of contracts one can hold "open" under the rules of the C.E.A.

POSITION TRADER — One who holds a long or short position open overnight or longer; as contrasted to the day trader and the scalper.

POSTED, ON THE BOARD — The point at which a given price, bid or offer is made known to the trade.

PREMIUM — The excess in price at which one delivery or quality of goods is selling over the value of another delivery, or quality, or the price relationship between cash and future.

PRICE AVERAGING — The practice of adding to losing positions; on the theory of "averaging" selling price upward, or buying price downward.

312

PRICE DIP — A sharp price drop.

PRICE FIX — See FIXING THE PRICE

PRICE PLATEAU — An area of congestion in trade where buying and selling forces remain in close balance and create a sideways pattern in a bar-chart.

PRICE RATIONING — The action of higher prices in discouraging consumption and encouraging production; and lower prices in encouraging consumption and discouraging production.

PRICE SPREAD — Price difference between commodities, maturities or geographical locations.

PRIMARY MARKET — The centers to which the producers bring their goods for sale, such as country grain elevators.

PRIVATE WIRE — A leased or owned communication link for the exclusive use of a single individual or brokerage house.

PRIVILEGES — In the stock market, the term for an option contract. See CALL, PUT, SPREAD

PROFESSIONAL SPECULATOR — Anyone who voluntarily owns valuable property over time, or assumes the **risks of such ownership** in the hope of earning a profit through price change.

PROGRAM-TRADING — Pursuit of a speculative program which calls for successive steps at designated price intervals; especially as the practice relates to pyramiding.

PUBLIC ELEVATORS — Grain storage facilities in which space is rented out to whoever wishes to pay for it; where grain is stored in bulk. These are licensed and regulated by the state and/or federal government, and **may** also be approved as regular for delivery on an organized commodity exchange.

PUBLIC SPECULATOR — A private person who trades in futures contracts through a brokerage house.

PURCHASE AGREEMENT — A form of Government price support in which the Government agrees to buy commodities from a farmer at a specified time at a designated loan price.

PURCHASE AND SALES STATEMENT (abbreviated P&S) — A statement sent by a commission merchant to a customer when his futures position has changed. It shows the amount involved, the prices at which the position was acquired and closed out, the gross profit or loss, the commission charges and the net profit or loss on the transaction.

PUTS AND CALLS — See PRIVILEGES. (Illegal in regulated commodity markets.) "Put" — an option permitting its holder to sell a certain commodity at a fixed price for a stated quantity, and within a stated period. Such a right is purchased for a fee paid the one who agrees to accept the goods if they are offered. The buyer of this right to sell expects the price of the commodity to fall so that he can deliver the commodity (the put) at a profit. If the price rises, the option need not be exercised. The reverse transaction is a "call" (q.v.).

PYRAMIDING — Using the profits on a previously established position as margin for adding to that position.

QUICK ORDER — See Fill or Kill Order.

QUOTATIONS — The changing prices on cash and futures.

RANGE — The difference between the highest and lowest prices recorded during a specified trading period.

REACTION — Downward tendency in prices following an advance.

REALIZING — Taking profits.

RECOVERY — Advance after a decline.

REGISTERED REPRESENTATIVE — See CUSTOMERS' MAN

REGULATED COMMODITIES — Those commodities over which the Commodity Exchange Authority has supervision are known as "regulated". This does not mean that the prices are controlled.

The C.E.A. simply concerns itself with the orderly operation of the futures market and at times investigates abnormal price movements. Under the Commodities Exchange Act, approved June 15, 1936, definite regulations were established providing for the safe-guarding of customers' money deposited as margin. Commodities currently supervised by the C.E.A. are wheat, cotton, corn, rice, oats, barley, rye, flaxseed, grain sorghums, bran, shorts, middlings, butter, eggs, potatoes, onions, wool tops, wool futures, lard, tallow, soybean oil, cottonseed meal, cottonseed, peanuts, soybeans and soybean meal.

RESTING ORDER — Instructions to buy at a figure below the present market price or sell at a figure above it.

RESTRICTED STOCKS — "Loan" stocks, etc. A separate segregation which, during recent years of "control", has been applied to supplies officially "off the market" for a definite or indefinite period.

REVERSAL POINT — The point on a price chart at which prices have reversed themselves in the past — and/or in the future are expected to do so.

RING — See PIT

ROUND LOT — A full contract as opposed to the smaller job lot. Round lots of grain are 5,000 bushels.

ROUND TURN — The completion of both a purchase and an off-setting sale or vice versa.

RULES — The regulations governing trading established by each exchange.

SAMPLE — In marketing, one or more units of a product given free (or sold at a price far below market) in order to induce prospective buyers to give it a trial, or to enable them to determine its characteristics by inspection or analysis.

SAMPLE GRADE — In commodities, (except grains) usually the lowest quality acceptable for delivery in settlement of a futures contract.

Glossary

SAMPLING — In statistics and research, a sampling is an approximation of the nature or magnitude of some characteristics of a universe arrived at through actual measurement of some of the individual units or elements of that universe, called a sample, which may be chosen at random or by other criteria.

SCALPER — A speculator operating on the trading floor who provides market liquidity by buying and selling rapidly, with small profits or losses and who holds his position for a short time. Typically, a scalper stands ready to buy at a fraction below the last transaction price, and to sell at a fraction above.

SECURITIES — The various classes of stocks which are issued by corporations and which represent equity ownership in the issuing firms.

SELLER'S MARKET — A condition of the market in which there is a scarcity of goods available and hence sellers can obtain better conditions of sale or higher prices.

SELLER'S OPTION — The right of a seller to select, within the limits prescribed by a contract, the quality of the commodity delivered and the time and place of delivery.

SELLING HEDGE — See HEDGE, HEDGING

SETTLEMENT PRICE — The daily price at which the Clearing House clears all the day's trades; also a price which may be established by the Exchange to settle contracts unliquidated because of Acts of God, such as floods, market congestion or other causes.

SHORT — The selling side of an open futures contract; also refers to a trader whose net position shows an excess of open sales over open purchases.

SHORT HEDGE — Sale of futures against the purchase of cash.

SHORT OF THE BASIS — This is said of a person or firm who has sold cash or spot goods and has hedged them with purchases of futures. He has therefore sold at a certain "basis" and expects to buy back at a better basis for a profit.

SHORT SQUEEZE — A sharp run-up of prices which forces shorts to offset (buy back open positions) in order to avoid larger losses.

SOFTEN — A slowly declining market price.

SOIL BANK — A Government program designated to take farmland out of productive use. The Government pays the farmer to not plant crops; instead, to plant the land in grass or trees.

SOLD OUT MARKET — A market in which liquidation of weakly held contracts has largely been completed and such offerings have become scarce.

SOLICITOR — A member or non-member who solicits business for a member.

SPECULATION — The owning of valuable property over time (or assumption of the **risks** of such ownership) in the hope of profiting from a change in market value.

SPECULATIVE CAPITAL — The portion of a speculator's assets which have been earmarked for use in the risk market.

SPECULATIVE INTERVAL — The period of time left in the life of a contract during which it can be traded; or the period of time which largely governs speculative activities of public speculators, position traders, day traders and scalpers.

SPECULATOR (PROFESSIONAL) — One who voluntarily deals in physical property (or risks) and relies on price change to produce a profit (risk premium) for him.

SPOT COMMODITY — See CASH COMMODITY. Goods available for immediate delivery following sale; improperly used to include a commodity bought or sold "to arrive". Also called "Actuals".

SPOT PRICE — The price at which a physical commodity is selling at a given time and place.

SPREAD or STRADDLE — These terms mean the same thing, but in practice the grain trade uses the term "spread" whereas other commodity interests use the term "straddle". A spread may be defined as the purchase of one futures against the sale of another future of the same commodity or a different commodity in the same or different markets. C.E.A. defines spreading only in terms of the same commodity, whereas exchanges define it to include different but related commodities.

STIPULATION OF COMPLIANCE — In commodity usage, formal assurance on the part of an individual or firm that an administrative request or order from C.E.A. or other regulative body will be followed.

STOCK SPECIALIST — Securities market principal who is required to buy or sell whenever public offerings to buy or sell are inadequate to maintain an orderly market.

STOCKPILE COMMODITIES — Commodities which are accumulated and held under government programs; gold, wheat, butter, etc.

STOP-ORDER or **STOP-LOSS-ORDER** — An order entered to buy or sell when the market reaches a specified point. A stop-order to buy becomes a market-order when the commodity sells (or is bid) at or above the stop-price. A stop-order to sell becomes a market-order when the commodity sells (or is offered) at or below the stop-price. The purpose of a stop-loss-order is to limit losses or protect a profit.

STRADDLE — See SPREAD

STRONG HANDS — Usually refers to commercial hedgers and well-financed professional speculators — who are hard to "shake loose" from an established market posture.

SUBSIDY — A sum of money offered by government to assist in the establishment or support of an enterprise or program which is considered to be in the public interest.

SUPPLY/DEMAND BALANCE — The known or estimated adequacy of supplies, in light of known or projected needs. Also called supply/demand equilibrium.

SWITCH — The liquidation of a position in one future of a commodity and the simultaneous reinstatement of such positions in another future of the same commodity. It may be done "at market" or at a specified difference.

TAPE TRADER — A speculator who follows current market prices somewhat constantly on a "ticker" or some other quotation device.

TECHNICAL RALLY (OR DECLINE) — A price movement resulting from conditions developing within the futures market itself and not dependent on outside supply and demand factors. These conditions would include changes in the open interest, volume, degree of recent price movement and approach of First Notice Day.

TENDER — Delivery against a futures position.

TERMINAL ELEVATOR — A grain storage facility at one of the major centers of agricultural product marketing.

TICKER TAPE — A stock or commodity quotation system. See BROAD TAPE.

TIME-LIMIT ORDER — An order to buy or sell, when time-of-day is the controlling consideration.

TRACK-COUNTRY-STATION — Usually involves a price designation; indicates the cost of a given commodity loaded in rail-car and ready for shipment from an interior location.

TRADING LIMIT — In virtually all North American commodity contracts there is a maximum price change permitted for a single session. These limits vary in the different markets. After prices have advanced or declined to the permissible daily limits, trading automatically ceases unless, of course, offers appear at the permissible upper trading limit or bids appear at the permissible lower limit.

TRADING RANGE — The interval between the highest and lowest price on a given contract or classification of goods, in a designated period: daily, weekly, life-of-contract, etc.

Glossary

TRADING RULES — Usually refers to the Rules and Regulations of an organized exchange, and which govern activities of both members and non-members who trade in the particular market.

TRADING SESSION — The period from the opening to the close, on a single day.

TRANSFER NOTICE OR DELIVERY NOTICE — A written announcement issued by a seller signifying his intention of making delivery in fulfillment of a futures contract. The recipient of the notice may make a sale of the future and transfer the notice within a specified time to another party on some exchanges directly, and on others through the Clearing association. The last recipient takes delivery of the commodity tendered. Notices on some exchanges are not transferable.

TREND — The direction in which prices are moving.

TRIER — See SAMPLE

UNDER-FILL — A trading error in which a smaller than intended purchase or sale is made.

UNDERSUPPLY — A situation in which demand for a commodity exceeds physical stocks offered for sale in the market. Result is usually seen in rising prices. See OVERSUPPLY

U.S.D.A. — United States Department of Agriculture

VARIATION MARGIN — The amount of money required to be kept constantly on deposit throughout the period a futures position remains "open", as a binder of performance on the contract.

VARIATION MARGIN CALL — A request for additional margin funds as collateral; occasioned by negative price movement against the held position.

VISIBLE SUPPLY — The amount of a particular commodity in store at loading centers. In the grain markets, the total stock of grain in store, in public and some private elevators in the principal primary markets, plus certain stock afloat.

VOLUME OF TRADING — The purchases and sales of a commodity future during a specified period. Inasmuch as purchases equal sales, only one side is shown in published reports.

WAREHOUSE RECEIPT — A document evidencing possession by a warehouseman (licensed under the U. S. Warehouse Act, or under the laws of a state) of the commodity named in the receipt. Warehouse receipts, to be tenderable on future contracts, must be negotiable receipts covering commodities in warehouses recognized for delivery purposes by the Exchange on which such futures contracts are traded.

WASH SALES — Fictitious transactions contrived by two or more brokers in order to create a market price for a security or for tax evasion. It may also consist of two or more outside operators who match their orders for purchase and sale so that a seeming market activity is given to stock. Illegal and prohibited by law and by the exchanges. Tax law usually considers a repurchase within 30 days at a loss to be a wash sale. In commodity futures, contracts left open after the last day of trading may be settled by "wash sales" in lieu of delivery.

WEAK HANDS — Usually refers to poorly capitalized public traders who cannot be expected to "stick to their guns" in the face of adverse price movement.

WEATHER MARKET — A market characterized by erratic price behavior based largely on weather developments or weather prospects, viz-a-viz particular growing crops, delivery conditions, etc.

WIRE HOUSE — Refers to a commission house with branch offices connected by telephone, teletype, telegraph or cable.

WORLD MARKET — Total global supply and demand; subject to such trading barriers as are erected by governments, from time to time.

Appendix

1967 UNITED STATES
CROP REPORTING DATES

Release Dates vary slightly from year to year.
(Released at 3:00 P.M., E.S.T., or 2:00 P.M., C.S.T.)

Mar. 20—Prospective plantings for 1967 as indicated by reported intentions for corn, durum wheat, other spring wheat, oats, barley, flaxseed, cotton, all sorghums, and soybeans; acreage for harvest of hay.

Apr. 10—Indicated production of winter wheat; indicated percentage of winter wheat seedings harvested for grain, United States; condition of rye and pasture; stocks of corn, wheat (all and durum), oats, barley, rye, flaxseed, soybeans, and sorghum grain on farms as of April 1.

May 10—Acreage remaining for harvest as of May 1, yield per acre and indicated production of winter wheat; percentage of winter wheat seedings harvested for grain for United States; condition of rye, hay, and pasture; stocks of hay on farms.

Crop Reporting Dates

June **9**—Indicated yield per acre as of June 1 for winter wheat; indicated production of winter wheat, spring wheat, condition of rye, hay, and pasture.

July **11**—Stocks of corn, wheat (all and durum), oats, barley, rye, flaxseed, soybeans, and sorghum grain on farms as of July 1, planted acreage of corn, winter wheat, durum wheat, other spring wheat, oats, barley, flaxseed, soybeans, peanuts, and sorghums; acreage for harvest, indicated yield per acre as of July 1, and indicated production of corn for grain, winter wheat, durum and other spring wheat, oats, barley, rye, flaxseed, and hay; acreage for harvest of soybeans for beans, and sorghums; indicated production of wheat by classes; condition of pasture.

Aug. **10**—Indicated yield per acre as of August 1 and indicated production of corn for grain, winter wheat, durum and other spring wheat, oats, barley, rye, flaxseed, soybeans for beans, and hay; indicated production of wheat by classes; condition of pasture.

Sept. **11**—Stocks of soybeans on farms as of September 1; indicated yield per acre as of September 1 and indicated production of corn for grain, winter wheat, durum and other spring wheat, oats, barley, flaxseed, sorghums for grain, hay, and soybeans for beans; acreage for harvest of sorghums for grain; indicated production of wheat by classes (U. S.); condition of pasture.

Oct. **10**—Stocks of corn, wheat (all and durum), oats, barley, sorghum grain, rye, and flaxseed on farms as of October 1; indicated yield per acre and indicated production of corn for grain, all wheat, durum and other spring wheat, flaxseed, sorghums for grain, hay, and soybeans for beans; indicated production of wheat by classes (U. S.); condition of pasture.

Nov. **9**—Indicated yield per acre as of November 1 and indicated production of corn for grain, sorghums for grain, soybeans for beans; condition of pasture.

Dec. 19—Annual summary of acreage, yield per acre, production of all crops for 1967 with comparisons.

Dec. 20—Seeded acreage and indicated production of winter wheat; and seeded acreage and condition of rye for crop of 1968.

(Note) On or about January 10, 1968 stocks of corn for grain, wheat, oats, barley, rye, soybeans and hay on farms as of January 1, 1968 will be reported.

1967 OILSEEDS REPORTS

Jan. 10—Soybeans for beans and flaxseed stocks on farms Jan. 1, with comparisons.

Jan. 24—Soybean and Flaxseed stocks in all positions. Reports as of Jan. 1.

Mar. 20—Prospective plantings for 1967—Flaxseed, Soybeans and Peanuts.

Apr. 10—Farm stocks Soybeans. Report as of Apr. 1.

Apr. 24—Soybean and Flaxseed stocks in all positions. Report as of Apr. 1.

July 11—Farm stocks Soybeans, Report as of July 1.

July 11—Acreage for harvest. Report as of July 1.

July 11—Indicated production Flaxseed; Planted acreage. Report as of July 1.

July 11—Acreage Peanuts; condition. Report as of July 1.

July 11—Revised estimates of the 1967 Peanut crop. Report as of July 1.

July 24—Soybean and Flaxseed stocks in all positions. Report as of July 1.

Aug. 10—Indicated production Flaxseed, Peanuts picked and threshed; Indicated production of Soybeans. Report as of Aug. 1.

Sept. 11—Indicated production Flaxseed, Soybeans, Peanuts. Report as of Sept. 1.

Sept. 11—Stocks of soybeans on farms.

Sept. 25—Stocks of soybeans in all positions.

Oct. 10—Farm stock Flaxseed; indicated production Flaxseed, Soybeans for Beans and Peanuts picked and threshed. Report as of Oct. 1.

Oct. 24—Flaxseed stocks in all positions.

Nov. 9—Indicated production Soybeans, Peanuts picked and threshed. Report as of Nov. 1.

Dec. 19—Annual production Soybeans, Peanuts and Flaxseed, Final. 1967 with comparisons.

SOYBEAN AND SOYBEAN PRODUCTS

Monthly reports are issued which include Soybean receipts at mills, crushed or used and Oil Mill Stocks of Soybeans on end of month. Exact publication dates for these reports are not available, but they are released approximately 23 days after the close of the reporting period.

This report also shows Soybean Oil Factory Production, Factory Consumption, factory and warehouse stocks on end of month. Soybean Meal Production, Shipments and Transfers, end of month stocks.

OTHER REPORTS
CONCERNING U.S. CROP PRODUCTION

Wheat Stocks on farms and off farms in all positions; Rye stocks in all positions: 3:00 P.M., E.S.T. January 24, April 24, July 24, and October 24.

Corn, Oats, Barley, and Sorghum Grain Stocks in all positions with comparisons, January 24, April 24, July 24 and October 24.

Soybean and Flaxseed Stocks in all positions: January 24, April 24, July 24 and Soybeans Sept. 25. Flaxseed Oct. 24.

1967 REPORTS ON COTTON

(Released at 11:00 A.M., E.S.T. or 10:00 A.M., C.S.T.)

May 8—Acreage, yield per acre, production of cotton lint and seed, value of production of lint, disposition and value of cottonseed, monthly marketing by farmers.

July 10—Acreage of cotton in cultivation on July 1.

Aug. 8—August 1, indicated yield per acre, indicated production and acreage for harvest.

Sept. 8—September 1, indicated yield per acre, indicated production.

Dec. 8—Yield per acre as of December 1, probable production, acreage for harvest, planted acreage, production of cottonseed.

GINNING REPORTS

Date of Report		Report as of Close of Business	
August (1967)	8	July (1967)	31
August	23	August	15
September	8	August	31
September	25	September	15
October	9	September	30
October	25	October	17
November	8	October	31
November	21	November	13
December	8	November	30
December	20	December	12
January (1968)	23	January (1968)	15
March (1968)	20	End of season	

Cotton Production in the United States. Crop of 1966.—Annual bulletin containing statistics on cotton production and ginnings, and active and idle gins, by States and counties, to be issued in July or August, 1967.

Crop Reporting Dates

Cotton Production and Distribution. Season 1965-1966—Annual bulletin, containing statistics on United States production, consumption and stocks, imports and exports of cotton, cottonseed and cottonseed products expected to be issued in summer of 1967.

Cottonseed and cottonseed products.—Monthly reports are issued on fats and oils which include receipts, crushings, and stocks of cottonseed and on production, shipments, and stocks of cottonseed products at mills. Exact publication dates for these reports are not available, but they are released in approximately 23 days after the close of the reporting period.

Poultry and Egg Production—Monthly. Numbers of layers on hand during month, eggs per 100 layers, total eggs produced by States, issued with monthly 'Crop Production' report, also numbers of layers and rate of egg production per 100 layers as of first of month by geographic divisions and United States.

BUTTER

Weekly creamery butter production—Tuesday of each week. Monthly creamery butter production by states: Jan. 26, Feb. 24, March 24, April 26, May 26, June 27, July 26, Aug. 25, Sept. 27, Oct. 26, Nov. 28 and Dec. 27.

AGRICULTURAL PRICES

Prices received by farmers for principal crops and livestock products, Index Numbers of Prices Received by Farmers, Prices Paid for feed, seed and other items bought by farmers, Indexes of Prices Paid by Farmers for Articles Bought and Parity Prices: January 30, February 28, March 30, April 28, May 31, June 29, July 31, August 30, September 29, October 30, November 30, and December 29.

Annual Summary—May or June.

CANADIAN
CROP REPORTING CALENDAR, 1967

Mar. 17—Intended Acreage of Principal Field Crops.

Apr. 14—Stocks of Grain on March 31.

May 10—Telegraphic Crop Report—Canada.

May 17—Telegraphic Crop Report—Prairie Provinces.

May 24—Telegraphic Crop Report—Prairie Provinces.

June 7—Telegraphic Crop Report—Canada.

June 14—Progress of Seeding: Winter-killing and Spring Condition of Winter Wheat, Fall Rye, Tame Hay and Pasture; Rates of Seeding.

June 21—Telegraphic Crop Report—Prairie Provinces.

July 5—Telegraphic Crop Report—Canada.

July 12—Telegraphic Crop Report—Prairie Provinces. (Including preliminary acreage report Prairie Provinces.)

July 19—Telegraphic Crop Report—Canada.

Aug. 4—Preliminary Estimate of Crop and Summer Fallow Acreages.

Aug. 9—Telegraphic Crop Report—Prairie Provinces.

Aug. 18—Stocks of Grain at July 31.

Aug. 23—Telegraphic Crop Report—Canada.

Sept. 1—August Forecast of Production of Principal Field Crops.

Sept. 13—Telegraphic Crop Report—Canada.

Oct. 4—September Forecast of Production of Principal Field Crops.

Nov. (date uncertain)—November Estimates of Production of Principal Field Crops, Area and Condition of Fall Sown Crops. Progress of Harvesting in the Prairie Provinces.

1967 REPORTS ON LIVESTOCK

(All Washington, D.C. reports released at 12:00 Noon except slaughter reports, which are released at 3:00 P.M.)

Jan. 13—Sheep and Lambs on Feed January 1, 1967. Number on feed, by States.

Feb. 13—Livestock and Poultry Inventory, January 1, 1967. Number, value, and classes by States.

Feb. 21—Calf Crop, 1966. Number of calves born during the year, by States.

Feb. 23—Lamb Crop, 1966. Number of lambs saved during the year, by States.

Mar. 14—Sheep and Lambs on Feed and Early Lamb Crop, 1967.

Apr. 24—1966 Revisions Commercial Slaughter by States and by Months and Total Livestock Slaughter, Meat, and Lard Production by Quarters.

Apr. 27—Meat Animals—Farm Production, Disposition and Income 1966. Data by States.

June 21—Pig Crop Report: December-May pig crop of 1967, and 1967 June-November farrowings indicated by breeding intentions, by States.

July 21—Lamb Crop, 1967. Number of lambs saved during the year, by States.

July 24—Calf crop, 1967. Expected number of calves born and to be born during the year, by States.

Nov. 14—Sheep and Lambs on Feed November 1, 1967. 7 States.

Dec. 22—Pig Crop Report: June-November pig crop of 1967, and December-May farrowings in 1968 indicated by breeding intentions, by States. Pig Crop Report: (Quarterly). Sows farrowing and inventory numbers, 10 States. March 21, June 21, September 21, December 22.

Crop Reporting Dates

Commercial Livestock Slaughter and Meat Production. Number of head and live weight of cattle, calves, hogs, sheep and lambs slaughtered in commercial plants by States, Meat Production by species and Lard Production for the United States: January 30, February 28, March 31, April 28, May 31, June 30, July 28, August 31, September 28, October 30, November 30, December 29.

Cattle and Calves on Feed as of 1st of the Quarter. Total number on feed by States; number on feed by classes, by weight groups, and by length of time on feed, leading States. Cattle sold for Slaughter at Selected Markets: January 17, April 18, July 18, and October 17.

Cattle and Calves on Feed as of 1st of the Month. Total number on feed in selected States. Cattle sold for Slaughter at Selected Markets; January 17, February 10, March 10, April 17, May 12, June 13, July 17, August 11, September 13, October 17, November 14, and December 12.

Shipments of Stocker & Feeder Cattle & Sheep. Number received in several Corn Belt States from Public Stockyards and directs during the preceding month by States. Monthly shipments from Public Stockyards by market origin and State of destination: January 26, February 24, March 24, April 25, May 25, June 26, July 25, August 25, September 25, October 26, November 24, December 26. Annual report of monthly data for 1966 in monthly issue of January 26.

Western Range and Livestock Report. Condition of ranges, cattle, and sheep, first of month by States, Western States: January 11, February 9, March 9, April 12, May 12, June 13, July 13, August 9, September 13, October 12, November 8, December 13.

Special Wheat Pasture Report: September 22, October 25, November 27, December 27.

1967 CROP WHEAT LOAN PROGRAM

Major provisions of the 1967 wheat program were announced on June 9, 1966 and are similar to those in effect for this year's program. The main features of the 1967 program compared with those for 1966 are:

1. Price-support loan level will be $1.25 per bushel; this is the same as for 1966.

2. Domestic marketing certificates on an estimated 520 million bushels will be valued at the difference between full parity as of July , 1967, and the $1.25 loan value, following the same formula in effect for 1966. (The certificate value for the 1966 crop, computed under this same formula, is $1.32 per bushel).

3. Marketing certificates to be issued represent expected production on 40 percent of the farm allotments on cooperating farms, which reflect the increased 1967 national allotment of 59.3 million acres announced on May 5. (For 1966, this allocation percentage was 45 percent on an effective national allotment of 51.6 million acres.) It not less than 90 percent of the farm's allocated acreage is planted, the producer is eligible for the full amount of certificates as in 1966.

4. Program participation requirements for 1967 will be the same as in 1966 except that there will be no required or additional diversion. (In 1966, a producer was required to set aside an acreage equivalent to 15 percent of his 1966 allotment. In addition, he could make a voluntary diversion of winter wheat up to 50 percent of the farm allotment or 25 acres, whichever was larger. For such diversion, wheat producers received a national average payment of about $15.65 per acre on 2.4 million acres.) Wheat growers, in order to be eligible for the price support loan, need to remain within their allotments and to cooperate in the program. By participating, they not only quality for price-support loans and purchases but also for domestic marketing certificates. Requirements for compliance between programs and farms also will be the same as in

1966. Since there will be no acreage diversion under the 1967 program, the production of alternate non-surplus crops will not be possible as was the case in earlier wheat programs. The Cropland Adjustment Program (CAP) as it applies to wheat will be announced later.

5. Wheat may continue to be planted on feed grain acreage on farms participating in both programs and feed grains may be planted on wheat allotment acreage. Producers will be able to substitute wheat for oats and rye on the same basis as in the 1966 program.

6. The "excess-wheat option" contained in the 1966 program will be continued in 1967. Under this option, a producer can plant in excess of his allotment acreage and be eligible for certificates and price support loans, provided: The wheat acreage does not exceed the allotment by more than 50 percent, and the excess production is stored and the farmer complies with other terms and conditions similar to those in effect in 1966.

1967 Voluntary Feed Grain Program Announced

With feed grain supply and demand in near-perfect balance, but with increased production needed in 1967, Secretary of Agriculture Orville L. Freeman announced 1967 feed grain program provisions designed to divert about half as many acres as in 1966.

The 1967 program will be basically the same as in previous years, the changes being a higher loan rate, higher total price support, and elimination of voluntary diversion for payment except on small farms which may earn diversion payments higher than in 1966.

"The 1967 feed grain program has these objectives: Improved farm income; livestock prices at a level fair to producers and consumers; full development of our export potential; and maintenance of adequate but not excessive reserves."

U.S. Government Farm Program

Major Provisions of the 1967 Feed Grain Program

1. Acreage. The program encourages farmers to divert 15-18 million acres as compared with 30 million acres of corn and grain sorghum land diverted in 1966.

2. Price support. For corn, the price-support loan is increased from $1 to $1.05, national average, and the payment stays at 30 cents a bushel on the projected yield of acres planted, up to 50 percent of the base acreage. For grain sorghum the loan is increased from $1.52 to $1.61 per hundredweight (national average), and the payment stays at 53 cents, computed as for corn. Loans are again available on all corn and grain sorghum produced on participating farms.

3. Minimum diversion. As in 1966, a farmer will divert 20 percent of his corn-grain sorghum base to qualify for price support payment and loans.

4. Diversion payment for small farms. Program provisions are exactly the same as for 1966; however, payments will be higher. Farms with feed grain bases of 25 acres or less will again be eligible for land diversion payments equal to 20 percent of support (loans plus price support payments for the qualifying diversion) (20 percent of base acreage) and 50 percent of support on any additional acres diverted, up to the total base. Producers who have bases of more than 25 acres and who divert 25 acres and plant no feed grains will be eligible for diversion payment on 5 acres at 20 percent of support and 20 acres at 50 percent of support.

5. Additional diversion for payment on other farms. Except on small farms, there will be no diversion payments. The Department seriously considered recommendations for a provision for additional diversion available to all farmers at a reduced rate. However, in view of the need for increased production and the possibility of encouraging the diversion of too much acreage, and in the interest of program simplicity the payment for additional diversion was dropped from the program.

334

U.S. Government Farm Program

6. Projected yields. Yields will be calculated on an up-to-date basis as provided for in the Food and Agriculture Act of 1965. For corn, the national average projected yield will be 75 bushels per acre as compared to the 72 bushels per acre projected for 1966.

7. Conserving base provisions. Conserving base and acreage substitution features continue as in 1966.

8. Soybean substitution. Soybeans will continue to be eligible for planting on permitted acreage without loss of corn-sorghum price-support payments.

9. Barley. As announced earlier, barley is not included in the 1967 program.

The program signup period began in early 1967. Wheat and cotton program signups will be held concurrently with those for the feed grain program.

1967 Soybean Price Support Level

Soybeans from the 1967 crop will continue to receive price support at $2.50 per bushel.

The 1967 level of soybean price support is 78 per cent of the February 1967 effective parity price of $3.22 per bushel.

Farm value of the 1966 soybean crop is estimated at about $2.7 billion, as compared to $2.2 billion in 1965, $1.8 billion in 1964, and around $1 billion in the late 1950s.

As in recent years, the soybean price-support level for 1967 is expected to be below the average market price.

Eligible producers can receive price support on their 1967-crop soybeans through loans and purchases, either as individuals or through their producer associations. Price support will be available through county ASCS offices. Loans will be available until one month before their July 31, 1968, maturity date.

335

U.S. Government Crop Support Programs for Crops 1966 and 1967

NOTE: See additional Crop Support Payment Data Available to Producers In The Program Diverting Acreages, bottom of page 337.

COMMODITY	Unit	NATL. AVG. FARM L. R. 1966	NATL. AVG. FARM L. R. 1967	APPROXIMATE TERMINAL MARKETS SUPPORT PRICES PRELIMINARY	Grade	1966	1967
WHEAT	Per Bu.	Minimum 1.25	Minimum 1.25	Chicago	No. 1 Hard R.W.	$1.49	$1.47
					No. 1 Soft R.W.	1.49	1.47
				Kansas City	No. 1 H.R.W.	1.43	1.43
					No. 1 S.R.W.	1.43	1.43
				Toledo	No. 2 S.R.W.		
				Minneapolis	No. 1 D.N.S. (Ord. Prot.)	1.56	1.55
				Duluth	No. 1 D.N.S. (Ord. Prot.)	1.56	1.55
RYE	Per Bu.	1.02	1.02	Chicago	No. 2 or better or grading No. 3 on the basis of test weight only.	1.32	1.32
				Minneapolis Duluth		1.23	1.23
				Kansas City		1.22	1.22
				Omaha		1.19	1.19
CORN	Per Bu.	1.00	1.05	Chicago	No. 2	Equivalent 1.12	1.17
OATS	Per Bu.	.60	.63	Illinois Points	Grade No. 3	61-65¢	64-68¢
				Wisconsin Points		59-63¢	62-66¢
				Minnesota Points		50-59¢	53-62¢
				Iowa Points		58-62¢	61-65¢
				So. Dakota Points		50-57¢	53-60¢

Commodity	Unit			Location	Grade		
BARLEY	Per Bu.	.80	.90	Chicago Kansas City Milwaukee Minneapolis	No. 2 or better	1.03 .98 1.03 .99	1.14 1.09 1.14 1.10
GRAIN SORGHUMS	Per Cwt.	1.52	1.61	Omaha Sioux City Kansas City St. Joseph St. Louis	No. 2 or better	1.68 1.64 1.78 1.78 1.92	1.75 1.71 1.85 1.85 1.99
SOYBEANS	Per Bu.	2.50	2.50	Chicago	No. 4 or better. Not more than 14% moisture.	Equivalent 2.70	2.70
FLAXSEED	Per Bu.	2.90	2.90	Minneapolis Los Angeles San Francisco Corpus Christi	No. 1	3.15 3.45 3.39 2.98	3.15 3.45 3.39 2.98
COTTONSEED	Per Ton	48.00 grade (100)	48.00 grade (100)				
COTTON Upland — 1 Inch Middling	Per Pound	21.00	20.25				

Crop Supports Payments To Producers In The Program Diverting Acreages.
1966 CROPS: Wheat per Bushel 75¢ for 45% domestic allotment. Corn per Bushel 30¢, Oats none, Rye none, Barley 20¢, Cotton 10.5¢ per pound for domestic allotment, Grain Sorghums Support Payment 53¢ per cwt., Soybean feed program participants may plant Soybeans on feed acreage and also receive the price support payments they would have earned if feed grains were planted.
1967 CROPS: Wheat per Bushel July 1 parity price minus loan rate $1.25. Corn 30¢ per Bushel, Oats none, Rye none, Barley none, Cotton 11.5¢ per pound domestic allotment and grain sorghums 53¢ per cwt.

U.S. Government Crop Support Programs
Crops 1966 and 1967

COMMODITY	Grades Eligible for Loan	Support is Available from Harvest through	Loans Mature
WHEAT	No. 3 or better or may grade No. 4 or 5 on the grading factor of test weight only.	Most States MARCH 31 Some States APRIL 30	Most States APRIL 30 Some States MAY 31
RYE	No. 4 on test weight only, and No. 3 or 4 on account of thin or smaller kernal grain.	MARCH 31	All States APRIL 30
CORN	All Grades	JUNE 30	All States JULY 31
OATS	No. 3 or better or No. 4 on test weight only.	Most States MARCH 31 Some States APRIL 30	Most States APRIL 30 Some States MAY 31
BARLEY	No. 2 or better	Most States MARCH 31 Some States APRIL 30	Most States APRIL 30 Some States MAY 31
GRAIN SORGHUMS	No. 2 or better	Most States JUNE 30 Some States MAY 31	JULY 31 All States Except JUNE 30 Oklahoma and Texas
SOYBEANS	No. 4 or better. Not more than 14% moisture.	JUNE 30	All States JULY 31
FLAXSEED	No. 2 or better	Most States MARCH 31 Some States APRIL 30	Most States APRIL 30 Some States MAY 31
COTTONSEED	Basis Grade (100) Farm Stored	Earliest Date Of Ginning Through February	JULY 31 Or May Be Called Earlier
COTTON Upland 1 Inch Middling	All grades based on grade staple and location		

338

CURRENT AND PREVIOUS YEARS PRICE-SUPPORT PROGRAMS

WHEAT — CORN — OATS

Crop	WHEAT Nat'l. Average Support Price Farm Basis Per Bushel	WHEAT (4) Quantity Placed Under Loan M. Bushels	WHEAT Wtd. Average Price Received By Farmers Per Bushel	CORN Nat'l. Average Support Price Farm Basis Per Bushel	CORN (4) Quantity Placed Under Loan M. Bushels	CORN Wtd. Average Price Received By Farmers Per Bushel	OATS Nat'l. Average Support Price Farm Basis Per Bushel	OATS (4) Quantity Placed Under Loan M. Bushels	OATS Wtd. Average Price Received By Farmers Per Bushel
1956	(2) $2.00	253,232	1.97	(2) $1.50	477,330	1.29	$ .65	36,122	.69
1957	(2) 2.00	256,333	1.93	(2) 1.40	369,026	1.11	.61	61,751	.61
1958	(2) 1.82	609,469	1.75	(2) 1.36	381,000	1.12	.61	84,598	.58
1959	1.81	317,451	1.76	1.12	529,467	1.04	.50	8,316	.65
1960	1.78	424,027	1.74	1.06	637,790	99.7	.50	19,670	.60
1961	1.79	271,200	1.83	1.20	658,576	1.08	.62	20,611	.64
1962	2.00	299,700	2.04	1.20	590,788	1.10	.62	32,017	.62
1963	1.82	172,366	1.85	1.07	395,000	1.11	.65	38,881	.62
1964	1.30	197,800	1.37	1.10	215,700	1.17	.65	42,600	.63
1965	1.25	169,900	1.35	1.05	214,900	1.16	.60	42,470	.62
1966	1.25	(1) 128,640	1.64	1.00	(1) 229,100	1.29	.60	(1) 21,621	.67
1967	1.25			1.05			.63		

CURRENT AND PREVIOUS YEARS PRICE-SUPPORT PROGRAMS

Crop	SOYBEANS Nat'l. Average Support Price Farm Basis Per Bushel	(4) Quantity Placed Under Loan M. Bushels	Wtd. Average Price Received By Farmers Per Bushel	RYE Nat'l. Average Support Price Farm Basis Per Bushel	(4) Quantity Placed Under Loan M. Bushels	Wtd. Average Price Received By Farmers Per Bushel	GRAIN SORGHUMS Nat'l. Average Support Price Farm Basis Per Bushel	(4) Quantity Placed Under Loan M. Bushels	Wtd. Average Price Received By Farmers Per Bushel
1956	$2.15	65,729	2.18	$1.27	3,170	1.16	$1.97	39,799	2.05
1957	2.09	90,552	2.07	1.18	7,665	1.08	1.86	293,407	1.74
1958	2.09	140,208	2.00	1.10	10,148	1.02	1.83	275,775	1.78
1959	1.85	52,384	1.96	.90	1,157	1.00	1.52	115,069	1.53
1960	1.85	25,617	2.13	.90	5,000	.88	1.52	202,884	1.49
1961	2.30	132,508	2.28	1.02	1,646	1.01	1.93	196,327	1.80
1962	2.25	68,759	2.34	1.02	6,114	.95	1.93	219,400	1.82
1963	2.25	72,829	2.51	1.07	1,549	1.08	1.71	141,400	1.74
1964	2.25	28,700	2.62	1.07	5,257	1.03	1.77	82,800	1.87
1965	2.25	86,509	2.54	1.02	5,850	.97	1.65	106,000	1.79
1966	2.50	(1)147,471	2.80	1.02	(1)2,157	1.08	1.52	(1)27,000	1.86
1967	2.50	......	......	1.02	......	......	1.61	......	......

(1) Through March 1967   (2) Commercial area.
(4) NOTE: Quantity placed under loan includes purchase agreements.

340

INDEX

Price, as cash-price reference, 109-110
Trading volume, unlimited, 34

G

Gambling vs. speculation, 1-2
Geographic price differentials, 104-108, 226
Glamour commodities, 83-84
Glossary, 291-321
Good-till-Cancelled (G. T. C.) order, 239
Government:
  Crop reports, 188, 323-331
  Policy, as price influence, 61-63, 70, 72
Grain market development, 18-19
Grain speculation, origin, 20
Gross Processing Margin (GPM), 233-234

H

Harvest, variability of, 206
Hedge:
  As substitute purchase, 106-108
  As substitute sale, 106-108
  "Basis," in decision-making, 111-114, 229
Hedgers, delivery choices, 35
Hedgers, use of the market, 5, 103, 111-114, 210
Hedging, as a selective practice, 110
History, as base for price analysis, 80

I

Ideological alignments, effects on trade, 76
Impatience, dangers of, 139
Insurance companies, speculative activity, 7

Inter-commodity spreading, 233-235, 245
Inter-market spreading, 104-108, 226, 232, 244-245
Internal Revenue Service, 136
International:
  Export subsidies, 69
  Prices, 70
  Wheat Agreement, 69
Inverses, possible extent of, 112-114, 232, 236
Investment vs. speculation, 1

J

Job-lot orders, 238

K

Kill-or-Fill order, 241

L

Last days of contract life, trading, 212, 281-282
Letters of Franchise, 15
Leverage, effect in pyramiding, 145, 271
Long-range speculative policy, 56-57
Long-squeeze, 99, 213
Long-term analysis, 68 et seq.
Losing position, close-out, 139

M

Manipulation, public and private, 76 et seq.
Margin:
  Amounts required, 42-45, 53, 250, 266
  Calls, answering, 266
  Funds, safety with broker, 257
  To bind performance, 19
  Varying broker policies, 250

Price behaviour:
  Cyclical, 55 et seq.
  Seasonal, 115, 229
Price:
  Convergence principle, 28
  Differentials between futures, 133-134
  Inversions, 132-136, 236
  Leadership in the market, 28-29
  Levels, as trading guide, 155
  Limit-order, 239
  Rationing, 73, 113-115, 227-229
  Relationships, inre supply/demand, 30
  Relationships, as speculative opportunity, 225, et seq.
  Reversal points, 143, 189
  "Tops" and "bottoms," 195
Prices, movement in "concert," 107
Priorities of use, related to price, 73
Production calendars, commodities, 79
Profit objective, in new position, 137
Profit, objective of all business, 47
Profit-seeking, morality of, 7
Public-interest, effects on prices, 96-98, 101
Public, tendency to be "long," 84, 96-98
Pyramiding, 191, 195

Q

Quality of news, as price influence, 83
Quality of trade decisions, relative, 65, 93
Quick-order (Fill-or-Kill), 241

R

Relative scarcity, normal condition, 37
Resting orders, 92
Reverse-crush, 233
Reversing position in market, 272
Risk-area concept, margin, 49-50, 54
Risk:
  Capital management, 128, 196
  Evaluation, 146-149
  Insurance, 5
  Shifting, 5
Risk-margin, earned by bearers, 6
Robber-baron, 14

S

Seasonal balance in hedging, 111-114, 210
Seasonal price behaviour, 55, 152
Securities, broker loans, 48
Securities vs. commodities margins, 47
Segregation, commodity margins, 257
Sell and buy situations, selection, 99-101, 192
Sellers' market, 16
  c.f. Buyers market, 16
Selling bulges, 194, 286-287
Selling weakness, 193
Short-range tactics, 58, 91 et seq.
Short-selling, 213, 270-271, 281-282, 286
Short-squeeze, 99, 213
Soybeans:
  Crush capacity, 80
  1965 crop and futures volume, 34
  Production trend, 80
  Recuperative abilities, 86

345

Specific-time-expiration order, 239
Speculation:
  Defined, 1, 288-289
  Effects of, 8-9
  In securities and commodities, 49
  Insurance simile, 22
  Nature of, 6
  Requirements for, 148
Speculative pitfalls, 263 et seq.
Speculative:
  Profits, a risk premium, 31
  Record-keeping, 130 et seq.
Speculator:
  Function, 121, 289
  Interests, 2-3
  Usually offsets, 35
  vs. hedger, 149
Special trading situations, 205 et seq.
Spot markets:
  Inefficiencies, 13-14
  Trade Fairs, 14
Spreading:
  Margin requirements, 235
  In normal market, 230
  In inverted market, 230-231
  Intra-market, 115-118
  Intra-market, 115-118, 232
  Inter-commodity, 115-118, 232-235
  Order placement, 243-244
Statistical projection, 55
Stock, as inflation hedge, 3
Stop-limit order, 240
Stop-loss:
  Moving the order, 196, 268
  On profitable position, 240, 272
  Placement, 138
  Use in market, 240
Stop-order, 240

Stoppages in distribution channels, 29, 72-73, 135
Strong-hands, in the market, 97-99
Supply/demand:
  As price determinant, 36
  Imbalances, regional, 222-226, 227-229
Surplus/deficit balancing, 26, 115-118, 227-229

T

Technical factors, effect on prices, 96-101
Ticker equipment, 92
Time, as risk element, 104
Time, price differentials, 225
Time dimension in trading, 15
Timed order, 239-240
Time-out between trade positions, 272-273
To-arrive contracts, 18
Trader motives, 93
Trading bulges and dips, 100-101, 162
Trading card facsimile, 125
Trading:
  Against the trend, 287
  Big markets, 287
  Dull markets, 286
  Errors, 258-259
  Nearby vs. deferred contracts, 136
  On "basis," 229
  On last days of contract life, 281-282
  On news, 274
  On the close, 280-281
  On the opening, 279
Trading range, as measure of risk exposure, 194
Trading recap sheet, 127